Psyche As Hero

Books edited by Lee R. Edwards

Alcuin: A Dialogue by Charles Brockden Brown
Woman: An Issue. With Lisa Baskin and Mary Heath
American Voices, American Women: A Collection of Fiction. With Arlyn Diamond
The Authority of Experience: Essays in Feminist Criticism. With Arlyn Diamond

Lee R. Edwards

Psyche As Hero

Female Heroism and Fictional Form

Wesleyan University Press
Middletown, Connecticut

The author gratefully acknowledges permission to quote from the following works:

Reprinted with permission of Macmillan Publishing Company from *The Dollmaker* by Harriette Arnow, copyright © 1954, renewed 1982 by Harriette Simpson Arnow.

Specified extracts from *Their Eyes Were Watching God* by Zora Neale Hurston (J. B. Lippincott Co.) Copyright 1937 by Harper & Row, Publishers Inc.; renewed 1965 by John C. Hurston and Joel Hurston. By permission of Harper & Row, Publishers, Inc. and J. M. Dent & Sons, Ltd.

The Woman Warrior, by Maxine Hong Kingston, © 1975, 1976 by Maxine Hong Kingston, by permission of Alfred A. Knopf, Inc., and Pan Books Ltd.

The Memoirs of a Survivor, by Doris Lessing. © 1975 by Octagon Press, by permission of Alfred A. Knopf, Inc., and Octagon Press.

Sula by Toni Morrison, © 1974 by Toni Morrison, by permission of Alfred A. Knopf, Inc.

Specified extracts (passim) from *Gaudy Night* by Dorothy L. Sayers (Gollancz), copyright 1936 by Dorothy Leigh Sayers Fleming. By permission of David Higham Associates Limited and Harper & Row, Publishers, Inc.

Mrs. Dalloway, by Virginia Woolf, © 1925 by Harcourt, Brace & World, Inc. Renewed by Leonard Woolf, by permission of Harcourt Brace Jovanovich, Inc., The Hogarth Press, and the Author's Literary Estate.

All inquiries and permissions requests should be addressed to the Publisher, Wesleyan University Press, 110 Mt. Vernon Street, Middletown, Connecticut 06457.

Distributed by Harper & Row Publishers, Keystone Industrial Park, Scranton, Pennsylvania 18512.

LIBRARY OF CONGRESS CATALOGING IN PUBLICATION DATA

Edwards, Lee R.
  Psyche as hero.

  Bibliography: p.
  Includes index.
    1. English fiction—History and criticism.
2. American fiction—History and criticism.
3. Heroines in literature.   I. Title.   II. Title: Female heroism and fictional form.
PR830.H4E38   1984   823'.009'352042   83-21841
ISBN 0-8195-6171-1 (alk. paper)

Manufactured in the United States of America

First published, 1984

Wesleyan Paperback, 1987; second printing, 1987

For my parents,
and for Bill & Amy, Craig & Hilary,
& Arlyn with love

We tell ourselves stories in order to live. . . . We inter-pret what we see, select the most workable of the multiple choices. We live entirely . . . by the imposition of a narrative line upon disparate images, by the "ideas" with which we have learned to freeze the shifting phantasmagoria which is our actual experience.

Joan Didion, *The White Album*

Yet fiction has, ironically, the rock-hard permanence that fact must lack.

Stephen Jay Gould, *Hen's Teeth and Horse's Toes: Further Reflections in Natural History*

Contents

Acknowledgments   xi

Prologue: *The Labors of Psyche: Women Heroes and Patriarchal Culture*   3

Part One
In Amor's Cave: Protoheroes and Early Novels

1   Psyche's Progress: The Heroine's World as the Hero's Maze   19

2   Lilies That Fester: The Divine Compromise in *Clarissa* and *The Scarlet Letter*   29

3   Heroes into Heroines: The Limits of Comedy in *Emma, Jane Eyre,* and *Middlemarch*   62

4   " 'Weddings be funerals' ": Sexuality, Maternity, and Selfhood in *Jude the Obscure, The Awakening,* and *The Portrait of a Lady*   104

Part Two
The Road to Olympus: Women Heroes and Modern Texts

5   Psyche's Ascent: A New Earth, A New Heaven   143

6   Love and Work: Reciprocity and Power in *The Odd Women, Daughter of Earth,* and *Gaudy Night*   150

7 Makers of Art, Makers of Life: Creativity and
   Community in *Sula, Their Eyes Were Watching
   God,* and *The Dollmaker*   188

8 Alternative Mythologies: The Metaphysics of
   Femininity in *The Woman Warrior, Mrs. Dalloway,*
   and *The Memoirs of a Survivor*   236

   Notes   285

   Index   301

Acknowledgments

Grateful thanks to those who saw me through my labors, whose help made this book possible: The National Endowment for the Humanities, which gave me a research fellowship and a year of precious time to think and write; Jeannette Hopkins and Alison Griffith, for tact and patience beyond the call of duty; friends and colleagues, for reading various versions of various drafts, for never failing to encourage and advise—Jules Chametzky, Margo Culley, Anne Halley, Cathy Portuges, Catharine Stimpson, Kathleen Swaim, Brook Thomas, Cynthia Wolff, Elizabeth Wood; three who were there at the beginning, who aren't here to drink champagne now that it's over, and whom I miss: Elizabeth Bruss, Robert Elliott, and Sheldon Sacks.

Psyche As Hero

The Labors of Psyche
Women Heroes and Patriarchal Culture

I think it was the great nineteenth-century paleontologist Cope who first clearly enunciated what he called "the law of the unspecialized," the contention that it was not from the most highly organized and dominant forms of a given geological era that the master type of a succeeding period evolved, but that instead the dominant forms tended to arise from more lowly and generalized animals which were capable of making new adaptations, and which were not narrowly restricted to a given environment.

Loren Eisely, *The Immense Journey*

Dreaming, we are heroes. Waking, we invent them. Conscious, unable to recreate the universe according to the patterns of desire, we require heroes to redeem a fallen world. Seductive figures, bold and daring, heroes promise power to the weak, glamour to the dull, and liberty to the oppressed. Their thoughts and actions cut channels into custom's rock. They cross borders, advance into new territory, inspire revolt. Dreamers' agents, necessary fictions, heroes enact our sleeping visions in the world, in daylight. We dream our heroes. In exchange, our heroes alter us.

Dreams are improvisations, private theatricals, unpredictable and fragmentary. Heroism, however, is a public drama, produced by a collective imagination, directed by a common will. Its narrative is formal, even stylized. Its principals have principles in common: each is unique, all are analogous. Heroes resemble one another in behavior, inner makeup, and relationship to their surroundings.[1] Yet, the specific details of heroic narratives—the actions they record, the heroes they depict—vary, like the content of our dreams, and reflect, as dreams do, a particular confluence of circumstance and psyche. Incarnations of abstract ideals and ineffable desires, heroes have no necessary attributes. They play a role, but cannot be typecast. Sex, class, status, occupation have great historical and social resonance, but not inherent meaning. A culture's heroes reflect a culture's values. Where values clash, heroic types conflict.

Western culture, for example, has represented heroes typically as military leaders: commanding, conquering, and above all, male. Erect before us, such figures are the Picts' perpetual descendants, woad-dyed warriors hoping that the spectacle of their naked physical magnificence will awe their enemies into submission. Sacking Troy, seeking the Grail, dying at the Alamo, in Flanders' fields, or on the Cross, their costumes change; their character remains. Even Christ, oddly peaceful in this company, must be remembered as the bringer of a sword; the crucifixion of God's son, not a carpenter's surprise, is the apotheosis of noblesse oblige. Within this context—patriarchal, hostile, preoccupied with rank—the woman hero is an image of antithesis. Different from the male—her sex her sign—she threatens his authority and that of the system he sustains. This is so not because of what men and women really are, if such imponderables are ever fully knowable, but because of the positions assigned to men and women in every society our culture has devised. Leading a fugitive existence, her presence overlooked, her identity obscured, the woman hero is an emblem of patriarchal instability and insecurity. From her perspective, all social contracts have been bargained in bad faith and must be renegotiated. History, she reminds us, has buried the Picts.

Western culture's opposing self, the woman hero uncovers fractures in the surface of reality, contradictions in its structure, gaps in its social ideology. Insofar as she resembles the male hero, she questions the conventional associations of gender and behavior. If, like the Bible's Judith or like Joan of Arc, she can do as he has done, then patriarchy's prohibitions are a lie. Restless, angry, often fierce, the woman hero forbids the presumption that women are innately selfless, weak, or passive. And where she differs from the male hero, she denies the link between heroism and *either* gender *or* behavior. Permitted, like others of her sex, to love and nurture, to comfort, to solace, and to please, the heroic woman specifies these impulses as human, not just female, and endows them with a value that counters their usual debasement. Assuming a position equal to that of the male hero, she challenges the compulsions of aggressivity and conquest, subverts patriarchy's structures, levels hierarchy's endless ranks. She stands at the border between domestic and public life, as Jo March does in Alcott's *Little Women*. Like Sophocles' Antigone, she reveals insupportable distinctions between spiritual imperatives and institutional prerogatives. She struggles to rectify imbalances between egalitarian and stratified societies, as Charlotte Brontë's hero dreams of doing in *Jane Eyre*. She tries, like Shakespeare's Cleopatra, to reconstitute relationships between the worlds of love and war. Toppling the walls dividing nature and unconscious life from consciousness and culture, as does Catherine in *Wuthering Heights,* she redefines culture, society, and self, producing a new synthesis of values.[2] Insisting that our civilization's typical heroic figure—biologically male and culturally masculine—cannot alone represent the prototype of heroism, she clashes with Titans.

Yet she is no sheep in wolf's clothing, no mere heroine in armor. A primary character, the hero inspires and requires followers; the heroine obeys, falls into line, takes second place. Although a hero can theoretically exist in a narrative without a heroine, the reverse is not the case. Hamlet's story is imaginable without Ophelia; Ophelia literally has no story without Hamlet.[3] Role, not sex, divides the two. The hero possesses vision, daring and power: to charm; move; break with the

past; endure hardship and privation; journey into the unknown; risk death and survive—at least in spirit. The hero
dances in the spotlight. The heroine is eclipsed, upstaged, in
darkness.

Changing the relationship of men and women to each
other, to heroism and society, might provide the bases of a
new cultural order, as D. H. Lawrence suggests in *Women in
Love*. In that novel, Ursula Brangwen's claims to self-determi-
nation run contrapuntally against Rupert Birkin's desire for
domination. Rejecting the constraints Rupert would impose
upon her, Ursula exclaims:

> "Yes — yes. . . . There you are — a star in its orbit! A satellite — a
> satellite of Mars — that's what she is to be! There — there — you've
> given yourself away! You've said it — you've said it — you've dished
> yourself!"[4]

Her anger here expresses the outrage heroes always feel at the
threat of convention and limitation, represented in this case
as synonymous with male authority. The novel's plot neither
resolves nor mediates the conflict.[5] Alternately battling and
embracing, Birkin and Ursula are opaque and enigmatic. Simultaneously fascinating and repellent, Lawrence's characters
reflect tensions unresolved in their society and, one suspects,
unresolved also in their creator's mind. *Women in Love* offers
the reader no final point of rest, no way to choose between
Ursula and Birkin or to incorporate her objections into his
vision. Permanent ambiguity holds the hero hostage.

Heroism, however, needs an initial instability, feeds on the
energy released when consensus dissipates and expectations
fail. Utopias do not generate the opposition that imperfect societies require. "Unhappy is the land that needs a hero," remarks Brecht's Galileo, wishing not to be one. Simone de
Beauvoir's declaration in *The Second Sex*—"I am interested
in the fortunes of the individual as defined not in terms of
happiness but in terms of liberty"—countervails, urges the acceptance of a need for will and strain. Unmasking misery,
risking present pain for the sake of a future ideal, heroes al-

ways emerge into uncertainty. What they promise is glorious, but what they ask is terrifying. And who they are is, initially, unknown. Villain and hero are each other's shadows. From the point of view of the conservative, the makers of a new cosmogony are heretics. Those who hear voices or march to the music of a different drum might more easily be witches or lunatics than saviors or saints. Only at the quest's end, when the whole story can be retrospectively revealed, is success or failure measurable. Only then is the hero distinguished clearly from the fraud.

Ambiguity disappears in retrospect. But then, of course, it is too late. For by the time the hero stands adored at society's center—parading down Fifth Avenue showered with rosebuds and confetti—the hero's *life* as a hero is effectively finished. The quest over, the hero rests and rusts, becomes an artifact, a statue, one of many ritualized objects guaranteeing social consensus, preserving stability, order, and a fixed notion of reality. With the threat of chaos overcome, a new convention is established. Heroism fades into memory. Nostalgia replaces the dangerous uncertainties of action. When stability fails, when this order in its turn is threatened, a new hero begins slowly to emerge, fueled as always by isolation, social confusion, and existential anguish.

Heroism, like a weed, need not be cultivated. It roots in borderlands, not garden plots. Heroes are volunteers, part of a category described by cultural anthropologist Victor Turner as "threshold people," "liminars" (from the Latin, *limen,* meaning threshold), "liminal personae."[6] Such figures, according to Turner, "elude or slip through the networks of classifications that normally locate states and positions in cultural space" (*RP,* p. 81). They are, like Lawrence's combatants, "necessarily ambiguous" (*RP,* p. 81). Regardless of sex or previous social status, their behavior is "normally passive or humble; they must obey their instructors implicitly, and accept arbitrary punishment without complaint. It is as though they are being reduced or ground down . . . to be fashioned anew and endowed with additional powers to enable them to cope with their new station in life" (*RP*, p. 81).[7] The status and social privilege that such a character might have by right of birth is stripped away.

Those persons whom Turner defines as "marginals," are like liminars in that they also dwell betwixt and between existing social groupings, but "unlike ritual liminars they have no cultural assurance of a final stable resolution of their ambiguity" (*DF&M*, p. 233). Liminality can be observed in numerous socially contained and sanctioned rituals—fraternity hazing, boot camp, the acceptable saturnalia and role reversals of Mardi Gras. Marginality, on the other hand, seems to lack this sense of ultimate connection to the fixed norms of a stable culture. Ritual liminality is a kind of antisocial state encysted within a durable surrounding structure. Transiently "divested of the outward attributes of structured position," liminars are momentarily "set aside from the main areas of social life" (*DF&M*, p. 232) and disturb its dignity and repose but briefly. Marginal beings, in contrast, belong to "two or more groups whose social definitions and cultural norms are distinct from and often opposed to, one another" (*DF&M*, p. 233). Their situation is more extreme than the liminar's, their dilemma more profound. Their absorption by society requires fundamental and permanent changes in the definitions of society or self. In patriarchal circumstances where woman's status is seen as categorically lowly, the tension between this reduction and heroic aspiration marks the woman hero as quintessentially marginal.

Male heroes within patriarchy are, in contrast, liminars. Because maleness is patriarchy's single absolute requisite, the male hero's isolation is impermanent, as well as less pronounced than that imposed upon his female counterpart. His heroism is contingent upon some factor—circumstantial or psychological—extrinsic to his sex. He may be poor, inwardly tormented, part of a racial, ethnic, or religious minority. His occupation may be unfashionable, like the Brave Little

Tailor's, or if fashionably employed, he must be debarred from duty, as Prince Hal is before he is crowned king. Like Oedipus, he may have violated an existing societal taboo or exceeded in some way the socially appropriate bounds of action. He may refuse to do what he is asked or seek to do more than is required. Capable of forcing society to change, he is nonetheless unable to negate the assumption at the culture's heart: the idea that society itself is inextricably bound up with prerogatives exercised exclusively, and necessarily, by men. A limit is marked when a representational strategy—heroism enacted by a male character—intersects with the cultural proposition that society *must* be patriarchal, *must* rest on male power. However marginal a male character may seem, however isolated, discontented, oppressed, or enraged, he can never remain male and be more than transiently un-manned. He can thus scarcely be used to pose the deepest threat to patriarchy's authority, to divide power from sex, gender from honor, strength from violence, and society from male supremacy.[8]

This is a job for the woman hero, for in patriarchy, femaleness is the ultimate and ineradicable sign of marginality. In relation to the female hero, male heroism is, in fact, a "strategy of containment," a device that provides local change and rearrangement at the price of preserving intact the central terms of order.[9] If, as Stanley Aronowitz suggests, "the revolutionary function of art is to work to smash the cultural conformity that contains consciousness within social rituals of domination,"[10] then the heroic woman is patriarchal culture's most puissant image of this radical aesthetic usage. Precisely because patriarchy has assigned women characteristics that are other than or alternative to those assigned to men, making femininity and masculinity complementary rather than overlapping categories, the woman hero can make use of culturally feminine traits in order to challenge the belief that society as an idea must rest on war and conquest. The lives we live, as Joan Didion suggests, depend on the stories we tell. Attending

to our tales of women heroes, we—men as well as women—
might make our future's history different from our past's.

Feminism, in recent years, has provoked an interest in
women heroes, but such figures have a lengthy history. Indeed, the Greek myth of Amor and Psyche, retold by Apuleius
in the second-century narrative, *The Golden Ass,* provides a
classic example of the female heroic paradigm. The story of
the love between a mortal woman and a male god, of Psyche's
passionate yearning for Amor, of Amor's evasions and manipulations, and Venus' jealousy of both the beautiful maiden
and her own son, emphasizes a quest that fuses power's needs
with love's.

Its surface is romantic, but Psyche's character, her deeds,
her relationships with the surrounding world—natural, social,
and supernatural—are typically heroic. Her beauty is both
curse and blessing, a sign of social value and a stigma that
thrusts her from society. Men worship her but will not marry
her. Women are jealous. Her parents are unable to protect her
from the oracle's prediction that she faces immediate extinc-
tion. Gods, both Amor and his mother, persecute and torment
her. Separated from parents, family, friends, and finally from
Amor, Psyche suffers a progressive isolation; it ends only when
her successful completion of seemingly impossible tasks restores the lovers to each other. Mediating between an alien
nature and an equally frightening, if more familiar culture,
she sorts the disordered seeds of Ceres, captures the sun's rams'
golden fleece, contains life's rushing waters in an urn. Contending against death, she pays her coins to Charon, throws
sops to Cerberus, and resists pity for those who would trap her
in the underworld, as Aeneas resists Dido's supplications and
Henry V leaves Falstaff in the dust.[11] With some supernatural
assistance, Psyche twice defies the gods, first when she uncovers
Amor's true identity, a second time when she takes for herself
a prize designed for Venus. Like Prometheus, she steals immortal secrets for humanity. The marriage with which the tale

concludes is a sign of triumph, not capitulation. Psyche's deeds have deified her, transformed Amor, fertilized life on earth, altered Olympus' eternal ethic. The promise of a new order, metaphysical as well as physical, is celebrated and continued in the birth of a daughter, not a son. Patriarchy's heir has been displaced.

Psyche's heroism, like all heroism, involves both doing and knowing. The pattern of the tale parallels the growth of consciousness. Each material advance marks an increase in psychic range, an apprehension of what was formerly forbidden and inaccessible. The possibility of the woman hero is contingent only on recognizing the aspirations of consciousness as human attributes; it is the absence of this understanding that has kept Psyche and her heroic daughters so long in shadow. For if heroism is defined in terms of external action alone and heroic actions are confined to displays of unusual physical strength, military prowess, or social or political power, then physiology or a culture that limits women's capacities in these areas thereby exclude women from heroic roles. But if action is important primarily for what it tells us about knowledge, then any action—fighting dragons, seeking grails, stealing fleece, reforming love—is potentially heroic. Heroism thus read and understood is a human necessity, capable of being represented equally by either sex.

Apuleius' tale is significant for being a myth of heroic questing and internal growth that concentrates on the possibilities of *human* development and change. In contrast to most myths the patriarchy has retained, "Amor and Psyche" resolutely makes the main representative vehicle a woman who represents not femininity but heroism. When, near the tale's end, Psyche defies Venus and discovers the secrets hidden by Persephone, her treatment violates mythological convention. Unlike Eve or Pandora, Psyche is neither punished nor reviled. She is not cited as the source of sin and human woe; instead she is hailed as a goddess, adored as the font and source of pleasure and delight. Psyche's immersion in the

archetypal patterns of heroic action supports a reading of heroism as an asexual or omnisexual archetype and suggests that
heroic actions may be culturally atypical. Psyche's labors and
those of Hercules are analogous and equal expressions of
heroic possibilities. Like the deeds of Achilles, Ulysses, Jason,
and Ahab, Psyche's actions resonate for all of us, men and
women alike. And as Psyche is—marrying, not murdering;
offering pleasure instead of pain; transforming the world
rather than subduing it—so might we all wish to be.

The goal of the quest in this tale is love: an expression and
an alteration of the possibilities of individual relationship.
Such love is born, the narrative's conclusion demonstrates,
only when the encounter is reciprocal. Amor and Psyche both
participate. The bond between them consciously acknowledges what was formerly unconscious or repressed. For Amor,
just as for Psyche, the prospect of intimacy means separation
from the mother and an end to childhood's idyll. The tale is
at pains to show that we are each—male and female, mortal
virgin and great god of love—our mother's frightened child,
potentially both her extension and her rival. In entering into
a relationship with Psyche, Amor is disobedient to Venus.
Psyche's encounter with the power of eroticism occurs in a
supposed paradise of love. A torrid, shadowed, and subterranean place that exists only at night, it is the creation of
Amor's desire, the expression of his insecurity. Having been
displaced by Psyche from this self-protective darkness, he returns for solace to his mother's perfumed bedroom. There,
wounded, passive, helpless, infantalized, he is imprisoned for
most of the tale. In thrall to Venus and to his own fears and
misapprehensions, he is rescued by Psyche when she makes
him rescue her from Persephone's spell. Gazing on divine
mysteries, Psyche chances death, learns the gods' secrets, empowers another, and lives. Bringing her treasure, as the hero
must, from a dream's darkness into daylight, she successfully
concludes her quest in a transforming act of love. At the tale's
end, she and Amor again embrace. No longer caught in a

deathly marriage where the first plunge into sexuality must be a fatal fall, the lovers now accept the risks attendant on self-revelation and the dispossession of old authorities by a new system of valuation that Psyche has created.

All heroism, in fact, appeals to love, makes love its end, relies on faith where knowledge is impossible. Even *The Iliad*, memorialized by Simone Weil as a "poem of force," concludes not with the spectacle of Hector's bloody body being dragged around the fallen city but with Achilles and Priam joined in prayer, reconciled, if only for a moment. Love, in this sense, is neither romantic nor sexual. A social rather than a private impulse, it seeks expression in a public form and brings about a change from an old idea of community to a new ideal, one Victor Turner calls "communitas." This term conveys a vision of community in its spiritual rather than its administrative or geographic sense. Communitas is "spontaneous, immediate, concrete . . . as opposed to the norm-governed, institutionalized abstract nature of social structure" (*RP*, p. 114). The participants in this relationship confront one another directly and create a "model of society as homogeneous and unstructured" (*RP*, p. 119). Communitas is the state brought to birth by Psyche's transformation of self and society, her union with Amor, and the offspring their relationship produces. Amor's hostility toward communitas—an expression of love freely given between individuals loosed from socially or divinely imposed restraints—reflects the extent to which Psyche's quest raises a living heroism against the dead hand of ritual.[12] Heroic power is inseparable from the love the hero expresses and inspires.

It is this connection between love and power, so often glossed over in narratives and interpretations of male heroism, that is the central structure of "Amor and Psyche." Psyche's child, always in utero referred to as a son, is born a girl and named Pleasure. The change is startling. Heroines typically have sons, hostages to patriarchy, signs that their marriages have been retreats and that they have been incorporated again into an unchanged world. But Pleasure—sensuous, unmanly, feminine—is love's product, a vital expression of communitas. Where instinct and intellect are fused, Pleasure is born. In a culture that sees love as expressive primarily of sexuality alone and as contained only in relationships that reinforce social and economic hierarchies, the need to liberate eros from this hidden bondage can best be perceived and represented by figures who are truly marginal to society, as women have been rendered marginal in patriarchal culture. Nonetheless, this quest is the prototype of all heroic action.

Psyche as Hero examines the fulfillment or frustration of heroic possibilities of plot and character in a variety of English and American novels arranged in rough chronological order from the mid-eighteenth century to the present time. Many of the works—*Clarissa, Emma, Jane Eyre, The Scarlet Letter, Middlemarch, Jude the Obscure*—are familiar literary classics. Others, like *The Awakening, Daughter of Earth, Gaudy Night,* and *The Dollmaker,* are less well known or less seriously regarded, in part because appropriate concepts for understanding their structural statements have not yet entered into critical circulation. The suggestion that heroism patterns all their plots and that a comprehension of its imperatives ought therefore to guide interpretive responses implies not just new readings but an as yet untried critical theory.

The hero, or even the potential hero, is an alternative to the more limited archetypes of angel, witch, hag, and madwoman limned so eloquently in Sandra M. Gilbert and Susan Gubar's *The Madwoman in the Attic.*[13] Gilbert and Gubar focus on the anxiety such figures must inevitably create in those who feel themselves, however illegitimately, so described within patriarchal culture. The hero provides a contrasting model: one that confronts and opposes institutions as they are and seeks to force society to honor this opposition, recognize its faults, and alter its structures. The hero is a figure who, at least *in potentia,* might oppose that most embracing of all cultural institutions, patriarchy itself. Gilbert and Gubar focus on "disguise" and on various other strategies of "fear and dis-ease" whereby women writers attempt to "transcend their anxiety of authorship," but the heroic female character (whether created by a female or a male author) strips away disguise, boldly revealing fundamental conflicts within patriarchy and the consequent need for alternative cultural syntheses. Where Gilbert and Gubar see covert reappraisals, I see overt and radical attacks. Admitting the possibility that heroism can reside in female characters and that heroic enterprise depends not on sex but on structure banishes the sense—cultural as well as private—that women are somehow invincibly limited in aspiration and accomplishment. The texts that make this case are not necessarily the conscious offspring of new feminist theories. But feminism provides the necessary context, for it alters literary interpretations no less than political goals and tactics.

Characters like Clarissa Harlowe, Emma Woodhouse, and Jane Eyre arouse intense feeling in readers. An understanding of the durability of the heroic paradigm and the peculiarly charged relationship it creates between character and audience can explain this emotional response and can also substantiate the conceptual relationship these characters bear to one another. Creatures who share a single habitat, some are more successful than others in exploiting its full resources. Some pay an acceptable coin to Charon, guaranteeing safe return from death's blighted realm; others are merely reformed, defeated, normalized, sunk in the warm waters society would have us think surround us.

Outside of this eternal interweaving of subjectivity and structure, but not really apart from it, the historical development of the topics treated in the novels considered within the following chapters provides its own justification for examining the functions female heroism performs within the genre, as well as outside it. Without confusing change and teleology, one must notice, nonetheless, sequential alterations in the treatment of the anomalous woman, the woman created as her own most compelling study. Resistance to various normalizing constraints is a shifting signal; a mask of deviance becomes heroism's requisite. This evolution is neither swift nor direct; quite the opposite, in fact. Until the twentieth century, most of the novels under discussion show nothing so much as heroism bought off with inappropriate rewards, defeated by the authors' sense that the tests involved are impossible for the would-be hero to perform, or subverted by narrative legerdemain that transforms the heroic plot back into one fit only for heroines. Each new trial, however, serves to make future narrative retreats more difficult. By revealing the obstacles which confront the hero, whether these are psychological, moral, or social barriers, a text plays out, as it were, one move in an ongoing game and makes the attentive reader conscious, as the hero is conscious, that future moves must require untried strategies. By the beginning of the twentieth century, novelists seem readier to abandon the project of entrapping the female heroic character and begin the task of inventing maneuvers whereby she can break out of familial, sexual, and social bondage into an altered and appropriate world.

This new world, of course, intersects with historical reality. It cannot be understood without some awareness of such matters as divorce laws, suffrage legislation, industrial developments, bills affecting married women's rights to property, access to reliable methods of contraception, and altered economic opportunities. The business world of George Gissing's odd women and the political chaos explored by Doris Lessing's survivor are not independent of events that actually occurred and that do not require the hero to verify their possibility. Events, however, are not heroic. Heroism specifies, instead, a relationship between the event and its participants; it connects tendencies in any given social world to imaginative constructs that suggest hypothetical consequences. As a transhistorical model, heroism mediates historical phenomena by giving individuals a way to incorporate change into private life, to move with confidence into a newly constituted world, and, inevitably, to dream beyond the borders of any momentary knowledge.

Part One

In Amor's Cave

Protoheroes and Early Novels

Chapter 1

Psyche's Progress

The Heroine's World as the Hero's Maze

*❧ What Psyche saw with the candle was not a god with wings
but a pigeon-chested youth with pimples, and that's why it
took her so long to win her way back to true love. It is easier
to love a daemon than a man, though less heroic.*

Margaret Atwood, "The Grave of the Famous Poet"

*❧ People like us are after the truth of life, and marriage is the
one thing that society won't take the trouble to learn the truth
about.*

Mary Hunter Austin, *A Woman of Genius*

Psyche's heroism starts in Amor's cave. Offering love but requiring submission, it is a place that makes ignorance the
price of adoration, that rewards obedience with opulence.
When Psyche arms herself with lamp and dagger, she disobeys
authority for the first time, discovering simultaneously Amor's
true identity and the connection between his divinity and her
constraint. Her paradise lost with her illusions, Psyche sets
out on her quest.

Between the time of Apuleius and the eighteenth century,
fictive conventions alter as profoundly as the surface of society. In modern times the novel serves as both a mythic genre
and a social metaphor. Its patterns reciprocally express and
motivate collective beliefs and behavior. Its situations record
the particular tensions and struggles of an emerging bourgeoi-
sie and the progressive crises of capitalism, urbanization, and
loss of faith in traditional authorities. *The Golden Ass* was no

more interested than *Pride and Prejudice* in "truth universally acknowledged," but to see Lizzy Bennet cast in Psyche's
mold clarifies the distinction between Pemberley and Mount
Olympus. The fable's certainty is the novel's dilemma.

Women undoubtedly "influenced" the novel. From Aphra
Behn's time to George Eliot's, they were among the most popular writers of the genre and constituted a major portion of
its audience. Yet the power of this influence appears to be as
limited in fiction as it has always been in life. Nominally
ceded the private sphere, women are supposed to leave the
public realm untouched. When Carlyle cries out for heroism,
lamenting its absence in the crass commercial world around
him, his imagination finds its object in Great Men, not Great
Women. But Great Men have moved outside of history and
are paralyzed like Melville's Ahab: "a Caryatid . . . uphold-
ing on his frozen brow the piled entablatures of ages."[1] Per-
ceiving the world as deracinated and uninhabitable, Ahab
prefers exile to revolution, chooses to contemplate an immense inhuman blankness rather than confront the darkness
of the cave where Psyche dwells. Ahab's gesture—brutal, self-
consciously masculine in cultural terms, ultimately solitary—
defines, but also limits, male heroism in its most familiar modern form. Refusing to live a landlocked life, Ahab sails away.
He would admit that men have made that world, but deny
that they must, therefore, dwell within it. Although a society
of *Pequods* is not entirely unimaginable, it could not be self-
sustaining, since the ship requires provisions (money, food,
and even sailors) extorted from the despised territory whose
competence and values it would reject.

Flight without the promise of a new social coalescence
leaves heroism incomplete. It is the obverse of totalitarian
closure without the possibility of change, but not a better alternative. Male hero and female heroine thus complement
each other. Their plots counterbalance, creating stasis out of
tension. Bourgeois aggressiveness and the needs of an industrial economy revolutionized society. But the demands for

libidinal restraint and commercial calculation corrupt the possibility of male heroism by making it—as the examples not just of Ahab, but of Twain's Huck Finn, and Conrad's Kurtz and Lord Jim attest—profoundly and deliberately nihilistic. Bourgeois and patriarchal structures, fused in their mutual insistence on female subordination, lock women into a coercive imaginative structure. The presumption of female piety and moral goodness is a staple of bourgeois ideology, as necessary as it is conservative. Safely at sea, Ahab is permitted to smite the face of an insulting God. Should it propose such a gesture in the bosom of the family, the hand that rocks the cradle would rock the foundations of the world.

When Psyche's tale enters the novel's history, she destabilizes both social and aesthetic structures. No longer an archaic generality—the youngest and most beautiful daughter of an unnamed king dwelling in the land of once upon a time and long ago—Psyche's identity becomes individualized. Her motives are psychologically complex, and also suspicious. Her narrative position is tentative, uncertain, because the questions she raises—questions about the intimate and institutional relationships of human beings to each other, to family, society, and God—cannot easily be answered. She may be, as the characters of Moll Flanders and Pamela Andrews testify, not only socially marginal and economically insecure—characteristics employed frequently as heroic markers—but also seemingly hypocritical. If Moll's final repentance is taken as sincere, and her happy marriage is read as a sign of God's benevolence, then God is either truly all-forgiving or a fool, and Moll's wonderful capacity to improvise a life outside the confines of convention's plot, is just a trick designed only to display her happy as a heroine at last. To see Moll as a hero, one must believe she mocks her piety even while proclaiming it; her amorality renders her heroic, sets her character and fate apart from those reserved for pious heroines. To accept Moll's heroism, as Ian Watt does, but describe her as therefore necessarily "masculine" is an evasion: clearly Defoe is at great pains to render her a woman. Sexuality and a spirit of adventure predominate in her character, and in *Moll Flanders* these are distinctly and appropriately female traits.[2] Pamela, too, is either a female Crusoe, fighting for survival in the wilderness of Squire B.'s estates or else she is a manipulative hussy and Squire B., like Defoe's God must be taken as someone taken in. In either reading, Moll and Pamela subvert the laws of God and society, although neither author's text declares its meaning or its viewpoint absolutely. The perspective each establishes permits no final judgments of their creations' status or their stature. Thackeray's similar ambivalence toward both Becky Sharp's adventures and her essential nature can be inferred from *Vanity Fair*'s subtitle: "a novel without a hero."

Women who assert the slightest claim to power assume the status of potential heroes because their assertion subverts the fundamental dialectic of power and submission that feeds society's dynamos. By creating an enormous countermovement of divine, societal, and psychological repression, the hint of aggressivity earns even heroines the punishments and suffering usually reserved for heroes. Jane Eyre's rebellion in the red room is justly famous because John Reed, a dictator disguised as an adolescent boy (unless the two terms are synonymous), deserves to be beaten by the one he tyrannizes over most. But Jane herself calls her reaction madness. Her rage, though just, has frightful consequences. The spectacle of Bertha Mason confirms her fears. In *The Wide, Wide World* (1851—the same year as *Moby Dick*), a novel unfamiliar in our time but enormously popular in its own, Ellen Montgomery (no protohero like Jane Eyre but a truly long-suffering heroine seeking only a world that will permit her to be good) dares to protest when her uncle takes away a book given to her by her cousin John. " 'But it is mine,' " Ellen asserts. " 'And you are mine,' " her uncle replies. Having "no right to choose for [her]self" whose authority to honor, she must obey her uncle and concede the point.[3] Her capitulation is necessary because she is judged by an ethos that requires women constantly to affirm their "natural" subordination to authority. When they question or, even worse, refuse its prohibitions and commandments, they undermine more than human law. It is precisely the agreement to submit—even if not always willingly or appropriately—to the whimsies and caprices of authority that makes authority itself seem natural and the figure of the heroine such a potent moral model. The threat posed by the woman who refuses to submit is correspondingly tremendous.

Novels like *The Wide, Wide World* or even like *Jane Eyre* schematize reality to suggest a chosen, moral end. The fates of their central figures (those, for example, of Brontë's Catherine Earnshaw; Eliot's Maggie Tulliver; Alcott's Jo March; Phelps's Avis Dobell; James's Olive Chancellor, Verena Tarrant, Kate Croy, and Daisy Miller) are sad and strangely similar. Dead or married, saved or damned, joyous or miserable, sane or crazed, the variety of their conditions is an illusion dissipated by the reality of their entrapment in the heroine's plot and the circumstances of domestic life. As in a chess game, fate is not arbitrary but depends on strategies and tactics. Action, however, is limited by rules prescribing movement, defining goals, limiting objectives. Free play takes place within an arena both circumscribed and sexualized. Only one female is admitted to the board's battleground: the queen.[4] The game's most valuable piece, she advances and retreats at will, moves in all directions. The supremely active subject, she is also the principal object of the opposition's desire. But, like every other piece, the queen owes her ultimate allegiance to her king. An inert monument, scuttling one square at a time, the king—unlike the queen—may not be captured or surrendered but only checked and mated. At that point, the queen falls with him. All play stops. The game is over. To liberate the queen from this ritual of bondage and subservience, the rules must be altered, the board redesigned, the game replayed.

Like chess players, novelists regretfully sacrifice their queens, typically in order to preserve the novel's plot and society's

rules. Their protoheroes feel their frustration as the chess-
board queens do not. They cry out for change, as Jane Eyre
yearns for "liberty." They require social rearrangement, as
Dorothea Brooke longs to rearrange the housing on her uncle's
estate. They contest fixity, whether as an ideal for social
reality or a description of it. Like the major figure in Mary
Braddon's *Lady Audley's Secret* (1862), they display a discon-
certing capacity to appear as "the sweetest girl that ever lived,"
while actually living as runaways, bigamists, and would-be
murderers.[5] It is hard to see how the former description is
compatible with the accompanying set of facts. Braddon's explanation could have come straight from the pages of *Jane
Eyre:* walled up in domesticity, she writes, women will " 'make
mountains of warfare and vexation out of domestic molehills;
and social storms in household teacups.' " Denied the escape
route given to her male counterpart, the aspiring woman hero
avenges her existence where she can: at home.

Such rebellions, embodied in a series of supremely energetic
and compelling women, become increasingly difficult to ignore, or to overrule by moral manipulations or authorial interventions in the plot. As the nineteenth century draws on, leading characters are endowed with increasing self-consciousness
and permitted to become more clearly radical in both thoughts
and behavior. Where Moll Flanders is on a merry-go-round
of endless marriage and repentance, Lucy Snowe in Charlotte
Brontë's *Villette* (1853) loses her future husband in a single
paragraph and, if she remains unhappily unwed, her economic
security—her work, her school—seems guaranteed. The extermination not just of husbands, but of sons as well, is ruthless
and generalized. In *The Story of Avis* (1877), Elizabeth Stuart
Phelps sacrifices both, to her hero's—Avis's—needs for self-
expression and an independent life. Avis's husband, Philip,
tries to make his wife his housekeeper, though he had promised
he would not. Her son, Van, weeps outside her studio door,
so inhibiting her painting; he finally wounds himself on her
palette knife. Each man dies. Avis had loved them both,

nursed them, sacrificed her life and art for her duty and her love. But Phelps transforms the heroine's plot by showing incontrovertibly that these three characters cannot all live together in it. For Avis to survive, the man and boy, who will not listen to her most reasonable petitions for a little time and a small amount of space to call her own, must vanish; they must suffer the fate usually reserved for the heroine herself. The point is not that either Phelps or her central character hate men (although books of this type, beginning with *Jane Eyre,* are often read—and objected to—on these grounds) but that the existing system of sexual and domestic relationships is itself deadly, and the private world is in a state of crisis, chaotic and besieged. Phelps's narrative concludes with Avis reading aloud her daughter's favorite story, the tale of the Round Table and its most noble knight, Sir Galahad. Like Lancelot, Avis sacrificed her quest for the sake of a blind, unworthy love; like Lancelot's successor, her daughter may live to find her grail.

Despite novelists' best efforts to make the world they invent safe for the women they imagine, the classic heroine's plot is increasingly distorted by the hero's demand for her own economic vocation and her sexuality. Although they insist that women ought to live sheltered from the forces loosed in the larger world around them, novelists cannot prevent themselves from seeing that the processes of social change free women from their traditional moorings no less than men. As Ian Watt remarks, "the patriarchal legal situation of married women made it impossible for them to realise the aims of economic individualism."[6] But if economic individualism prevails, all must feel its compulsions and respond to them. It is only a successful career in prostitution that permits Defoe's Roxana to decline a noble marriage with the observation that " 'I was as well without the titles as long as I had the estate, and while I had £2,000 a year of my own I was happier than I could be in being prisoner of state to a nobleman, for I took the ladies of that rank to be little better.' " Amoral enterprise marks the heroic figure. Heroines, more pious than Roxana, are also less well endowed and either toil at home with no financial recompense; or starve in one of the few jobs permitted to respectable women, whatever their class; or languish idly, pent-up, restless and increasingly vicious, for want of any proper occupation to entertain their energies and talents.

Economically imprisoned, inside and out of marriage, heroines are sexually immured as well. If unrestrained male power is brutal, domesticated males—"feminine heroes" or "women's men," as Elaine Showalter names them[7]—are curiously sexless. Passion is impossible; sex is either rape or duty. Roxana, Moll, and Becky Sharp are occasionally hoist on others' petards, but married to "good" men, women heroes, like their spouses, become neuters. Fully sexualized women are supremely menacing, since their needs, like the demand for an independent economic life, can be met neither within marriage nor outside it. In the dark, Amor is a god; exposed to Psyche's light, he's just a little boy.

Between the earliest eighteenth-century examples and the later works of Meredith, Hardy, James, and Dreiser, the novel on both sides of the Atlantic evinces a growing and horrified awareness not only that female sexuality does exist but that its existence is incompatible with existing moral and aesthetic structures. The possibility that women might properly experience pleasure and desire desire jeopardizes God's commandments, dissolves domestic authority, and calls into question both the codes that govern inheritance and the legitimacy of the inheritors. If the iron laws of sexual economy are revised, the laws of social economy must undergo a corresponding revolution. Even while conniving at Milly Theale's death, Kate Croy realizes that the demise of the virtuous heroine means that the world the survivors inhabit shall never again be as it was.

Like all heroic acts, the escape from Amor's cave links defiance of the gods to societal upheaval. Would-be heroes in pre-twentieth-century fiction rebel against the interdependency of metaphysical imperatives and mundane institutions. Where the facts of marriage are seen to contradict its formal idealization, this idealization loses its mythic function; it becomes not just a fiction but a lie. A related and parallel decline is suffered by a theological ideal that requires female submission to masculine authority as an asymmetrical sign of God's power and humanity's sinfulness.[8] No bower of bliss or sacred temple, Amor's cave becomes a charnel house, an emblem of the world filled with as much existential potency as Twain's Mississippi or Melville's whaling grounds. Where God and husband are separable but fused, the divine father and the domesticated lover are Psyche's enemy no less than Ahab's or Huck Finn's.

No longer used merely to question domestic customs and the arrangements of private life, women like Sue Bridehead are permitted to envision a world founded on entirely different organizing principles: Greek joyousness is called on to replace Christianity's emphasis on human suffering and female sinfulness. Clarissa Harlowe never reigns on her own estates, but Isabel, at the end of James's *Portrait of a Lady*, has knowledge and fortune sufficient to allow her to overrule Osmond and liberate Pansy, and nothing to lose by doing either. The perturbations such characters create survive, informing future characters and novelistic situations.

The question faced by women in the plots and societies of novels changes from "How to catch a man?" to "How to avoid the perils of matrimony and still survive?" Problematic in reality, this shift in focus is equally perplexing in fiction. Life is experienced willy-nilly, but fiction's patterns, even when ambiguous, imply meaning. If marriage is the traditional "happy ending," and death its only, and unsatisfactory, alternative, novelists must devise ways to render happiness without them. If it is necessary to choose between marriage (or death) and happiness, they must determine both the resolution and its grounds. Can the structure of marriage be changed in fiction, in order to suggest the possibility of and necessity for a corresponding change in life? Can the author imagine another form

of human affiliation that would not impose the same restraints? If Melville's Bartleby declines to work on Wall Street,
how is the woman hero to walk that street and not be tainted
by its values? Does society make whores of everyone, and must
the hero, like Roxana, provoke society's awareness of that unpleasant fact? Or can there be a reorganization that will invest
society with meaning, now that Pan and Jehovah both have
fled?

The radical implications of such questions provoked enormous resistance. Protoheroes, coerced into voluntary surrender,
are transformed into heroines; otherwise they suffer for their
intellectual and sensuous desires. The very qualities—curiosity, eagerness, wit, passion—that seize the imagination of
author and reader alike, are annihilated, sublimated to serve
the needs of social order and fictive stability, or rendered monstrous, as a sign of their destructive power. The novel's conventions display and replicate a society walled in and blank.
Since male heroes evade this society and the women who appear to be a necessary part of it, it is the aspiring women
heroes left behind who truly reveal the bourgeois world's
sterility and whose needs mandate the construction of new
social and aesthetic forms.

Until the end of the nineteenth century, Psyche, confined
in Amor's cave, explores the territory the gods have given to
her and experiences as truth the equivalence of death and
marriage. Psyche's progress (within two centuries of novels)
takes her to the limits of the heroine's world until finally she
breaks its barriers and stands ready to venture into the larger
realm outside its walls. The first part of this book displays the
details of this labyrinthine exploration in a variety of representative fictions, tracing the progress of Psyche's ultimate
emergence from her subterranean and suffocating confinement.

Chapter 2

Lilies That Fester

The Divine Compromise in *Clarissa*
and *The Scarlet Letter*

Since the better is always the enemy of the good, every drastic innovation is an infringement of what is traditionally right and may sometimes be a crime punishable by death.
C. G. Jung, *Symbols of Transformation*

Sexual symbolism . . . is always available to make statements about social experience and to reflect (or conceal) contradictions within it. . . . In the little world of the family, with its conspicuous tension between intimacy and power, the larger matters of political and social order . . . find ready symbolization.
Natalie Zemon Davis, "Women on Top,"
Society and Culture in Early Modern France

In *Clarissa* (1748) and *The Scarlet Letter* (1850), the heroism of the novels' central female characters threatens primary social structures and challenges the moral and ethical imperatives animating domestic and communal life. Although Hester and Clarissa seem superficially quite different, at a deeper level they are strikingly alike in opposing societies they see as psychologically invasive and physically enclosing. Despite Richardson's and Hawthorne's inescapable allegiance to conventional Christian morality, they create fictions in which this morality is severely strained and its limits rigorously exposed.

Brilliant and beautiful, Clarissa and Hester are more importantly alike in their relatively high level of material and spiritual freedom from their surroundings. An heiress with her own estate and a potentially independent income, Clarissa starts out with a reputation as a moral paragon. Her virtue combines with her wealth, looks, and social position to endow her with a high degree of apparent power and authority. But, as the novel shows, the society that provides her power also forbids its use; only in flight and isolation can Clarissa gain a measure of autonomy. Hester Prynne, in contrast to Clarissa, begins her life as a social outcast; she is infinitely poorer than Clarissa, though equally self-sufficient. Yet she, too, uses a position of involuntary isolation to gain freedom from social limitations and restrictions. If neither character is conventionally virtuous, their moral lapses, their violation of the orthodox, force a renewed understanding of the chasm between spiritual realities and the pious conventions which purport, but fail, to represent the soul. Both characters stand in lonely defiance, stubbornly opposing a code that requires, from one party, passivity and asexuality, and from the other, tyranny and violence. Richardson and Hawthorne use Hester and Clarissa as devices to test the strength and limitations of the social forms in which the characters are embedded—patriarchal forms enforced by Puritan metaphysics. Having shown that the balance and maintenance of the customary world requires a reciprocal relationship of dominant men and submissive women, the authors use their tales to expose the rapacity and inhumanity of unchecked power and to suggest the necessary heroism of any opposition.

The story of *Clarissa* begins with its central character at her most virtuous and passive. Even against such background stasis, however, Richardson uses Clarissa to contest the claims of strong men to righteous authority. These men—Clarissa's father, brother, uncles, and suitors—emerge as mightily bloated, crazed with the conviction that their ability to impose their wills and enforce their wishes guarantees the correctness of their hearts' desires. The women these men command or inspire—Clarissa's sisters, her aunts, her mother and

Mrs. Howe, Mrs. Sinclair and her whoring "daughters"—are complementarily enmeshed, supine, excessively inert. A hierarchical framework meant to mirror God's relationship to mankind sets father above daughter, brother over sister, makes husband master wife, and pimp rule whore. In Richardson's novel, however, such a system reduces flexibility, denies freedom, makes will impossible. Rendering authority synonymous with tyranny, *Clarissa* suggests that divinity disguises dictatorship. Lovelace mourns his sex and class when he begins to realize that, in his need to dominate Clarissa and break her will, he has ossified: "I hate compulsion in all forms; and cannot bear, even to be compelled to be the wretch my choice has made me: So now . . . I am a machine at last, and no free agent."[1]

Hawthorne, too (through his persona as the narrator of *The Scarlet Letter*) seizes on a certain codified rigidity, a brutality focused particularly—if not exclusively—on women as characteristic of masculine authority in Puritan culture. If Lovelace exploits the norms that bound *Clarissa*'s world, the Hawthornes are the moral arbiters of *The Scarlet Letter*; their descendant, the narrator, who represents his "first ancestor" as

a soldier, legislator, judge; he was a ruler in the Church; he had all the Puritanic traits, both good and evil. He was . . . a bitter persecutor; as witness . . . his hard severity towards a [Quaker] woman . . . which will last longer, it is to be feared than any record of his better deeds. . . . His son, too, inherited the persecuting spirit and made himself so conspicuous in the martyrdom of the witches, that their blood may fairly be said to have left a stain upon him.[2]

Led by such self-proclaimed "patriarchs," the Puritans are "a people amongst whom religion and law were almost identical. . . . Meagre, indeed, and cold, was the sympathy that a transgressor might look for, from such bystanders at the scaffold" (chap. 2, p. 40).

The authority described in both novels amounts to little more than a system of legitimized oppression and victimization, degrading to all parties. The excesses of domestic dictatorship are replicated throughout all social institutions and are consistently represented in terms of an encroaching masculinity encountering an incapacitated femininity. A corrective alternative would have to revise the meaning of the terms "masculinity" and "femininity" and rework their relationship to one another and to society in general. Although the developmental strategies of *Clarissa* and *The Scarlet Letter* suggest and support this hypothesis, neither fiction accomplishes this task completely; neither Richardson nor Hawthorne can give up his limpetlike hold on the rock of Christian theology on which the entire social superstructure rests. Nevertheless, the magnitude and appeal of the opposition that their principal women offer to traditional Puritanic mores is suggested by the degree to which both authors shape their characters in the mold of heroic conflict and endeavor.

In the case of Clarissa, heroism bursts from orthodoxy: Clarissa is initially characterized as the epitome of female subordination and submissiveness, particularly praiseworthy because she refuses an opportunity for freedom by renouncing control of her grandfather's estate.[3] Virtue so negatively defined can be safe only in a virtuous world whose desires it can reflect but not compel. In the scheme of the novel, however, the model of Christian virtue is an endangered paradigm; individual integrity is increasingly at odds with social value. In consequence, the maintenance of private honor—defined first as virginity but later encompassing psychic coherence and, indeed, psychic identity—necessitates passive resistance, followed, when that fails, by open rebellion. Not surprisingly, Clarissa, who has been acclaimed for her success in the role of the conventionally good girl, must be "pushed into blaze" and becomes reluctantly "the subject of the public talk." Her worth as a social commodity declines. She suffers. Yet suffering refines what it does not destroy; the fire re-forms its subject. Clarissa metamorphoses from an obedient, predictable child into a "lion-hearted lady," a being whom Lovelace, Belford, and Anna Howe agree to call "heroic" (IV, letter 5, p. 217; V, letter 4, p. 42; VI, letter 96, p. 424).

Two factors precipitate this suffering in Clarissa: her looks and her wealth. The heroic character is, after the beautiful Psyche's example, always physically remarkable. Her status is partly conveyed by her capacity to draw the crowd's attention to her person. Often, as we shall see later, she is remarkably *un*-beautiful and is pitied and scorned for her presumed inability to experience the "joys" of ordinary women. Emphasis on physical attributes is, in either case, a convenient shorthand, an easy way to indicate the character's capacity to provoke ambivalent responses: admiration tinged with resentment; repulsion at odds with fascination. Clarissa belongs to the positive side of the equation, the side of excessive beauty. Similarly, her inheritance and financial status also stand for more than they can directly embody. Her material wealth, her goods, property, and money serve as talismans.[4] The woman who controls money and is capable of living free of subordinate relationships with men is distinguished, in all the fictions we shall be examining, not merely from the generality of her sex but from its very definition. A woman with an income of her own can, potentially at least, evade the psychic reduction which is the price a bourgeois world exacts for economic dependence.[5] And a single woman with money of her own is always potentially heroic because her resources are not committed to the existing social enterprise until she marries and surrenders both her person and her wealth first to a husband and then to a male heir.

In Clarissa's case, her grandfather's will, by providing her with an estate independent of her father's, renders her entire social position immediately anomalous. A younger daughter and an unmarried woman, Clarissa should be outside the line of normal inheritance; her father, her uncles, or her brother are all more suitable heirs than she, and all resent her usurpation of their prerogatives. To be sure, Clarissa tries to deny her independence by ceding control of her estate to her father or his representative. Such a negotiation, however, implies that alternative action is, or might be, possible and thus suggests that vested authority might have had to exert itself to recapture what ought to belong to it by right. Should Clarissa marry and use her property as part of her dowry or marriage portion, the delicate balance of economic power and social authority would be restored. In that case, her grandfather's legacy (or, as Solmes and young John Harlowe suggest, another "equivalent" estate) although nominally remaining in Clarissa's hands, would revert to masculine control. Richardson illuminates the relationship between social power and economic independence by focusing the first two volumes of *Clarissa* on the Harlowe family's efforts to rid themselves of social embarrassment by marrying off Clarissa and depriving her of the only privilege that might be hers in normal circumstances: not the right to choose the man that she will marry, but the choice of refusing to marry someone whom she finds repugnant.

The nature of marriage is not in question. Clarissa describes even her *"best prospects"* as follows:

Marriage is a very solemn engagement . . . : To be given up to a strange man; To be engrafted into a strange family; To give up her very Name, as a mark of her becoming his absolute and dependent property. To be obliged to prefer this strange man to . . . everybody: — And his humours to all her own — Or to contend perhaps, in breach of a vowed duty, for every innocent instance of free-will — To go no-wither; To make acquaintance; To give up acquaintance; To renounce even the strictest friendships perhaps; all at his pleasure, whether she thinks it reasonable to do so or not.

(II, letter 33, p. 223)

Unexpectedly, perhaps, and certainly significantly, this view complements Lovelace's:

I would have the woman whom I honour with my name . . . forego even her *superior duties* for me. I would have her look after me when I go out . . . and meet me at my return with rapture. I would be the subject of her dreams, as well as of her waking thoughts. I would have her think every moment lost, that is not passed with me: Sing

to me, read to me, play to me when I please; no joy so great as in
obeying me . . . Thus of old did the contending wives of the honest
patriarchs.

(IV, letter 41, pp. 264–65)

Rake and heroine agree. Contemplating marriage, each describes an institution which, subsuming the woman's interest
in the man's, guarantees that power and property will con-
verge, by force if necessary, in the ruling figure of the husband. The obsession with marriage in this book, and in
many others where a woman is the principal figure, does not
necessarily indicate an author's narrow preoccupation with the
romantic, the domestic, or even the sexual, although these
elements may play into a larger configuration. Focused on marriage, choice of mate, and intimate sexual and familial relationships, the novel's lens studies social power, exposes autoc-
racy at work in daily life, and illuminates, as well, the dangers
of enforced passivity and of an order that systematically con-
fuses virtue and inertia.[6] In this context, the struggle between
Clarissa and her family over whether or not she will behave
correctly and marry Solmes serves a dual purpose. As her relatives articulate their positions, they define the terms of the system that surrounds Clarissa and provides her with a conventional social and moral identity. They isolate Clarissa and
punish her for her inability to harmonize the demands of social organization with her own requirements for personal happiness, integrity, and authenticity. Clarissa, in response, is
forced to undertake a series of radical actions that shock and
surprise her as much as they do her relatives. She, who begins
the book as her family's pampered, acquiescent darling and
society's example of womanly excellence, is transformed by
ostracism and exile into society's objective, if unwilling,
enemy.

Richardson marks this shift from society's center to its periphery in a variety of ways. Clarissa starts out as a rich young
lady and potential commander of her own independent fortune, house, and land. Although she is the youngest person in

her family and a mere girl at that, it is clear that she is her world's emotional and intellectual center. People turn to her for advice and moral counsel. She is in touch with everyone by letter and by a regular system of visits back and forth. She is loved. As the book progresses, this orderly pattern of communication and affection is destroyed. Her letters go unanswered, as her correspondents are forbidden or refuse to write to her, or as their letters and her own are misdirected. At Harlowe Place she is confined to her room because her family fears that Lovelace will seize her or that she will use any unguarded opportunity to run off with him and put herself in his power rather than theirs. This fear is borne out, but her flight transforms Lovelace from apparent supplicant to overt jailer. Locking Clarissa up in Mrs. Sinclair's back rooms, Lovelace lies to her about the nature of the house and its owner, intercepts and censors her letters and Anna Howe's, and frustrates all Clarissa's attempts to understand her situation or secure her freedom. Ultimately Clarissa escapes, only to be arrested and jailed once again, this time literally. Regarded now as a criminal rather than a paragon, a warning rather than an example, she is "guilty," appropriately, of economic failure: Mrs. Sinclair has her seized by officers—by men, as Clarissa wails—and sent to prison for nonpayment of debts supposedly owed for her earlier whorehouse lodgings. As in Clarissa's family, so in the larger world, women cooperate with and enforce the strategies of men; the relations between Lovelace and Mother Sinclair mirror those between Clarissa's parents, as well as those between Clarissa's brother, James, and his other sister, Arabella.[7] Finally freed from prison, Clarissa withdraws to her smallest, poorest quarters. Her contacts with her former familiar world broken by her terror of revealing her position to Lovelace, she retreats from room to coffin, an abode chosen consciously to mark the boundary between earthly existence and heavenly life and to indicate her desire to leave the one in favor of the other.

Clarissa's progressive isolation is clearly and significantly related to her emerging heroism. If heroes are to act on life or change the world in any way, society's hold must logically be less than total. To exert leverage on communal values requires, as Turner's models of liminality and marginality suggest, an eccentric vantage point. The closer to the center the heroic character's origins, the farther this initial outward journey must be. Although social ostracism alone is no guarantee of heroism, the hero must be tested by isolation, and hero and society must discover in mutual separation what each lacks that the other might provide. Social inclusion at the beginning of a project is, in any event, precarious and largely illusory for women heroes, real or fictional, because such inclusion is ideologically predicated on a rigid separation of the female and the active principles. Consequently, the slightest exertion, the smallest effort to strive, struggle, even think is immediately isolating. The primary difficulty in imagining a woman hero is compensated by the paradoxical ease of rendering her circumstances: a full-scale plot for a female hero can turn on almost any action, or even on the wish for action, precisely because any movement will do when all are forbidden.

In Clarissa's case, trial by isolation is the backbone of a structure that includes a variety of other references to heroic motifs. Most prominent are the numerous more or less direct references to what has been labeled earlier as the monstrous marriage, the marriage of death. Initially, these references to the connection between marriage and death apply to the proposed union between Clarissa and Solmes. Clarissa calls Solmes "a man I never can endure. . . . My eye is . . . disgusted and my reason not convinced— . . . and I am to be wedded to a *monster*—" (I, letter 17, p. 116). In another letter, Clarissa assures Anna Howe that she has already informed Lovelace that "I would sooner chuse death, than Mr. Solmes" (II, letter 18, p. 127). Hardhearted Arabella suggests that her sister's wedding dress ought to match her funereal mood: "As it will be a solemn wedding what think you of *black* Velvet, child?" (I, letter 45, p. 345). Immediately before Clarissa's flight from Harlowe Place she has a dream whose prophetic power transfers the association of marriage and death from Solmes to Lovelace. In this dream, Clarissa's brother, her Uncle Antony, and Mr. Solmes are plotting to destroy Lovelace who, discovering the plot and thinking Clarissa has had a hand in it, scatters her spurious protectors. Then, as she writes to Anna Howe, "afterwards seizing upon me, [he] carried me into a churchyard; and there, notwithstanding all my prayers and tears, and protestations of innocence, stabbed me to the heart, . . . tumbled me into a deep grave . . . throwing in the dirt and earth upon me with his hands, and trampling it down with his feet" (II, letter 39, p. 283).

Clarissa's fear of marriage is neither an infantile rejection of all physical contact nor a snobbish overvaluation of her own self-worth. Solmes, to be sure, both repels and bores Clarissa, but Clarissa's view of him is not challenged by anyone else in the book. As a lover, he is literally monstrous, counterpart of the snake that Psyche's sisters tell her she has married, the being who shames the hero through incongruous relationship. But Lovelace, on the other hand, is erotically fascinating and compelling, as Anna Howe immediately notes and Clarissa herself finally admits. Clarissa is not Richardson's portrait of a prude. The structure of the book suggests, however, that her rejection of both suitors is based on her accurate perception that marriage *is* destructive, because men appeal to its sanctity as a way of disguising their desires to own a wife, to control her, and to confine her permanently in the net of their own wishes. Clarissa's personal superiority—her looks, mind, money, and morality—subverts the claim of the surrounding society for men's intrinsic, unearned, and generic superiority. Unmarried, independent, resistant, Clarissa's very existence violates the norms of female nature and upsets the division between male power and female impotence that supports the entire communal edifice.

Throughout the novel, the play of marriage makes woman's role subordinate. Clarissa's father overwhelms her mother.

Anna Howe's mother, a widow, refuses to marry because on again becoming a wife, she would have to give up the powers and privileges of independent status. It is domination—not sexuality—that Clarissa is truly opposing when she refuses to wed.[8] Lovelace himself is voluble on the subject of his desire to control not just Clarissa but all women as a means of expressing masculine superiority and conquest. For him—and thus for her—sexuality and domination are inseparable. The lover's language is a tyrant's discourse:

Thou [Belford] knowest, that I have more than once, twice, or thrice, put to the fiery Trial young women of Name and Character; and never yet met with one who held out a month; nor indeed so long as could puzzle my invention. I have concluded against the whole sex upon it. And now, if I have not found a Virtue that cannot be corrupted, I will swear that there is not one such in the whole Sex. Is not then the whole Sex concerned that this trial should be made?

(III, letter 14, pp. 91–92)

Is it to be expected, that a *woman of education,* and a *lover of form,* will yield before she is attacked? . . . I doubt not but I shall meet with difficulty. I must therefore make my first effort by surprize. There may possibly be some *cruelty* necessary: But there may be *consent in struggle;* there may be *yielding in resistance.* But the first conflict over, whether the following may not be weaker and weaker, till willingness ensue, is the point to be tried. . . . We begin, when Boys with Birds; and when grown up, go on to women; and both, perhaps, in turn, experience our sportive cruelty.

(IV, letter 4, p. 12)

The institutions in Clarissa's world are homologous; Lovelace's language echoes everywhere. Human relationships can scarcely be expressed except as manifestations of power and hierarchy. Describing Clarissa's early situation, Anna Howe writes:

Do not you observe, how much your Brother's influence has overtopped yours, since he has got into fortunes so considerable; and since you have given some of them an appetite to *continue* in themselves the possession of your Estate, unless you comply with their terms?

I know your dutiful, your laudable motives; and one would have

thought, that you might have trusted to a Father who so dearly loved
you. But had you been actually in possession of that Estate, and living up to it, and upon it . . . do you think that your Brother . . .
would have been practising about it, and aiming at it? . . . You will
be more than woman, if you can extricate yourself with honor, having
such violent spirits and sordid minds in some, and such tyrannical
and despotic wills in others, to deal with. Indeed, all *may* be done,
and the world be taught further to admire you for your blind duty and
willess resignation, if you can persuade yourself to be Mrs. Solmes.

(I, letter 15, pp. 97–98)

Much of Lovelace's fiendishness comes from his conviction
that, by deliberately playing on the convention that demands
Clarissa's obedience, he can compel her complicity with vice
and still remain socially acceptable. Clarissa describes him as
a living contradiction, an emblem of a world where belief has
no necessary relation to behavior, where actions disguise motives one dare not display overtly:

At first, I saw something in your [Lovelace's] Air and Person that
displeased me not. . . . You acted not ignobly . . . Every-body said
you were brave: Everybody said you were generous. A *brave* man, I
thought, could not be a *base* man: A *generous* man could not, I believed, be *ungenerous,* where he acknowledged *obligation.* . . . You
seemed frank, as well as generous: Frankness and Generosity ever at-
tracted me: Whoever kept up those appearances, I judged of their
hearts by my own; and whatever qualities I *wished* to find in them,
I was *ready* to find; and *when* found, I believed them to be natives
of the soil. . . . I honoured Virtue: —I hated Vice: —But I knew
not, that you were Vice itself.

(V, letter 36, pp. 331–32)

Clarissa's heroic quest, then, has three goals: to expose the
incongruities of the present social structure; to realize an alternative system based on a morality independent of conventional ideas about economic, physical, or sexual power; and,
as a necessary corollary, to discover or create a set of particular
social circumstances that will allow her to act as her conscience dictates. Her attack is initially restricted; in a world
where action itself is tainted, Clarissa seeks merely the power
to refrain: "Let me but be permitted to avoid the man I *hate*;

and I will give up with cheerfulness, the man *I could prefer*.
. . . This is a sacrifice which a child owes to parents and
friends" (II, letter 15, p. 100).

Because the existing social structures are interdependent
and threatened by even such minimal petitions, their unyielding rigidity forces Clarissa to adopt ever more extreme measures. The issue throughout the novel is the contradictory relationship between social power enforced by economic and
sexual tyranny and the freedom to enact a personal choice.
Domestic relations merely reflect and enforce prevailing social
norms.[9] As Clarissa observes, in a late letter to Mrs. Norton:

Shall we wonder that Kings and Princes meet with so little control in
their passions, be they ever so violent, when in a private family, an
Aunt, nay, even a Mother in that family, shall chuse to give up a once
favoured child against their own inclinations, rather than oppose an
aspiring young man, who had armed himself with the authority of a
Father, who, when once determined, never would be expostulated
with?

(VII, letter 64, pp. 244–45)

Neither within the family nor outside it, are women strong
enough to protect themselves or other women against masculine incursions. No woman has the right combination of command and compassion to exert herself effectively in Clarissa's
favor: Anna Howe, Clarissa's most vigorous and assertive sup-
porter, is kept from action by her youth and her position as
an unmarried daughter in her mother's house; Clarissa's maid,
Hannah, becomes ill after she is discharged from service; Mrs.
Howe, for most of the novel, stands on the side of patriarchal
authority over daughters' fates and against Clarissa's violation
of its codes; Mrs. Norton must stay at home nursing a sick
son; Mother Sinclair and her infamous progeny are merely the
last of a long line of powerless or co-opted women. Friendship
among men—male bonding, if you will—is a contrasting expression of socially licensed sexual self-interest; its participants,
concerned only with preserving power, recognize only their allegiance to each other. " 'You gentlemen,' " Clarissa remarks to

Belford, "had rather see an innocent fellow-creature ruined, than be thought capable of an action, which, however generous, might be likely to loosen the bands of a wicked friendship' " (I, letter 8, p. 49).

For all its power as a social indictment, Richardson's novel is no revolutionary text. Its plot, instead, contrives to "save" Clarissa by containing her rebellion within terms that her society professes still to honor (however much, in practice, it violates these norms). At the book's beginning, Clarissa declares her bewilderment at her family's insularity and the selfishness of each individual's behavior within a unit that has come increasingly to define its collective interests against those of any larger entity or moral schema. "In my opinion," she observes to Anna Howe, "the World is but one great family. Originally it was so. What then is this narrow selfishness that reigns in us, but relationship remembered against relationship forgot?" (I, letter 8, p. 49).

The relationship remembered by Clarissa is, of course, the traditional connectedness or communitas of Christianity: the spiritual, moral, and emotional network that joins—or ought to join—people as a result of their primary relationship to God. Clarissa's character, as has often been noted, is created and maintained within a dense web of Christian references. Her personal qualities having often been associated with heaven and angels, in the end she is referred to as a dying saint[10]; a balancing cluster of references associates Lovelace and his entourage, their plots and machinations, with Hell and the devil. (See, for example: I, letter 10, p. 63; III, letter 61, p. 339; VII, letter 92, p. 392; V, letter 36, p. 332.) Richardson solves the dilemma posed by Clarissa's deviance from prevailing definitions of femininity and social standards not by postulating an alternative sexual or social vision, but rather by appealing nostalgically to Christian possibility. The threat that Clarissa's struggles present to the social community is contained and given meaning by the overarching ethical and metaphysical framework that Christianity, specifically Puritanism, seems to provide.[11]

Richardson uses this unworldly moral framework to redeem Clarissa after Lovelace rapes her, just as he uses the rape itself to suggest the extreme logical consequence of a man's implacable pursuit faced with a woman's equally obdurate refusal to yield or compromise. Rape is the final rite marking Clarissa's initiation into the possibility of evil. No longer a virgin, no longer innocent, she is irretrievably outcast. Unclassed, dishonored, and disgraced, she no longer has any place within the social structure. Having been abandoned and cursed by her earthly father, deprived of her own estate and her childhood home, Clarissa might—in another book—have remained a solitary traveler wandering into ever more uncharted and desolate spaces, seeking disciples as a guard against loneliness and a sign of progress. Richardson's deployment of the Christian moral framework saves Clarissa from this narrative possibility. Communitas is not found on earth; the realities of earthly life render such an ideal impossible to achieve. Richardson accordingly turns Clarissa toward God and makes her seek a final resting place in one of her heavenly Father's many prefabricated mansions.

The rape awkwardly divides the world of the book as it calamitously shatters Clarissa's life. Up to this point, Clarissa has survived as a social being, wishing primarily for the social integration she could effect were she able to continue to live at home, unmarried and at peace with her family. Her relatives' attitudes and actions bewilder her precisely because they seem unconventional, unsuitable, and unwarranted. Clarissa tells Arabella:

I will claim the protection due to a child of the family, or . . . know why I am to be thus treated, when I offer only to preserve to myself the liberty of *refusal*, which belongs to my Sex; and, to please my Parents, would give up my *choice*. . . . You are but my Sister: My Brother is not my Sovereign. And while I have a Father and Mother living, I will not be thus treated by a Brother and Sister, and their servants. . . . I will know, in short . . . whether I am to be considered as a *child* or a *slave*?

(I, letter 43, p. 332)

She responds to her family's initial pressures and confinements with an attempt to maintain her daily habits because "people in adversity . . . should endeavor to preserve laudable customs, that if Sunshine return, they may not be losers by their trial" (II, letter 24, pp. 158–59). Reluctant to leave her father's house, she does finally flee because, outflanked on every side, she is yet too proud to surrender.

After the rape, when we, along with Lovelace, might expect Clarissa to be most powerless because she is socially most vulnerable, Richardson empowers her, allows her to assert herself, grants her final control over her destiny. From a creature pitifully convinced of her own impotence or wickedness, she is transformed into a defiant being capable of telling Lovelace: " 'I am not now in your power: That consideration will comfort me for all' " (V, letter 18, p. 117); and " 'Compulsion shall do nothing with me. Tho' a slave, a prisoner, in circumstance, I am no slave in my will: —Nothing will I promise thee—With-held, compelled—Nothing will I promise thee—' " (VI, letter 6, p. 27). Now it is Lovelace's turn to respond to an implacable intransigence, to realize that feelings, beliefs, and convictions have lives of their own and that these subterranean states have as much reality as physical circumstances. Belford hears Lovelace confess that he never knew "what fear . . . was . . . till I became acquainted with Miss Clarissa Harlowe; nay, what is *most* surprising, till I came to have her in my power" (VI, letter 19, p. 85). Lovelace's surrender indicates a more general turning in the structure of the book: moral authority, personified by Clarissa, has conquered and replaced Lovelace's physical, sexual, and social power.

The terms of this triumph have great significance for understanding how female heroism can be represented in fictions that work within a patriarchal metaphysical, as well as social, context. Clarissa's victory turns upon her transformation from erring woman into Christian saint. But this transformation ironically depends upon the substitution of one system of patriarchal authority for another, and upon Clarissa's death. The pattern of Clarissa's heroism is completed by theologizing the plot and thereby shifting the arena of significant activity from this world to the next. Clarissa's early fear of Solmes as a monster and of Lovelace as a murderer gives way to a positive longing for death as a relief from the chains and oppressions of this world:

> When Honour's lost, 'tis a relief to die:
> Death's but a sure retreat from infamy.
>
> (V, letter 36, p. 333)

Heroic plots typically include a transitional time, a time of withdrawal from the world, a time to contemplate eternity directly. At the end of this time, there are several narrative options available. The hero may return with renewed vigor — as Moses did when he came from Sinai with the Ten Commandments—determined and able to make the final effort in favor of a new community. Or, on the contrary, the hero may abandon the old society completely and, like Huck Finn, light out for some new territory which may prove more amenable to the heroic vision. Alternatively, the hero, frightened by the cold and windy spaces of eternity, can simply give up all claims to heroism and return to the old society, compromised but accommodated; comic plots involving potentially heroic women often turn, as we shall see in the next chapter, on such a transformation. In many instances, however, the hero dies and accomplishes through death what could not be accomplished in life; that is, death, which removes the direct affront the living hero offers to society, also frees society to honor, if only in principle, certain of the hero's claims: Christ is Western culture's prototype for this version of the hero. Although Richardson intends Clarissa as an example of the Christ-like hero, the terms of such heroism, far from freeing Clarissa, are part of the system which has trapped her. Christian heroism, for a woman bound by patriarchy, constitutes little more than rationalized suicide. Martyrs and heroes are both defined by death, but heroes must return from the underworld to teach and change society, to transform the world with knowledge and revelation. Clarissa's heroism, however, is limited by the doubling back at the end of the book to the unresolved motif of the deathly marriage, by Clarissa's deliberate courtship of death. Richardson is unable to use morality to aid a new incarnation of social possibility.

On leaving Harlowe Place, Clarissa's life in London becomes a kind of limbo, where she undergoes a liminal period of death-in-life, a "gradual . . . weaning-time from the world . . . that . . . in a manner annihilates all other considerations and concerns" (VII, letter 82, p. 340). The familiarity of this image does not negate its significance; it is, indeed, characteristic of women heroes to see themselves—or to be seen—as not receiving nourishment at the world's breast. The deficiencies of patriarchal culture are contained by means of this implied metaphor in a larger system of negation, denial, and withdrawal: the world, imaged as a lactating woman, withholds nourishment from her children—in these cases, specifically her daughters. The natural process of weaning is perverted; its effect in this particular usage is to suggest the complicity of mother earth in the excesses of masculine society. The daughters of earth have enormous difficulty breaking this linkage, circumventing male social authority by an appeal to either a female community or a transcendent female force. Instead, they transcend only by capitulating, as Clarissa gives herself over to God, to death, to heaven.

By weaning Clarissa away from the world's maternal breast and making death benign rather than threatening, Richardson replaces the hostile tyranny of earthly life with heaven's supportive love. In so doing, Clarissa's threat to social patriarchy is negated by her support of the great metaphysical fatherhood of God. The process is intended not to deny but rather to enhance the qualities that made Clarissa heroic in the first place. Her intelligence, her will, her inner core of being remain intact throughout the novel and survive its end. Clarissa tests qualities that the society inside the novel (as well, perhaps, as Richardson himself) preferred not to contemplate in their logical extremes. Clarissa's fidelity to the dictates of her conscience and her refusal to sacrifice her inner feelings for the sake of social expediency or economic gain are undeniable (and never, in the particular context provided by the novel, less than admirable). Yet these same qualities conflict powerfully with social and economic imperatives to which Clarissa's relatives respond as representatives—although extreme ones—of their time, place, and class. Not as virtuous or admirable as Clarissa, her family, nevertheless, is never entirely dismissed, and the legitimacy of its claims to some measure of controlling authority is never breached. Richardson solves his narrative and emotional dilemma by supporting Clarissa's claims to heroic status at the same time as he makes the framework which ultimately surrounds her religious rather than social. Thus, Clarissa's personal heroism is abstracted and enlisted, finally, in aid of a socially regressive, deified patriarchy. The Christian community that Clarissa remembers and endorses cannot, apparently, be established in this world—her memory is powerless even to prevent her cousin Morden from murdering Lovelace and continuing the cycle of blood and power. Although the heroic manner of Clarissa's life and death alters individual lives and feelings, it does not provoke social or structural reform.

The force of Clarissa's heroic nature is blunted, and the heroic pattern of her story limited, by Richardson's apparent inability or unwillingness to use his character to challenge the fundamental precepts of the society he has created. Clarissa's status is used in the end to support the structure of male power and female submission that her initial circumstances and attitude seemed to undermine. If Mr. Harlowe is a bad father, God is a good one; this fact both sanctions and restricts Clarissa's heroism, because as long as the good father is presumed to exist somewhere, Clarissa presents no ultimate challenge to the claims of masculine authority.

Like Clarissa Harlowe, Hester Prynne initially opposes Puritanism's strict and patriarchal codes. Her story, like Clarissa's, demonstrates that strong-willed and independent women inevitably violate the rules and traditions of a patriarchal order and reveals the psychological and social ambivalence surrounding such violation.

In the case of *Clarissa,* the author's ambivalence may be inferred from the overall construction of his narrative. By embedding Clarissa in a cast of characters that ranges from the ineffectual to the monstrous, Richardson seems to be endorsing Clarissa's behavior as both necessary and correct within the circumstances. Yet the extraordinary hostility and venality of these characters and circumstances, in conjunction with Clarissa's extraordinary scruples and her reservations about her own actions, suggest the limits of Richardson's sympathy for this unusual behavior. Had her parents and relatives been either reasonable or compassionate, had her friends been more protective, then Clarissa might well have been able to spend her life in voluntary obedience to their desires. As Clarissa repeatedly tells Anna Howe, only her extreme isolation, the entire absence of any external prop or protection, justifies the course she enters into on her own behalf. In ordinary circumstances, such as Anna's, society's expectations for obedience are still justified and ought to prevail.

Although the relationship of tale to teller is more direct in *The Scarlet Letter,* the attitude conveyed by this relationship is no less ambivalent. In choosing to tell Hester's tale and in the manner of his revelations, the novel's narrator reveals the insecurities of his own position. The heir of those soldiers, legislators, and judges who made up the top level of the old Puritan hierarchy, the narrator has grave reservations about their narrow sympathies and harsh judgments: "I know not whether these ancestors of mine bethought themselves to re-pent, and ask pardon of Heaven for their cruelties; or whether they are now groaning under the heavy consequences of them, in another state of being. At all events, I, the present writer, as their representative, hereby take shame upon myself for their sakes, and pray that any curse incurred by them . . . may be now and henceforth removed" ("The Custom-House," p. 11). So *The Scarlet Letter* is offered by the narrator to expiate the sins of his fathers and atone for their guilt—this despite the fact that he believes his forebears would understand neither the necessity for restitution nor the method and manner of his offering. As an artist, the narrator is caught between his sense that those "stern and black-browed Puritans" would have seen their descendant as "an idler . . . worthless, if not positively disgraceful," and his apprehension that, nevertheless, "strong traits of their nature have intertwined themselves" with his ("The Custom-House," p. 12). This divided legacy, he feels, has alienated him from his art. A participant in the culture's materialism, he wonders if he hasn't bartered his imagination "for a pittance of the public gold" ("The Custom-House," p. 30).

Because *The Scarlet Letter*'s revelation of Hester's character and social position consistently reflects back on the narrator's view of his own nature and surrounding circumstances, the book illuminates Hawthorne's perception of the limited function and precarious social position of the creator—the visionary, the person of imagination—within American society. Hester, too, is an artist and pariah. She does not merely wear the scarlet *A*, she flaunts it and her adultery, by embroidering the letter and making Pearl conspicuous. The narrator's account of the Puritan governors as primitive, limited, "not often brilliant," and "distinguished by a ponderous sobriety rather than activity of intellect" (chap. 22, pp. 168–69) is contrasted and balanced by his view of Hester's radiance, elegance, and "mind of native courage and activity" (chap. 18, p. 143). Finding Hester in a wilderness freed of social rules, customs, and conventions, the narrator calls her a creature whose "fate and fortunes had . . . set her free" (chap. 18, p. 143). Hester sins, but is creative; the Puritan fathers are sterile in their purity. Still, the claims of Puritan moral codes cannot be evaded here, any more than in *Clarissa*. Puritanism's inheritor, as well as its antagonist, the narrator uses his tale of Hester Prynne to embody and enact a blend of the admired and the forbidden. If Hester is the artist behind the scarlet letter, the narrator is the artist behind *The Scarlet Letter*. The complicated and unresolved forces focused on Hester suggest, first, that it is psychologically possible for a male, whether artist or not, to distance himself from heroic commitment to living change by expressing certain types of heroism through the vehicle of female character or image. Second, this distancing reveals the limits implicitly imposed on such heroism by virtue of its apparently "feminine" qualities. Simultaneously Hester's accomplice, her judge, and her defender, Hawthorne's narrator particularizes society's generally doubtful attitude toward heroism by rendering society as patriarchal and the hero as a woman.

Hester's power enthralls the narrator because he sees that exercising it requires that "the whole system of society . . . be torn down, and built up anew. Then, the very nature of the opposite sex, or its long hereditary habit, which has become like nature, is to be essentially modified, before woman can be allowed to assume what seems a fair and suitable position" (chap. 13, p. 120). The "opposite sex" in *The Scarlet Letter* is principally represented through Hester's husband, Roger Chillingworth, and her lover, the minister Arthur Dimmesdale. Chillingworth, like Lovelace and his rakish cronies in *Clarissa,* embodies the worst excesses of patriarchal power and authority: its ultimately asexual tendency toward tyranny and self-aggrandizement. Again like Lovelace, Chillingworth enacts the part of the monstrous lover, the deadly male analogous to the life-threatening woman often encountered by male heroes. Dimmesdale, on the other hand, is described as weak and "feeble" (chap. 12, p. 108); Pearl accuses him of being neither bold nor true; Hester observes that the minister's "nerve seemed absolutely destroyed" and his "moral force was abased into more than childish weakness" (chap. 13, p. 115). When Hester offers Dimmesdale the opportunity to escape, his strength suffers further decline: " 'Thou tellest of running a race to a man whose knees are tottering beneath him! I must die here' " (chap. 17, p. 142). Refusing to acknowledge his own sexual experience, Dimmesdale cannot grow through it as Hester does, but remains stuck in a kind of perpetual adolescence, crippled by shame, made impotent by his own—and his community's—hypocrisy. The divergence between his moral opinions and his behavior renders his actions either trivial or evasive. His goodness has no independent status but exists merely as a formal necessity to balance Chillingworth's evil. In narrative terms, the elderly husband and the youthful clergyman are two halves of a single defective being; one's death necessitates the other's. Yet if Dimmesdale and Chillingworth convey between them the total context of relationships open to a character like Hester, it is little wonder that Hawthorne has such difficulty imagining a social or sexual reality able to contain her.

It is easier to understand the pattern of relationships among Hester, Dimmesdale, and Chillingworth if we see this triad of two men and a woman as mirroring the more usual configuration of a man and two women. In cases where the heroic or potentially heroic figure is male, he is typically flanked by two women, one good, one bad. The bad woman is dark, seductive, and sexually expressive; the good one blonde, chaste, and vapid. This structural division into good and bad survives the shift in the hero's sex, but Hawthorne uses this structure to associate *both* the vicious and the virtuous figure with sexual denial enforced by an authority symbolized as male.

Although Hester ultimately finds a moment of freedom and release in the forest and longs to found a life there, on Chillingworth's first appearance in the book he has been "redeemed" out of his "captivity" in this same wilderness (chap.

3, p. 48); he despises it and rejects anything the forest might have taught him about human capacities for joy or pleasure. In emotional terms, Dimmesdale is redeemed by Hester, in the forest, not by his confession on the scaffold. Deciding at last (although temporarily) to depart from Boston, the minister exults:

The decision . . . made a glow of . . . enjoyment throw its . . . brightness over the trouble of his breast. It was the exhilarating effect . . . of breathing the wild, free atmosphere. . . . His spirit rose . . . with a bound, and attained a nearer prospect of the sky, than throughout all the misery which had kept him grovelling on the earth. . . . "Do I feel joy again? . . . O Hester, thou art my better angel! I seem to have flung myself—sick, sin-stained, and sorrow-blackened—down upon these forest leaves, and to have risen up all made anew, and with new powers to glorify Him that hath been merciful. This is already the better life!"

(Chap. 18, pp. 144–45)

This single passionate utterance reveals the heart of the relationship between Hester and Dimmesdale. If he is to be fully alive, he must follow her. Reciprocally, Hester needs Dimmesdale, because opposition to society becomes significant only when it is no longer solitary. Since society's illness is associated, as it was in *Clarissa*, specifically with customs enforced by men and labelled patriarchal, the opposing figure logically must be a woman. This construction in turn suggests that the conventionally pious, repressed, and passive role typically played by a woman must here be taken by a male, as must the countering, sinister role. If Hester Prynne is the hero of *The Scarlet Letter*, Chillingworth is the dark lady and Arthur Dimmesdale is the heroine.

Hawthorne's fiction, like Richardson's, represents the opposition between antisexual authority and psychological and sexual autonomy in a clash between subordinated male figures and a heroic female character. Richardson plays out Clarissa's heroism by shifting the narrative field from the earth to the heavens. Hawthorne does not allow Hester such transcendence or escape. Dimmesdale follows Clarissa in renouncing the claims of the material world, while Hester remains in Boston. Where Clarissa's actions, socially futile, must be read against a celestial reevaluation of the meaning of all earthly connections, the success of Hester's position depends on a redefinition of social relationships.

Hawthorne's narrator reveals the boundaries of his own vision by withholding a full measure of approval from the most radical effects of Hester's inspiration. Even in his account of Dimmesdale's rejuvenation at the prospect of a future life with Hester, the narrator refers to Dimmesdale's escape into an "unredeemed, unchristianized, lawless region" (chap. 18, p. 144). However attractive this place is in some ways, the language used to describe it here suggests why its appeal is ultimately denied. Unable to flee society, Hester is forced back upon it. The terms of society's punishment can be altered only by society; its understanding of the meaning of Hester's acts can grow only from within.

At the beginning of *The Scarlet Letter,* Hester is Turner's quintessentially marginal being, an outsider camped on society's threshold. At a distance from a society that nonetheless continues to define her, Hester occupies "a small vacant area—a sort of magic circle . . . into which . . . none ventured, or felt disposed to intrude." This "magic circle" is a "forcible type of the moral solitude in which the scarlet letter enveloped its fated wearer" (chap. 21, p. 166). Reborn into this numinous space, Hester's objective task is to define her new identity in a way that will force society to stretch itself in order to accommodate her in a visibly altered relationship:

It was as if a new birth, with stronger assimilations than the first had converted the forest-land, still so uncongenial to every other pilgrim and wanderer into Hester Prynne's wild and dreary, but life-long home. . . . As is apt to be the case when a person stands out in any prominence before the community, and, at the same time, interferes neither with public nor individual interests and convenience, a species of general regard had ultimately grown up in reference to Hester Prynne. . . . She was self-ordained a Sister of Mercy . . . The letter was the symbol of her calling.

(Chaps. 5 and 13, pp. 60, 116–17)

Hester is driven to the fringes of society because the Puritan community, priding itself on its goodness, wishes to exclude the sinner from its midst. But society, Puritan no less than others, is full of sinners, suffering and uneasy. Hester's knowledge of her own ambiguous position refines her awareness of this general condition and lets her sympathize with the pain of the afflicted. Society and Hester are thus bound together, the needs and incapacities of neither being expressible within Puritanism's strict and prohibitive codes.

Hester's circumstances, as well as those of Puritan Boston, are bracketed by unacceptable alternatives. The Old World, with its richness, robustness, physical sensuality and splendor has been rejected as decadent; and the new community has been established on the borders of a gigantic wilderness, equally dangerous and repellent. Hester cannot escape her situation, in large measure because the narrator clings to the Puritan community as the only viable New World model of human association. When Pearl finally escapes, she does not set out for a new frontier but rather returns to Europe, and even this maneuver is conditional upon her earlier acceptance into her parents' society. For the narrator and, therefore, for Pearl, Hester and Dimmesdale's natural relationship must finally be bounded by social norms. Community reigns, but not communitas.

In rejecting the Old World, the Puritans limit themselves by their own moral scruples. However necessary, even virtuous, their original vision, the narrative shows the result of their self-limitation to be dulling and depressing. Human activity is coldly regulated, rather than impelled by spontaneous feelings. Interpretation of these actions, like their generation, is governed by external and abstract canons, not weighed against an internal balance of emotional or physical pleasure. The sensuous, the emotional, the spontaneous are all distrusted because they threaten the pilgrims' strict standards and formal rules. The narrator sees the town beadle as the one who "prefigured and represented . . . the whole dismal severity of the

Puritanic code of law" (chap. 2, p. 42), and observes that the community owes "its origin and progress, and its present state of development, not to the impulses of youth, but to the stern and tempered energies of manhood, and the sombre sagacity of age; accomplishing so much, precisely because it imagined and hoped so little. The . . . forms of authority were felt to possess the sacredness of divine institutions" (chap. 3, p. 50).

In this minimal world of aging manhood where the predominant colors are black and white, gray and brown, Hester's flamboyance signifies her threat. She menaces because she enthralls: beautiful, in a society that inhibits and devalues beauty, she is bold when authority calls for submission, passionate in a world that distrusts such passion as it can remember, and female in a hierarchy that places men on top. Furthermore, Hester refuses to recant. Although compliant with society's punishment of her actions, she holds fast to her own private assessment of her motives and their meaning. " 'What we did,' " she tells Dimmesdale, in one of the book's most memorable lines, " 'had a consecration of its own' " (chap. 17, p. 142). Most significantly, she expands the space of the book by considering alternatives to Boston, worlds within the wilderness, waiting to be formed:

Whither leads yonder forest-trace: Backward to the settlement . . . !
Yes; but onward, too! Deeper it goes . . . into the wilderness. . . .
There thou art free! So brief a journey would bring thee from a world where thou has been most wretched, to one where thou mayest still be happy!

(Chap. 17, p. 142)

But Dimmesdale cannot leave; and without him, neither can Hester. Like a Moses who can see the Promised Land but never enter it, Hester cannot realize her vision. The reasons for this failure are at least partly historical. Hawthorne is, after all, discovering the origins of what he saw as the materialistic and emotionally stunted world of nineteenth-century New England in seventeenth-century Puritan culture. The truth of this judgment depends on Hester's failure either to

start a new society or even to alter the old one very much.[12]
More interestingly, however, Hawthorne's treatment of Hester
within *The Scarlet Letter* suggests *why* the historical circumstances developed as they did—why it was, in fact, necessary
that Hester's heroism fail.

Hester is heroic in the name of love, connectedness, responsiveness to emotion. She stands (as I suggest all heroic figures
do) for freedom in human relationships—a morality, enacted
first in the hero's life, which strikes out against the narrow-
ness of the old, in this case Puritan, society. Hester is most
herself standing with hair loosed in the sunshine of a forest
clearing, urging Dimmesdale away from "all these iron men
and their opinions" (chap. 17, p. 142). To the existing social
world, this heroic stance is part of Hester's sinfulness, the
inner substance of her adultery. This conflict between society's
attitude and the hero's vision is an inherent part of all heroic
narratives; a measure of suspicion is built into all assessments
of the hero. For such a character to succeed in establishing
a new vision in place of the old reality, this mistrust must be,
if not entirely abandoned, at least overbalanced by the creator's or society's eventual endorsement of the hero's postures
and activities; the sense of need must be so great that the pull
of security is overcome.

In the case of Clarissa, Richardson claims Clarissa's life in
exchange for his contingent approval of her behavior. Hawthorne, too—or at least his narrator—shares the Puritans'
ambivalence in judging the status of his central character. If
it seems that Hester's capacity to commit herself to Dimmesdale and to love is both educational and redemptive, it is
equally certain, the narrator asserts, that Hester has learned
many things which are not true. Not always a creature of the
sunlight, of consciousness combined with sentience, Hester is
described as having replaced puritanical gloom with another
kind of darkness:

She had wandered, without rule or guidance, in a moral wilderness;
as vast, as intricate and shadowy, as the untamed forest. . . . Her

intellect and heart had their home . . . in desert places, where she roamed as freely as the wild Indian in his woods. For years past she had looked from this estranged point of view at human institutions, and whatever priests or legislators had established; criticizing . . . the judicial robe, the pillory, the gallows, the fireside, or the church. The tendency of her fate and fortunes had been to set her free. The scarlet letter was her passport into regions where other women dared not tread. Shame, Despair, Solitude! These had been her teachers, — stern and wild ones, — and they had made her strong, but taught her much amiss.

(Chap. 18, p. 143)

The book is vague, if suggestive, in describing Hester's error. Her greatest mistake seems to be her belief that she will be empowered by decamping from the Puritan settlement. In offering her love to Dimmesdale, she turns "the wood's heart of mystery" into "a mystery of joy" (chap. 18, p. 146). Banishing shame and anguish, she pledges a love which "must always create a sunshine, filling the heart so full of radiance, that it overflows upon the outward world" (chap. 18, p. 146). Perhaps. But in the "outward world" of the book, in Boston, that is, we see Hester's love as functioning and productive not because it is based on joy, free union, and affiliation but rather because it is grounded in oppression, despair, and suffering. It is her very victimization that gives Hester insight and liberty—insight into sinful and suffering humanity, inner freedom within an outer ring of socially mandated constraint. Hester's heroism is in large part gauged by her willing acceptance of social burdens:

Hester . . . was quick to acknowledge her sisterhood with the race of man, whenever benefits were to be conferred. None so ready as she to give of her little substance to every demand of poverty. . . . None so self-devoted . . . when pestilence stalked through the town. In all seasons of calamity . . . the outcast of society . . . found her place. She came . . . as a rightful inmate, into the household that was darkened by trouble.

(Chap. 13, pp. 116–17)

Hawthorne thus divides Hester's character, splitting it between the revolutionary and the ameliorative, between the sensual hero and the domestic heroine. In the forest, Hester seeks and briefly finds freedom and a place that endorses her desires; stepping outside society, she claims satisfaction for herself and Dimmesdale. In the town she is reduced, subdued, a caretaker who depends, by definition, upon a sinful, suffering society. In Boston "it was only the darkened house that could contain her. When sunshine came again, she was not there" (chap. 13, p. 117). But it is the care-taking Hester whom the narrator supports, denying, if not the attractions of freedom and happiness, then certainly the possibility that they can exert a social claim equivalent to that of Puritan order.

The division within Hester is mirrored by divisions within Hester's child, Pearl, and between Pearl and the surrounding community. Like Psyche's Pleasure, Hester's child is a daughter; and, like her antecedent, Pearl seems to personify life, energy, and joy devolving down the line begun by a female hero. She expresses a power that validates the heroic enterprise of her mother's life, incorporating the fiery passion and responsiveness that joined her parents in producing her. Hester's offspring, Pearl conveys the possibilities of Hester's self. She is called "lovely," (chap. 6, p. 66), a "creature that had nothing in common with a bygone and buried generation, nor owned herself akin to it" (chap. 10, p. 98). Marked by a "never-failing vivacity of spirits," she "had not the disease of sadness, which almost all children, in these latter days, inherit . . . from the troubles of their ancestors" (chap. 16, p. 133). Despite these attractions, the narrator regards Pearl's state as deficient. However beautiful and brilliant she may be, she is tainted by the same ambiguity that divides his view of Hester's character. The elements of her nature are "all in disorder" because they lack "reference and adaptation to the world into which she was born" (chap. 6, p. 67). This lovely child is seen as an "imp of evil, emblem and product of sin." Pearl and Hester stand together "in the same circle of seclusion from human society" (chap. 6, p. 70).

As the Puritan children reject Pearl, she rejects them. She plays at inventing a new society, but she can invent only Pilgrim fantasies and, in revulsion, smashes and destroys her creations: "the pine-trees, aged, black, and solemn . . . needed little transformation to figure as Puritan elders; the ugliest weeds of the garden were their children, whom Pearl smote down and uprooted, most unmercifully" (chap. 6, p. 70). Like Hawthorne's narrator, Pearl is alienated from the social products of her imagination and, like Hester, she seeks respite from her troubles in nature. The forest becomes "the playmate of the lonely infant," putting on "the kindest of its moods to welcome her" (chap. 18, p. 146). Small birds, a squirrel, a fox acknowledge her right to be among them. Even a wolf is reputed to have "offered his savage head to be patted by her hand" (chap. 18, p. 147). Here again, as in *Clarissa*, this nature and its promised nurture are inadequate. In Richardson's fiction, nature starves the weanling; in Hawthorne's tale, the popular imagination has erased the older egalitarian order of this alternative domain, which includes the human and much more within its territory. It has been endowed with negative power, a realm subservient to the devil and the Black Man, powerful beings who turn women into witches and who compete with God without challenging the coercive bases of patriarchal authority. As in *Clarissa*, as in *Jane Eyre* and *The Awakening*, as in so many fictions treating women heroes, mother earth cannot nourish her daughter. Anarchic rather than free, the forest's sunshine becomes the fires of Hell.

Pearl, the creature most at home in this alien terrain, is socially defined as necessarily inhuman, as either imp or animal. And, according to the narrator, Pearl needs what Hester needs to establish a living connection between herself and a specifically social and human kind: not happiness, but rather the experience of sorrow. "She wanted . . . a grief that should deeply touch her, and thus humanize and make her capable of sympathy" (chap. 16, p. 133). Pearl's kiss, granted to Dimmesdale on the scaffold after having been withheld from him in the forest's clearing, indicates that she, too, has participated in the general scene of sorrow and entrapment that precedes and precipitates Dimmesdale's theological salvation and his death.

Pearl, like her mother, is both humanized and diminished by her suffering. Forcing Hester and Dimmesdale back to the Puritan community, Pearl gains a human father in exchange for a reaffirmed submission to his laws and God's. It is true that Pearl, unlike her parents, may not have to live and die in Boston. Still, her flight displays no forward motion, but is rather a journey backward, a return to an old, already rejected world. It is possible that in Europe Pearl can live richly and at peace with herself and her surroundings, but the wild energy, the uncanny insightfulness, the singular perceptions that characterize her early life all seem to vanish with her transformation from outcast to aristocrat. Yet since her future is surmised and hypothesized, rather than concretely rendered, alternatives are still possible. The narrator provides the terms. Either "the elf-child had gone . . . untimely to a maiden grave; or . . . her wild, rich nature had been softened and subdued, and made capable of a woman's gentle happiness" (chap. 24, p. 185).

Die as a hero; or live as a woman. The choice is dramatic, radical, and final. Hawthorne concludes *The Scarlet Letter* with the narrator's assurance of his and Hester's firm belief that, "at some brighter period, when the world should have grown ripe for it, in Heaven's own time, a new truth would be revealed in order to establish the whole relation between man and woman on a surer ground of mutual happiness. . . . The angel and apostle of the coming revelation must be a woman . . . lofty, pure, and beautiful; and wise, moreover, not through dusky grief, but the ethereal medium of joy; and showing how sacred love should make us happy, by the truest test of a life successful to such an end!" (chap. 24, p. 186).

Hawthorne may believe in the possibility of such happiness and even in the eventuality of such a future, but, like Richardson, he can neither incarnate nor release this vision. Both authors represent heroism as antithetical to social stability, as appropriately female in a world where authority rests with the male. The conflict between an individual's claim to autonomous control of self and sexuality against society's claim that such assertion violates not just social custom but metaphysical imperatives is left unresolved in both texts. Although Clarissa Harlowe and Hester Prynne follow heroic patterns as they express their defiance of patriarchal norms, both are contained by plots which resist social reform. Clarissa's heroism is partially fulfilled by the absorption of earthly rebellion into a heavenly schema. Her trouble is not finally predicated on patriarchy as a system, but originates in the corruption of an ideal in a series of bad earthly fathers. Hawthorne, whose doubts about even cosmic patriarchy are overtly and self-consciously expressed by his narrator, cannot allow Hester even such a restricted triumph as Clarissa's. Hester gains a measure of social influence, but only by accepting her status as a sinful woman; the comfort she bestows resigns people to society, rather than inciting them to permanent rebellion. Neither Hester nor her daughter becomes the central point of a new birth growing from joyful self-expression instead of gloomy self-restraint. Without such correspondence between metaphysical and social centrality, the characters' heroic possibilities remain in some sense undeveloped and unfulfilled.

Chapter 3

Heroes into Heroines

The Limits of Comedy in *Emma, Jane Eyre,* and *Middlemarch*

> ℰ *Solomon says "there is nothing new under the sun" for which reason I will not marry, for I don't want to be tied to this nasty world, and old maids are of so little consequence. . . . —It is a happy thing to be a mere blank, and to be able to pursue one's own whims, where they lead, without having a husband and half a hundred Children at hand to teaze and controul a poor woman who wishes to be free.—Some may follow St. Paul's advice "in doing well," but I, like a true born Englishwoman, will endeavour to do better.*
>
> Mary Wollstonecraft, Letter to Jane Arden c. 1782

Comedy mediates between once upon a time and happily ever after. Its stories tell how the weak repel the strong, how the poor dispossess the rich. Showing the isolated and the orphaned gaining access to community, comedy reveals society's capacity to be transformed by love and virtue. Its structure makes revolution needless, suggesting instead that tyranny declines naturally with age and that elderly oppressors are inevitably supplanted by more youthful, humble, and humane authorities. Its rhythm is a dance, not a dirge. Its season is spring. Its heroes are young people, Turner's liminars, crossing the threshold that separates irresponsible childhood from a more powerful, if burdensome, maturity.

Northrop Frye outlines comedy as follows:

What normally happens is that a young man wants a young woman, that his desire is resisted by some opposition, usually paternal, and that near the end . . . some twist in the plot enables the hero to have his will. . . . The movement of comedy is usually a movement from one kind of society to another. At the beginning . . . the obstructing characters are in charge of the . . . society, and the audience recognizes that they are usurpers. At the end . . . the device in the plot that brings hero and heroine together causes a new society to crystallize around the hero, and the moment when this crystallization occurs is the point of resolution in the action. . . .

The appearance of this new society is frequently signalized by some kind of party or festive ritual. Weddings are most common.[1]

Frye's account suggests immediately that traditional romantic comedy is at least as problematic a vehicle as tragedy for female heroism and woman heroes. Tragedy isolates. Women can be allowed to assume the burdens of tragic heroism because the price of such activity is death or social ostracism. The challenge offered by a Clarissa Harlowe or a Hester Prynne is tolerated and even, to some extent, honored because these characters ultimately vacate the premises, sparing society the pain of either enforced change or consciously acknowledged inadequacy. The pattern of comic heroism leaves no such loopholes; the comic hero must be rewarded in fact as well as in principle, materially as well as theoretically, by society as well as by God. Precisely because comedy assumes a continuing relationship between the hero and the world, the form has tended to be more cautious than tragedy about the social challenges it considers, including, of course, the challenge that female autonomy offers to male authority. It is no accident that Frye's comic hero is, by definition and unalterably, male.

The boundaries of comedy are further defined by a tendency to assume a continuing and knowable relationship between natural and social forms. As time inevitably passes and the seasons inexorably change, so, comedy suggests, does one human generation give way to the next. By thus analogizing natural and social processes, the form of comedy controls and limits change: social relations are less progressive than cyclical. Human relations, determined by the age and sex of the par-

ticipants rather than by their characters, recapitulate themselves from generation to generation; this recurrence essentially neutralizes the effects of historical development or even
the idea of social progress. So, for all its apparent emphasis on
change, comedy actually develops out of an ideology of stasis,
and human relationships are correspondingly limited to what
is regarded as natural and unvarying. It is not surprising that
comic relationships between men and women are read in pre-
dominantly sexual terms, that happiness through mating is the
goal, that men chase and women are chased.

But comedy accomplishes the shift from nature to society in
terms of marriage, and marriage is more than merely mating.
In society, if not in nature, women are presumed to be not
merely chased but chaste; a wedding is more than a rite of
spring. The social consequences of marriage are significant
and predictable: marriage establishes legitimacy through the
male line; provides for the orderly transfer of money and
property from one generation to the next; and together with
other social institutions, sanctions and perpetuates female
subordination. For male heroes, nonetheless, comedy is apparently a liberating structure, rewarding each new generation of
young men in turn. A kiss turns a toad into a prince who marries a princess and thereby gains access to her land, or her
father's. A handsome youth, killing the dragon at the gates of
the capital, wins both a bride and a kingdom. No one sup-
poses that the princess might see herself as more closely tied
to the beast than to the prince, or that she might have had
other plans entirely for her life. In the classic version of the
comic plot, the princess, as heroine, exists only in relation to
the hero, who, having slaved or suffered to attain her hand,
sees her as his just reward, the symbol of both social status and
success. One can hardly object; the prince is always a nice
young man, and only a churl would wish the situation otherwise.

Some questions, however, still remain. What happens if the
roles are reversed? How much of comedy's structure can sur-

vive when the principal and active figure is a woman? Could comedy metamorphose this hypothetical female as it does her male counterpart? Can toadishness be used to disguise royal femininity, and will Princess Charming free and wed her prince? Does marriage function for potentially heroic women as it does for men, to signal triumph and symbolize command? In short, can the gestures of comedy transcend Frye's narrow sexual specifications and legitimize women's aspirations for psychic autonomy, sexual release, and social power, as well as men's? Or do comedy's requirements ultimately subvert, rather than support, the claims of female heroism? "Amor and Psyche" suggests one answer; the bourgeois novel implies another.

As particular cases to test these questions, let us consider three fictions—Jane Austen's *Emma* (1816), Charlotte Brontë's *Jane Eyre* (1847), and George Eliot's *Middlemarch* (1871–72).[2] These are neither random nor even surprising choices. On the contrary, they were chosen on account of their familiarity, their obvious membership in the genre, and because individually and in relation to each other they set a standard as representative, if uniquely valuable, texts. These novels exemplify the most complex mid-nineteenth-century responses to the hypothesis that traditional comic forms might be adequate to reconcile female demands for personal happiness and socially sanctioned power. The evolving demonstration that this hypothesis is null, that these imperatives cannot, in fact, be reconciled for women within comedy's conventional gestures makes further, more radical innovations both necessary and possible. Emma Woodhouse, Jane Eyre, Dorothea Brooke are too big for the plots that must contain them. Their metamorphoses into Emma Knightley, Jane Rochester, and Dorothea Casaubon Ladislaw mark no progression from captivity to royal rule, but rather a surrender of heroic claims and appetites in favor of the more limited and contingent existence of the heroine.

Like Clarissa Harlowe, Emma Woodhouse initially appears

as fortune's darling and her father's best-loved child. Handsome, clever, and rich in her person; undistressed and unvexed by her circumstances; she is Hartfield's mistress and, despite her youth, its undisputed ruler. As for the surrounding community—embodied in Highbury, the town to which Hartfield belongs—it too "afforded her no equal" (chap. 1, p. 37). Her chief attractions are her irrepressible energy and wit. By virtue of these qualities, she excites our curiosity and interest no less than Mr. Knightley's. And yet, like him, we are uneasy. For in the miniature worlds of Hartfield and Highbury, what forms can contain Emma's energies, what gestures express her values, what subjects present themselves as objects for her wit? In this realm of unequals, who are her playmates? Confined to a nutshell must Emma, no less than Hamlet, have bad dreams?

For what, indeed, can such a woman do with herself? Mr. Knightley's anxiety about Emma's future is appropriate, since possible activities are severely limited, and Emma is, in any case, indifferent to them. Rejecting the tiny range of ordinary female accomplishments, that familiar, tedious list of drawing, painting, singing, piano playing, and polite conversation, Emma deceives society—"her reputation for accomplishment often higher than it deserved" (chap. 6, p. 72)—but bores herself. Animals in zoos occasionally reject the terms of their captivity: they withdraw, refuse to eat or mate, groom themselves excessively or not at all, and sometimes even die. Others accept entrapment, eat the food provided, walk many miles daily in their cages, survive, and reproduce. Emma, enmeshed by Austen in society's cage, is pushed to such an accommodation. She adjusts to her captivity, moves from a position of social withdrawal and exclusion to one of acceptance, moderates outrage, and adopts the standards of her keeper.

Austen makes Emma adapt even though the book as a whole neither disguises nor ignores the limitations of her world, the vista Emma sees from the door of a shop in the center of town:

Much could not be hoped from the traffic of even the busiest part of Highbury;—Mr Perry walking hastily by, Mr. William Cox letting himself in at the office door, Mr. Cole's carriage horses returning from exercise, or a stray letter-boy on an obstinate mule, were the liveliest objects she could presume to expect; and when her eyes fell only on the butcher with his tray, a tidy old woman travelling homewards from shop with her full basket, two curs quarrelling over a dirty bone, and a string of dawdling children round the baker's little bow-window eyeing the gingerbread, she knew she had no reason to complain, and was amused enough. . . . A mind lively and at ease, can do with seeing nothing, and can see nothing that does not answer.

(Chap. 27, p. 241)

There is a peculiar sadness to this last sentence, a sense of unjustified assertion that raises more questions than it answers. The narrator, unwilling or unable to regard street life in Highbury as "something," offers internal perception as compensation for an external void.

Can "a mind lively and at ease" make do with seeing nothing because its eye habitually turns inward? If so, why look out at all? And why, then, should Emma be culpable, as she often seems to be, for chronically ignoring what she sees in favor of what she thinks, wishes, or imagines? Conversely, why *should* a mind be satisfied with so little outside stimulus? Why should it not crave for something bigger and grander, and invent what it can't find? Isn't any mind, especially a lively one, diminished when forced to dwell exclusively among the known and the familiar? Emma Woodhouse may be an heiress with £30,000, but her wealth cannot extend the limits of her horizons. Living on an island, she has never seen the sea;[3] nor has she ever traveled even the seven miles to Box Hill. A scant half mile beyond Highbury, gypsies lurk; like the dragons on the corners of old maps, these vagabonds and estateless persons mark the farthest bound of the known world and frighten straying ladies back to safety.

The formal symmetries of *Emma* grow out of and depend upon the extraordinary restrictions imposed on its hero. The male comic hero, regardless of his initial status, leaves home to win his way; Emma, in contrast, is barely allowed to visit neighbors for fear of getting her feet wet. Her aspirations cannot be represented by a journey: social limits on respectable women nullify the possibility of a female quest. Locked inside society, Emma cannot hope to alter it, for change implies leverage, which in turn requires the existence of an independent reference point. "Give me a lever and a place to stand," said Archimedes, "and I will move the world." Lacking the second term, Emma cannot compel the third. The book's trajectory traces the exchange of Emma's independence for a corresponding measure of guaranteed social prestige and security.

Possessed of a will and the wit to use it, Emma is confined in a tiny space. It is no wonder that she turns tyrant. Nor is it surprising that she is extraordinarily sensitive to decorum, status, and all those self-regarding rituals by which society defines precedence and assigns rank. Far from being shocking, Emma's rudeness to Miss Bates is the predictable signal of her fugitive feelings and capacity for genuinely subversive action. An act of heroism, a breach of manners for the sake of truth and power, it is equally a revelation of why society must moderate such unrestraint.

Emma's words to Miss Bates are true, however antisocial or unkind. Such mockery provokes both relief and horror; a natural force threatening civilization's dams, it is simultaneously splendid and frightening. An old maid, as Emma herself has declared she will be, Miss Bates casts a dark shadow over Emma's future. She is the self Emma might become, despite the defending power of her money. To put distance between her youth and this depressing vision of lonely female old age, Emma, incited to giddy restlessness by the disturbing presence of Frank Churchill, makes a scapegoat of Miss Bates. Churchill, too, has a relationship to the dark side of Emma's psyche. Witty, teasing, and manipulative, he, like she, cannot easily accept Highbury's conventions and restraints. As a man, however, he can be treated more leniently by Austen; he can be given more license than Emma, can travel more widely in every way than she without finally sacrificing his right to claim a social niche.

Although the structure of the book ultimately implicates the audience in enforcing Highbury's values, it is possible nonetheless to understand Emma's flare-up as frustration's inevitable eruption, the breaking out of a spirit that has become destructive because it is allowed no other outlet. Our sense of Emma's heroic potential is born from the tension between understanding this frustration and condemning its results. As John Stuart Mill points out in the last part of his essay "The Subjection of Women" (1869):

An active and energetic mind, if denied liberty, will seek for power: refused the command of itself, it will assert its personality by attempting to control others. To allow to any human beings no existence of their own but what depends on others, is giving far too high a premium on bending others to their purposes. Where liberty cannot be hoped for, and power can, power becomes the grand object of human desire; those to whom others will not leave the undisturbed management of their own affairs, will compensate themselves, if they can, by meddling for their own purposes with the affairs of others. . . . The love of power and the love of liberty are in eternal antagonism. Where there is least liberty, the passion for power is the most ardent and unscrupulous.[4]

Power sought under these circumstances debases itself, testifies to weakness rather than strength, meanness not magnanimity. Emma's assertion of ego in talking to Miss Bates is, like her interference with Harriet Smith and speculation about Jane Fairfax, vain and dangerously frivolous, but comprehensible.

Emma is, of course, wrong in seeking to appropriate other women's lives for her own ends. Existentially violent, Emma's relationships to other women in the book are travesties of the primary female relationship between mother and daughter. When Miss Taylor—a weak, if loving, mother surrogate—decamps to marry Mr. Weston, her departure precipitates the psychological crisis around which the plot revolves. In becoming Mrs. Weston, Miss Taylor betrays Emma, who consequently enters into new, ambivalent relationships with women who are younger or more vulnerable than she. Miss Taylor, like Mr. Woodhouse (biologically Emma's father, but emotionally a much more conventionally feminine and thus maternal figure) has indulged and spoiled Emma. She is therefore untrained for the role of female guide or mentor. Emma's assertions of authority are, at best, embarrassing. Cruel when she should be kind, Emma is controlling rather than empathetic, and light-minded when circumstances require rational assessment of realistic possibilities and values.

Attempting to force the souls of others, Emma herself is the victim of socially imposed constraints. Once again her heroic potential is negatively realized. Her almost unrestricted power in her own house—"I believe few married women are half as much mistress of their husband's house, as I am of Hartfield; and never . . . could I expect to be so truly beloved; so always first and always right in any man's eyes as I am in my father's" (chap. 10, p. 109)—allows her to suppose, logically if incorrectly, that she can extend and generalize this authority. With her overblown idea of her own majesty, she is, like the fisherman's wife who wants the magic flounder to turn her into the pope, a ripe candidate for deflation.

A strong woman can check a weaker one. Emma can interfere with Harriet Smith, condescend to Jane Fairfax, and scoff at Miss Bates. But no woman, however strong, can finally control a man. Harriet must marry Robert Martin. He is more worthy as well as more generous than she, the attractions of prettiness and docility being poor compensation for a lack of property and status. Frank Churchill secures Jane Fairfax's social position when he marries her; the initiative is his, although in matters of character she is his superior. And Mr. Knightley humiliates Emma by making her fully conscious of her unkindness to Miss Bates. The power of even ineffectual men is demonstrated in the novel by Emma's relationship with her father. Indeed, her deference to his whims and considerations of his comfort suggest throughout that she may be socially redeemable. She evades his prohibitions but does so without defiance or even bad temper, and finally she gives in to him, beginning married life not in her own house or even in her husband's but at Hartfield, so as to spare her father suffering. As the narrator remarks, when Emma is similarly patient with the equally provoking John Knightley, "Her heroism reached only to silence" (chap. 13, p. 135). If the attack on Miss Bates shows Emma's capacity to threaten society, her failure to turn on foolish or irritating men indicates her capacity for rehabilitation.

Miss Bates, a poor old maid, is tolerated because her poverty and simplicity combine to make her harmless: "'Nobody is afraid of her: that is a great charm,'" Emma correctly observes (chap. 10, p. 110). But a rich old maid and a willful one, an aunt who may model her relationships to her nieces after the pattern of her attentions to Harriet Smith is worrisome indeed. Thus society's need to contain Emma intersects with Emma's equally compelling need for such power as can be socially legitimized. The intersection of these needs prepares the way for Emma's wedding.

Far from being altered, society is reinforced by the union of Emma and Mr. Knightley. To say this is in no way to deny Austen's success in making us feel the correctness of this marriage. She is at great pains to show us the developing consciousness of relationship between the two characters, the difficulty with which they both realize and finally acknowledge their love for each other, the pleasure with which they contemplate their future. In this respect, the novel has educated Mr. Knightley's feelings no less than it has Emma's. As Mrs. George Knightley, Emma can accede to the social position that is rightfully hers and retrieve from the usurping Mrs. Elton the title of Highbury's ruling matron.

In this limited way, the structure of *Emma* satisfies the minimal requisites of comedy. Illusion yields to insight; the young assume social responsibility; the main character is justly happy. The terms of this happiness, however, negate rather than fulfill Emma's original aspirations. Emma has grown up, but in the course of doing so, she has had her wings clipped and her talons trimmed. An acceptance of the necessity of marriage and reproduction has replaced a wish for perpetual celibacy. A desire for sons to inherit Donwell Abbey has taken precedence over a wish for nieces to manage and indulge. "A small band of true friends" witnesses the wedding, but whether we hear the accent falling more on the smallness of the band or the truth of the friendship, on a limited and highly structured community or a looser and more spontaneously human communitas is an open question. Such social expansion as might be thought to take place is due largely to Mr. Knightley's exertions, not to Emma's; it is he who, consistently seeing the virtue in Robert Martin's character, finally forces Emma to acknowledge his presence as necessary to Highbury society. Her father's daughter still, Mrs. Knightley presumably continues as Emma Woodhouse began: protecting Hartfield from intruders, pilferers, and chicken stealers. Although these are not unworthy occupations, they originally seemed too small to consume all of Emma's energies.

Jane Eyre's world is both larger and more brutal than Emma Woodhouse's: much of the distance between the two characters can be measured simply in the difference between a woman who is handsome, clever, and rich and one who is poor, plain, and without powerful social connections. Not a "sanguine, brilliant, careless, exacting, handsome, romping child," Jane attracts only disapproval and sinks into a "habitual mood of humiliation, self-doubt, [and] forlorn depression" (chap. 2, pp. 15–16). As an outcast Jane is miserable; but misery, however great, is insufficient to make her compromise her principles, give in to what she sees as tyranny, and hypocritically endorse values and behavior she finds repugnant:

I was a discord in Gateshead Hall; I was like nobody there; I had nothing in harmony with Mrs. Reed or her children, or her chosen vassalage. If they did not love me, in fact, as little did I love them. They were not bound to regard with affection a thing that could not sympathise with one amongst them; a heterogeneous thing, opposed to them in temperament, in capacity, in propensities; a useless thing, incapable of serving their interest, or adding to their pleasure; a noxious thing, cherishing the germs of indignation at their treatment, of contempt of their judgment.

(Chap. 2, p. 15)

A pariah from choice as much as from status or ascription, Jane seems to be searching for a situation that will validate rather than alter her essential self. We might therefore expect that Jane's success, the conclusion of her life as comedy, would necessarily involve Charlotte Brontë in a much more radical reshaping of the surrounding social, moral, and metaphysical universe than that required by Jane Austen.

Emma's power was wrongly used insofar as it was detached from a recognition of her obligations to a network of interlocking social responsibilities. Attractive as a reservoir of untapped energy, Emma is condemned as a potentially anarchic force. Our positive feeling for the character conflicts with our negative judgment of her. In considering *Jane Eyre*, however, we are conscious of no such split in our attention or our loyalties. Since Jane tells her own story, our experience of her life is initially controlled by the suspended judgment governing our response to autobiography. The narrative structure of *Jane Eyre* enhances our capacity to empathize with her, to value her for the same reasons and in the same terms as she values herself; the distance required for differentiated judgment is sacrificed temporarily in favor of the immediacy and power of identification.

Sharing Jane's sense of herself, we participate in her circumstances, accept as our own her outrage at society's injustice and her boredom at social routine. We likewise endorse her longing for freedom. The most passionate moments in *Jane Eyre* are those in which, enraged by her present circumstances, Jane longs for an unembodied future. Her war cry on Thornfield's battlements is justly famous:

I am not writing to flatter paternal egotism, to echo cant, or prop up humbug; I am merely telling the truth. . . . when I add . . . that . . . I longed for a power of vision which might . . . reach the busy world, towns, regions full of life I had heard of but never seen; . . . I desired more of practical experience than I possessed; more of intercourse with my kind, of acquaintance with variety of character, than was here within my reach. I valued what was good in Mrs. Fairfax and . . . Adèle; but I believed in the existence of other and more vivid kinds of goodness, and what I believed in I wished to behold. . . . My sole relief was to . . . allow my mind's eye to dwell on whatever bright visions rose before it . . . to let my heart be heaved by the exultant movement, which, while it swelled it in trouble, expanded it with life; and, best of all, to open my inward ear to a tale that was never ended—a tale my imagination created, and narrated continuously; quickened with all of incident, life, fire, feeling, that I desired and had not in my actual existence.

It is in vain to say human beings ought to be satisfied with tranquillity: they must have action; and they will make it if they cannot find it. Millions are condemned to a stiller doom than mine, and millions are in silent revolt against their lot. Nobody knows how many rebellions besides political rebellions ferment in the masses of life which people earth. Women are supposed to be very calm generally; but women feel just as men feel; they need exercise for their faculties, and a field for their efforts as much as their brothers do; they suffer from too rigid a constraint, too absolute a stagnation, precisely as men would suffer; and it is narrow-minded in their more privileged fellow-creatures to say that they ought to confine themselves to making puddings and knitting stockings, to playing on the piano and embroidering bags. It is thoughtless to condemn them, or laugh at them, if they seek to do more or learn more than custom has pronounced for their sex.

(Chap. 12, pp. 105–6)

Brontë here is allowing Jane to mythologize her life and express a longing for a new birth into freedom. Defining herself as equally opposed to the self-serving hypocrisy of "paternal egotism" and the oppressive domesticity of the house (both a traditional female image and a space that is for the moment literally inhabited only by women) Jane propels herself upward. Pacing the corridors, climbing the stairs, opening the trap door and finally emerging from the attic, Jane then looks outward from the rooftop. She has moved from a material world in which poverty, impotence, and femininity are inextricably intertwined to an unsubstantial realm where imagination sheds shackles imposed by sex and class and makes life rich.

But this awareness of the dissociation between her self and

her environment inspires no vision of affiliation. Jane's revolt, for all its eloquence and grandeur, has no positive goal and consequently does not seem to promise attainment of a new community. Material and psychic deprivations cripple Jane's desires even as they limit her circumstances. The articulation of limits becomes itself an impediment to progress. Recall, for example, Jane's position as she abandons Lowood School for Thornfield immediately following Miss Temple's marriage to the Reverend Mr. Naysmith. At that time a bitter consciousness of isolation provokes Jane to desire a great world but accept a small one:

[M]y mind . . . put off all it had borrowed of Miss Temple . . . and . . . now I was in my natural element, and beginning to feel the stirring of old emotions. . . . I remembered that the real world was wide, and that a varied field of hopes and fears, of sensations and excitements, awaited those who had courage to go forth into its expanse, to seek real knowledge of life amidst its perils. . . . I desired liberty; for liberty I gasped; for liberty I uttered a prayer; it seemed scattered on the wind then faintly blowing. I abandoned it and framed a humbler supplication; for change, stimulus: that petition, too, seemed swept off into vague space: "Then," I cried, half desperate, "grant me at least a new servitude!"

(Chap. 10, pp. 82–83)

Jane's most extravagant and particular claims of status and freedom emerge in her relationship with Rochester and involve her assertions of essential parity with him. In order to compel an acknowledgment that she has a self which exists independently of others' views of her, Jane must hypothesize circumstances in which the social framework is collapsed, its fabric disintegrated. Thornfield, like Amor's cave, is a self-contained world, and Rochester exploits Jane's ignorance of his situation, and perhaps his nature, in the same way that the god of love imposed darkness to guarantee his power. Resisting Rochester's attempted manipulations, Jane demands divine equality:

"Do you think, because I am poor, obscure, plain, and little, I am soulless and heartless? You think wrong!—I have as much soul as you,—and full as much heart! . . . I am not talking to you now through the medium of custom, conventionalities, or even of mortal flesh:—it is my spirit that addresses your spirit; just as if both had passed through the grave, and we stood at God's feet, equal,—as we are!"

(Chap. 23, p. 240)

This outburst, like the two preceding ones, is operatically intense but incomplete. Her existential opposition to society depends on a sense of unjust deprivation rather than on a desire to erase all inequalities of rank. Although Jane resents those— especially women—who are physically imposing, rich, and well-born, she defends the metaphysical reality of hierarchy; equal to each other, she and Rochester are superior to the rest of the world.

No social revolutionary, Jane is rather a displaced spiritual aristocrat, unfortunate in being born into the wrong body and the wrong economic niche. Her heroism is compromised. Her desire to evade or change society conflicts with her wish to force society to honor her. We are prepared for Jane's transformation from Eyre to heir by her despairing sense that Rochester's wealth and her own poverty unbalance their relationship, making Jane the loser in a sexual power struggle where mastery accrues to masculinity in part because money is power. Thinking back to her early conversation with Mr. Lloyd, the apothecary who ministers to her in the red-room, Jane recalls that "poverty for me was synonymous with . . . degradation. . . . I could not see how poor people had the means of being kind; and . . . I was not heroic enough to purchase liberty at the price of caste" (chap. 3, p. 24). Her only defense is her hope that her Uncle John in Madeira will one day acknowledge and enrich her: "If I had but a prospect of one day bringing Mr. Rochester an accession of fortune, I could better endure to be kept by him now" (chap. 24, p. 255).

Psychologically ambivalent, Jane is torn between a desire to defy society and an equally compelling need to make peace with it by altering both her external circumstances and her inner being. As an orphan whose substitute parents and siblings are either relatively ineffectual like Mr. Reed, Miss Temple, and Helen Burns or unusually hostile like Mrs. Reed, the young Reeds, and Mr. Brocklehurst, Jane grows up with an inordinate craving for personal affection. When Helen Burns asserts the alternative power of an innocent conscience to comfort and console the person who is friendless and misunderstood, Jane denies this hope:

"I know I should think well of myself; but that is not enough: if others don't love me, I would rather die than live—I cannot bear to be solitary and hated . . . [T]o gain some real affection from . . . any . . . whom I truly love, I would willingly submit to have the bone of my arm broken, or to let a bull toss me, or to stand behind a kicking horse, and let it dash its hoof at my chest."

(Chap. 8, p. 67)

The extremity of these imagined acts testifies to the desperation of Jane's need. It is hardly surprising, then, that her sense that love is beyond her reach motivates her progress: Miss Temple's wedding makes Lowood unendurable; the revelation of Rochester's prior marriage sends Jane away from Thornfield; the absolute certainty that St. John will never love her figures significantly in her flight from Moor House. The happy possibility of marrying Rochester makes Jane wonder "why moralists call this world a dreary wilderness: for me it blossomed like a rose" (chap. 25, p. 266). Transfigured by Rochester's affection, Jane examines her face in the mirror and feels it as "no longer plain: there was hope in its aspect, and life in its colour: and my eyes seemed as if they had beheld the fount of fruition, and borrowed beams from the lustrous ripple" (chap. 24, p. 244). Conversely, the knowledge that she and Rochester must part entirely blights Jane's world:

A Christmas frost had come at midsummer; a white December storm had whirled over June; ice glazed the ripe apples, drifts crushed the blowing roses; on hay-field and corn-field lay a frozen shroud: lanes which last night blushed full of flowers, to-day were pathless with untrodden snow; and the woods which twelve hours since waved leafy and fragrant as groves between the tropics, now spread, waste, wild

and white as pine-forests in wintry Norway. My hopes were all dead—
struck with a subtle doom, such as, in one night, fell on all the first-
born in the land of Egypt. I looked on my cherished wishes yesterday
so blooming and glowing; they lay stark, chill, livid corpses, that
could never revive.

(Chap. 26, pp. 280–81)

The ripe fertility that the promise of Rochester holds out
gives way to a deprived, shrunken world in his absence.[5]
Both worlds, however, are equally fictitious, equally visionary,
equally dependent on Jane's internal weather: the earth does
not literally bloom when Jane is loved or freeze when she is
denied, however much Jane may feel this is true. There is always a potential disjunction between the psyche's experience
and society's perception. In the case of Jane Eyre, the disjunction is enormous; cruel reductions are necessary on both sides
of the equation for Jane's psyche and her chosen society to be
mutually accommodated.

Since Jane is initially positioned at society's periphery rather
than its center, she can journey and adventure where Emma
Woodhouse must stand still and endure. Moving from Gateshead to Lowood to Thornfield, and then to Moor House and
Morton, Jane's bravery and resolution are, like Psyche's, not
so much chosen as thrust upon her as artifacts of her circumstances. Moved by rage or feelings of suffocation, Jane bursts
out; each stage between the Reeds' house and the Riverses'
prefigures the next. In the rhythm of the narrative, negativism
and fear give way first to pleasure but later to boredom, betrayal, a renewed sense of isolation, and a need to move on
in search of new attachments. Contemplating her first move
from Gateshead to Lowood, Jane reflects:

If Bessie's accounts of school-discipline . . . were somewhat appalling, her details of certain accomplishments . . . were . . . equally
attractive. . . . Besides, school would be a complete change: it implied a long journey, an entire separation from Gateshead, an en-
trance into a new life.

(Chap. 3, pp. 24–25)

After Miss Temple's marriage, the charm of this "new life" evaporates, and Jane again feels cramped: "What do I want? A new place, in a new house, amongst new faces, under new circumstances" (chap. 10, p. 83).

On first coming to Thornfield, Jane had felt herself to be an "inexperienced youth . . . quite alone in the world, cut adrift from every connection, uncertain whether the port to which it is bound can be reached, and prevented by many impediments from returning to that it has quitted. The charm of adventure sweetens that sensation, the glow of pride warms it; but then the throb of fear disturbs it; and fear with me became predominant" (chap. 11, p. 91). Yet even Thornfield's atmosphere, initially both frightening and enchanting, palls:

I did not like re-entering Thornfield. To pass its threshold was to return to stagnation; to cross the silent hall, to ascend the darksome staircase, to seek my own lonely little room, and then to see tranquil Mrs. Fairfax, and spend the long winter evening with her, only, was to quell wholly the faint excitement wakened by my walk,—to slip again over my faculties the viewless fetters of an uniform and too still existence; of an existence whose very privileges of security and ease I was becoming incapable of appreciating.

(Chap. 12, p. 112)

The prospect of marriage to Rochester appeals because his is "an existence more expansive and stirring than my own: as much more so as the depths of the sea to which the brook runs are than the shallows of its own strait channel" (chap. 25, p. 266). Having resolved to leave Rochester once Bertha's presence is acknowledged, Jane conquers her earlier fear: "I was not afraid. . . . I felt an inward power; a sense of influence, which supported me. The crisis was perilous; but not without its charm: such as the Indian, perhaps, feels when he slips over the rapid in his canoe" (chap. 27; p. 287).

Fleeing with no money and no goal except the resolute refusal to break faith with herself and the doubtful hope of mere survival, Jane undergoes her most radical experience of psychic reduction. She is utterly isolated, removed from any social role, and she faces the possible disintegration of self under such deprivation. Alone, homeless, destitute, starving, Jane records her position: "Not a tie holds me to human society at this moment—not a charm or hope calls me where my fellow-creatures are—none that saw me would have a kind thought or good wish for me. . . . I drew near houses; I left them and came back again, and again I wandered away: always repelled by the consciousness of having no claim to ask—no right to expect interest in my isolated lot" (chaps. 27, 28, pp. 304, 311). Without hope for the future, Jane longs for death. As Jung points out, "this death is no external enemy, it is [the hero's] own inner longing for the stillness and profound peace of all-knowing non-existence, for all-seeing sleep in the ocean of coming-to-be and passing-away. . . . If [the hero] is to live, he [sic] must fight and sacrifice his longing for the past in order to rise to his own heights."[6]

At this juncture, like Hester in the forest, Jane turns for support to a female nature, contrasting it with the world of men.

I touched the heath: it was dry, and yet warm. . . . I looked at the sky; it was pure: a kindly star twinkled just above the chasm ridge. The dew fell, but with propitious softness; no breeze whispered. Nature seemed to me benign and good; I thought she loved me, outcast as I was; and I, who from man could anticipate only mistrust, rejection, insult, clung to her with filial fondness. To-night, at least, I would be her guest—as I was her child: my mother would lodge me without money and without price.

(Chap. 28, p. 307)

As nature is maternal, so, too is night: "Night was come, and her planets were risen: a safe, still night; too serene for the companionship of fear" (chap. 28, p. 307).

Disclosed by night, the moon consistently emerges as both source and image of female illumination. The moon is absent from Gateshead; it exists there only as a "cold and ghastly" image in Bewick's *History of British Birds*, where it reveals a sinking wreck that seems associated with Jane herself. The moon shines on Jane and Helen Burns at the moment when

Miss Temple gives them food and sympathy. When Jane is out walking in the neighborhood of Thornfield, Rochester makes his first appearance as a "rude noise" and a "metallic clatter" that intrudes on a peaceful moonlit scene (chap. 12, p. 108). As he departs, after Jane has revealed her strength by helping him back on his horse, the moon reappears, and Jane feels herself reluctant to return to the house and go inside:

Both my eyes and spirit seemed drawn from the gloomy house . . . to that sky expanded before me . . . the moon ascending it in solemn march; her orb seeming to look up as she left the hill tops . . . and aspired to the zenith . . . and for those trembling stars that followed her course; they made my heart tremble, my veins glow when I viewed them. Little things recall us to earth: the clock struck in the hall; that sufficed; I turned from moon and stars, opened a side-door and went in.

(Chap. 12, p. 112)

The moon rouses Jane to action when it wakes her to attend to Mason after his sister's attack. Finally, after Jane has learned that Rochester is already married, she sleeps and dreams of herself in the red-room again. This time the moon appears transformed into a living being who seems to appeal to her:

The gleam was such as the moon imparts to vapours she is about to sever. I watched her come—watched with the strangest anticipation; as though some word of doom were to be written on her disk. She broke forth as never moon yet burst from cloud: a hand first penetrated the sable folds and waved them away; then, not a moon, but a white human form shone in the azure, inclining a glorious brow earthward. It gazed and gazed on me. It spoke to my spirit: immeasurably distant was the tone, yet so near, it whispered in my heart—
  "My daughter, flee temptation!"
  "Mother, I will."

(Chap. 27, p. 303)

The moonlit heath provides the book's most powerful vision of a female territory that might sustain and succor the hero. At night Jane lies outdoors "nestled to the breast of the hill; and ere long, in sleep, forgot sorrow" (chap. 28, p. 308).

Daylight, however, reveals the moor as "a golden desert," capable of nourishing bees and lizards, perhaps, but not people: "I was a human being, and had a human being's wants: I must not linger where there was nothing to supply them" (chap. 28, p. 308). The imagery of daylight, sunshine, hot flames and flashing fires that has been consistently opposed to the cool, liquid, lunar landscape finally displaces it entirely. Rochester's hope that he and Jane might live together on the moon is vanquished. As Adèle has earlier pointed out to Rochester, the desire for moon life is founded on an impossibility: " 'She [Jane] is far better as she is . . . she would get tired of living with only you in the moon.' " Besides, " 'You can't get her there: there is no road to the moon: it is all air; and neither you nor she can fly' " (chap. 24, p. 253). Her logic here is unassailable, if mundane; her punning on Jane's name (Eyre=air) Brontë's irony, if not her own.

If nature and moonlight are inadequate to fill Jane's needs, so too are literal relationships with other women. Helen Burns, described as "a martyr and a hero" (chap. 7, p. 65), nonetheless abandons Jane for death, as Miss Temple abandons her for marriage. The vital friendship that exists between Jane and the Rivers sisters is diffused by Jane's inheritance; the charms of wealth are more seductive than the possibilities of female independence; rich ladies, unlike poor ones, must be married.

Brontë shows, throughout the book, how the frames around Jane resist alteration, although Jane's position within society can be changed in accordance with her relative poverty or wealth. The pressure that Jane seems to be exerting outward, as against the bars of a cage, at the book's beginning, is, in the course of her development, increasingly turned inward. Unable to locate or make an accommodating universe, Brontë instead turns Jane's energies upon her self. Faced with an intractable world, Jane's heroism is deflected from the social to the psychic sphere.

Jung suggests that by hiding "in the lap of nature," the

hero reawakens "the relationship to the mother, and to something older than the mother, and it is therefore to be expected that [the hero] will emerge reborn in some other form."[7] Jane's experiences on the heath are indeed transforming. Since Brontë portrays nature as starving Jane (much as the forest failed Hester and the breast of the world offered Clarissa no nourishment), she suggests that Jane transforms herself, that the self is that "something older than the mother." Within the Jungian paradigm, the hero is "psychologically an archetype of the self."[8] Brontë's emphasis on autogenesis within *Jane Eyre* is, like her development of the motifs of wandering and sexual ambivalence, characteristic of heroic narratives in general.

While Jane is Adèle's governess and Rochester's fiancée, she has recurrent dreams in which she is responsible for caring for a child. In these dreams both Jane's responses and the infant's are fluid, labile: sometimes "hushed in [Jane's] arms, sometimes dandled on [her] knee, sometimes watched playing with daisies on a lawn; or again, dabbling its hands in running water. It was a wailing child this night, and a laughing one the next: now it nestled close . . . and now it ran" (chap. 21, p. 209). Whatever the temperament or aspect of the most recent dream images, they always make the waking Jane "nervous as bedtime approached and the hour of the vision drew near" (chap. 21, p. 209). On the night that Bertha tears Jane's wedding veil, Jane dreams again, this time seeing the infant as an obstacle to her relationship to Rochester and an impediment in her progress toward him:

For some time after I went to bed, I could not sleep. . . . On sleeping, I continued . . . the wish to be with you, and experienced a strange, regretful consciousness, of some barrier dividing us. During all my first sleep, I was following the windings of an unknown road; total obscurity environed me; rain pelted me; I was burdened with the charge of a little child: a very small creature, too young and feeble to walk and which shivered in my cold arms, and wailed piteously in my ear. . . . My movements were fettered; and my voice . . . died away inarticulate; while you, I felt, withdrew farther and farther

every moment. . . . Wrapped up in a shawl, I still carried the unknown little child: I might not lay it down anywhere, however tired
were my arms—however much its weight impeded my progress, I
must retain it. I heard the gallop of a horse at a distance on the road:
I was sure it was you; and you were departing for many years, and
for a distant country. I climbed the thin wall . . . eager to catch one
glimpse of you from the top: the stones rolled from under my feet,
the ivy branches I grasped gave way, the child clung round my neck
in terror, and almost strangled me: at last I saw you like a speck on a
white track, lessening every moment. The blast blew so strong I could
not stand. I sat down on the narrow ledge; I hushed the scared infant
in my lap: you turned an angle in the road; I bent forward to take
a last look; the wall crumbled; I was shaken; the child rolled from my
knee, I lost my balance, fell, and woke.

(Chap. 25, pp. 267–68)

The child who cannot be abandoned despite its inconve-
nience clearly represents Jane's image of her inner core of
being. Lacking a mother and failing to find an adequate one
in either the local world or the cosmos, Jane tries literally to
mother herself; not surprisingly, she feels this effort as burdensome, and the claims of the self are experienced as isolating
rather than integrating forces. Yet the need to acknowledge
this self is imperative exactly in proportion to the weakness
and fragility of Jane's social identity, the degradation of her
social role.

In the last third of the book, Brontë neutralizes the conflict
between Jane's struggle to preserve her self and the wish to
abandon it that is represented in the ambiguous falling away
at the end of Jane's dream. The book's conclusion gives Jane
a new and secure social identity, severely limits the extent of
the social world in which Jane will have to function, and provides Jane with a lover who is her mother as much as she
is his.

Brontë shows that female nature, represented by the heath,
would let Jane die, just as Jane would finally let the baby roll
away from her, presumably to perish. As was true in *The Scarlet Letter,* however, a male God contains this nature; experi-
encing Him Jane feels that she must live: "Sure was I of His

efficiency to save what He had made: convinced I grew that neither earth should perish, nor one of the souls it treasured. I turned my prayer to thanksgiving: the Source of Life was also the Saviour of spirits" (chap. 28, p. 308).

The dynamics of this revelation recapitulate in metaphysical terms the human workings of an earlier scene: the house party at Thornfield. On this occasion Rochester, disguised as a fortune-telling Gypsy woman, reveals to Jane the torment growing in her own soul from her need to reconcile "the dictates of conscience" with a "harvest . . . in smiles, in endearments, in sweet" (chap. 19, p. 191). Nature's inadequacies are also women's; God's compensations men's. No human female in *Jane Eyre* has sufficient power, insight, and kindness to combine an understanding of Jane's conflict-ridden sense of personal identity with an ability to help her connect it with the world at large. Although Rochester at this point still retains power over Jane—he is, after all, disguised, and she is not—his mask paradoxically allows him to reveal Jane to herself. Brontë shows us here a Rochester who sees Jane as more than a specimen of what he thinks women ought to be and generally are. In Jane, Rochester finds neither vanity nor insatiable passion nor a propensity for betrayal; instead he sees her as another self, a self that, like his own, battles with the world and has a right to an acknowledged subjectivity. Rochester's capacity for such perception is both revealed and facilitated by his costume. Dressed as a woman, he can see as a woman and can speak to Jane as she would have it, as spirit to spirit. Jane's addressing Rochester as "mother" is not deluded but prophetic. This odd scene sets the terms which will express Jane's final compromise with heroism: by the end of the book, Jane's cry for action has modulated into an assertion of happiness secured by her inheritance, defined by her consciousness of caste, and framed by her reformulated relationship to Rochester.

In some ways this ending is surprising, coming as it does after Jane has survived her ordeal on the heath and had a

glimpse of various prospects for an independent life: as a
teacher at Morton; as a wealthy woman living either on her
own or with her cousins; as a missionary in India. Each of
these possibilities tantalizes, seeming to satisfy some of the requirements for her life Jane specified as she paced back and
forth in controlled agitation on Thornfield's heights.

In the end, none pleases, and all are rejected. Far from feeling inspired and freed by her ability to earn her own money
as a teacher, Jane feels hedged in, degraded, déclassée: "I
doubted I had taken a step which sank instead of raising me
in the scale of social existence" (chap. 31, p. 341). The contrast
between Jane's description of her life as a schoolmistress and
her fantasy of existence with Rochester is almost ludicrous, so
heavily is the emotional balance tipped in favor of Rochester,
however much conscience may claim otherwise.

Which is better?—To have surrendered to temptation; listened to
passion; made no painful effort—no struggle;—but to have sunk
down in the silken snare; fallen asleep on the flowers covering it;
wakened in a southern clime, amongst the luxuries of a pleasure
villa: to have been now living in France, Mr. Rochester's mistress;
delirious with his love half my time . . . a slave in a fool's paradise
at Marseilles—fevered with delusive bliss one hour—suffocating with
the bitterest tears of remorse and shame the next—or to be a village
schoolmistress, free and honest, in a breezy mountain nook in the
healthy heart of England?

(Chap. 31, p. 341)

Jane must choose in favor of both school and chastity: "I was
right when I adhered to principle and law, and scorned and
crushed the insane promptings of a frenzied moment" (chap.
31, p. 341). But this choice fools no one about the real answers
to Jane's questions. The attractions of Amor's cave are all too
apparent here.

The supraerotic intensity of Jane's feelings also helps to explain why life as a member of a sisterly triumvirate is not possible for her. St. John, however, offers Jane more than a school
in a remote corner of rural England, more than the rigid conventions governing proper female life would usually allow.

Recognizing that Jane is perishing of boredom, he promises her that larger world her vision has so persistently yearned to discover:

"I am sure you cannot long be content . . . to devote your working hours to a monotonous labour wholly void of stimulus; any more than I can be content . . . to live here buried in morass, pent in with mountain—my nature, that God gave me, contravened; my faculties, heaven-bestowed, paralysed—made useless. . . . God has given us . . . the power to make our own fate; and when our energies seem to demand a sustenance they cannot get . . . we need neither starve . . . nor . . . despair; we have but to seek another nourishment for the mind . . . and to hew out for the adventurous foot a road as direct and broad as the one Fortune has blocked up against us."

(Chaps. 30, 31, pp. 338, 343)

Jane's resistance to St. John's importunings cannot be adequately accounted for in terms of the often noted contrast between Jane's fire and St. John's icy nature. The contrasts, to be sure, are there, but they are embedded in a wider and more interesting conflict, that of Jane's relationship to the imperatives of heroism. "He wanted to train me," Jane remarks, "to an elevation I could never reach; it racked me hourly to aspire to the standard he uplifted" (chap. 34, p. 378). Jane, who views St. John as explicitly heroic, weighs his virtues and limitations:

The humanities and amenities of life had no attraction for him—its peaceful enjoyments no charm. Literally, he lived only to aspire—after what was good and great, certainly: but still he would never rest; nor approve of others resting round him. . . . I saw he was of the material from which nature hews her heroes—Christian and Pagan—her lawgivers, her statesmen, her conquerors: a steadfast bulwark for great interests to rest upon; but at the fireside, too often a cold, cumbrous column, gloomy and out of place.

(Chap. 34, pp. 372–73)

In rejecting St. John's heroism, Jane rejects her own as well. The disjunction between the wish for action and the need for love that so divides Jane's inner being at the beginning is finally resolved: she abandons action for love, and the larger world is displaced by an idealized but hermetic domesticity.

As the plot is consummated, Jane is rendered increasingly passive. Even the money that secures her rise on the social scale comes to her not in response to her own exertions but rather through the belated kindness of her father's brother. Although this inheritance empowers Jane, it does so only by tying her to a socially acceptable family. Emphasizing the connection between Jane's wealth and social adhesion, Brontë has Jane immediately assign four fifths of her money to her cousins. Even £5,000, however, represents a considerable amount of potential freedom; it is, after all, the equivalent of almost 170 years of work at her annual teacher's salary of £30. Her social responsibility acknowledged, Jane might still be expected to move out into that active world she once claimed to crave. But of course she doesn't move out; she moves back to Rochester. And even this turning, this rejection of St. John and India, the only fully articulated alternative the fiction offers, is presented as not so much a freely chosen action as an irrational compulsion. At the point of giving in to St. John, Jane hears a mysterious voice calling to her through the air and claiming her for itself. Finding Rochester again, Jane discovers a man who has been changed, not by her, but by the exertions of a female lunatic, a woman whose rage against male authority is boundless but safely dissociated from Jane's own feelings. Bertha has often been analyzed as Jane's "dark shadow," or unacknowledged self. Undeniably Brontë requires the character of Bertha, to do for Jane what she cannot allow Jane to do in her own person.

The demonic side of heroism, so visible in Jane's descriptions of her younger self and echoed in her accounts of St. John's terrible power, is bleached away by the conclusion of her tale. Through the fairy tale motifs dominating the resolution of *Jane Eyre*, Brontë reinforces our consciousness of Jane's increasing inertia; the end of the book sees the transformation of an agent who asserts herself against the limitations conventionally imposed on women's lives into someone who is merely the derivation of a formula. The character who once observed that "human beings never enjoy complete happiness in this world. . . . To imagine such a lot befalling me is a . . . daydream" (chap. 24, p. 245) concludes by asserting simply that "my Edward and I, then, are happy" (chap. 38, p. 429).

Charlotte Brontë herself may not have been soothed by this ending: the novel that she wrote may well be more complex and ambivalent than we are able to perceive if we assume that the text belongs to Jane and that her responses govern ours. Although the book asks to be read as autobiography it is, of course, fiction. Ambivalence, then, must be inferred indirectly and read against the protestations of happiness Jane Eyre offers on her own behalf.

"Reader, I married him," states Jane (chap. 38, p. 426). The announcement is triumphant. "I know what it is to live entirely for and with what I love best on earth" (chap. 38, p. 427). Yet the society presided over by this happy couple is even more reduced than Emma Knightley's Highbury. The "small band of true friends" who witness the marriage that concludes Jane Austen's book is, in the case of *Jane Eyre,* whittled down to a single clerk; and the world, represented in the former by the dozen or so permanent residents of Highbury, at Ferndean numbers only two servants and one male child.

Ferndean itself seems an odd location for a marriage that is meant to be regarded as wholly blissful. We first learn of it when Mr. Rochester tells Jane about his disastrous first marriage to Bertha. Having brought a mad wife back to England from the West Indies, Rochester was faced with the problem of lodging her. At that time he specifically rejected Ferndean because " 'a scruple about the unhealthiness of the situation . . . made my conscience recoil from the arrangement. Probably those damp walls would soon have eased me of her charge: but to each villain his own vice; and mine is not a

tendency to indirect assassination, even of what I most hate' "
(chap. 27, p. 285). Since much is made of Bertha's strength and
power, one wonders how what could be expected to prove
fatal to her should be healthy for Jane. When Jane returns to
Rochester after Bertha has incinerated Thornfield, she describes her new home in language which echoes Rochester's
earlier description:

> The manor-house of Ferndean was . . . deep buried in a wood. I
> had heard of it before. Mr. Rochester often spoke of it. . . . His
> father had purchased the estate for the sake of the game covers. He
> would have let the house: but could find no tenant, in consequence
> of its ineligible and insalubrious site. Ferndean then remained unin-
> habited and unfurnished.
>
> (Chap. 37, p. 408)

Hardly a love nest, Ferndean is, as far as we can tell, unredeemed by Jane and Rochester's choice of it as home. The
estate remains as it always was: bleak, forbidding, inhospi-
table.

The chapter that begins by announcing Jane's marriage
concludes with a description of St. John Rivers's life in India
and a forecast of his impending death. The terms of this account implicitly contrast with the limited framework of the
Rochesters' domestic bliss. St. John, like Clarissa, remains
heroic to the end.

> A more resolute, indefatigable pioneer never wrought amidst rocks
> and dangers. Firm, faithful, and devoted; full of energy, and zeal,
> and truth, he labours for his race: he clears their painful way to im-
> provement: he hews down like a giant the prejudices of creed and
> caste that encumber it. He may be stern; he may be exacting; he
> may be ambitious yet; but his is the sternness of the warrior Great-
> heart, who guards his pilgrim convoy from the onslaught of Apol-
> lyon. . . . His is the ambition of the high master-spirit, which aims
> to fill a place in the first rank of those who are redeemed from the
> earth . . . who are called, and chosen, and faithful.
>
> (Chap. 37, p. 429)

Brontë, like Richardson, discovers the requirements of heroism to be incompatible with the claims of life. Faced with this

choice, she plots for her initially heroic character a different course. Happiness is ransomed by heroism. In marriage, Jane (and Rochester) are diminished even as they are rewarded.

Middlemarch, like *Emma* and *Jane Eyre,* is a novel about imaginative energy—the mental power to envision a self and a society as yet unformed in the given world—as this force is related to will and to society. Like Jane Austen and Charlotte Brontë, George Eliot uses her fiction to record the inability of will to call up energy sufficient not just to envision but to create new social forms. In *Middlemarch,* energy initially resides in many characters: in Lydgate, Fred Vincy, Rosamond, even Casaubon, but above all, in Dorothea Brooke. Indeed, it is the force of this last character's imagination, her questing nature and desire to be simultaneously wise, useful, and good, that illuminates the book.

More serious than Emma Woodhouse and more secure than Jane Eyre, Dorothea Brooke is related to her predecessors through her rejection of those norms and stereotypes held to govern female nature and development. At the very beginning of her narrative, George Eliot defines Dorothea against the grain of social femininity:

To her the destinies of mankind, seen by the light of Christianity, made the solicitudes of feminine fashion appear an occupation for Bedlam. She could not reconcile the anxieties of a spiritual life involving eternal consequences, with a keen interest in guimp and artificial protrusions of drapery. Her mind was theoretic, and yearned by its nature after some lofty conception of the world which might frankly include the parish of Tipton and her own rule of conduct there; she was enamoured of intensity and greatness.

(Chap. 1, p. 6)

By describing Dorothea's obsession with her future life as initially focused on vocation rather than marriage, Eliot again isolates her central character from the generality of women and makes us aware of Dorothea as a boundary breaker and potentially a heroic character.

There had risen before her [Dorothea] the girl's vision of a possible future for herself to which she looked forward with trembling hope, and she wanted to wander on in that visionary future without interruption. . . . What could she do, what ought she to do? . . . With some endowment of stupidity and conceit, she might have thought that a Christian young lady of fortune should find her ideal of life in village charities . . . with a background of prospective marriage to a man who . . . might be prayed for and seasonably exhorted. From such contentment poor Dorothea was shut out. The intensity of her religious disposition, the coercion it exercised over her life, was but one aspect of a nature altogether ardent, theoretic, and intellectually consequent: and with such a nature, struggling in the bands of a narrow teaching, hemmed in by a social life which seemed nothing but a labyrinth of petty courses, a walled-in maze of small paths that led no whither, the outcome was sure to strike others as at once exaggeration and inconsistency. The thing which seemed to her best, she wanted to justify by the completest knowledge; and not to live in pretended admission of rules which were never acted on. Into this soul-hunger . . . all her youthful passion was poured.

(Chap. 3, pp. 20–21)

Where Charlotte Brontë envisions Jane Eyre's rebellion against social limits and constrictions in terms of a rejection of the house, a prototypically female image, conceived of as both a psychic prison and a domestic space, George Eliot sets Dorothea wandering like Theseus in Minos' maze.[9] The house, of course, finally reclaims Jane: Mrs. Rochester is immured in Ferndean Manor. So, too, in *Middlemarch,* the Minotaur ensnares Dorothea, as the motif of the labyrinth fuses with the image of the deathly marriage: Edward Casaubon, Dorothea's first husband, is literally a monster, a condition that Dorothea perilously ignores, obvious though it is to everybody else in the book. The labyrinth is a double image; it describes both the monster's hidden lair and the path traversed by his destroyer. (Amor's darkened cave is a similarly ambiguous territory; the night which defends him from Psyche's vision serves also to nourish her misgivings.) Dorothea's relationship with Mr. Casaubon deranges both participants; the pieties of marriage disguise a dreadful combat.

If Dorothea's needs delude her into mistaking a husband

for a tutor and married life for a university education, so Casaubon's needs for all-accepting and unquestioning love lead him to confuse Dorothea with the perfect wife and regard an intelligent woman as an idolater. Dorothea's power to destroy Casaubon is thus equal to his capacity to imprison her. George Eliot pities both these figures; for Dorothea, however, she reserves a measure of suspicion absent from her consideration of Casaubon's flaws. From the beginning of the book, *Middlemarch*'s narrator undercuts Dorothea's longings for immortality, mocks them, questions their utility and their foundations. At one time, Dorothea is pictured as a young hero; at another, she's a young fool or, worse, an unmitigated social danger, an anarchic force that must be restrained not liberated. By the novel's end, Dorothea's energy, initially so great as to constitute a threat to her society, has been confined. Like Emma and Jane Eyre, she is, in a very real sense, not the same character at the book's conclusion that she was at its beginning; at first a latent epic hero, she is ultimately a comic heroine. Although she leaves Middlemarch, she still has a home there and in claiming it, she is diminished.

In effecting this reduction, George Eliot is by no means unambivalent, as we can see from the structure of the narrative. *Middlemarch* is peculiarly divided, divorcing its emotional centers—Dorothea and Lydgate, and their foils Casaubon, Ladislaw, and Rosamond—from its ethical pivots. It is the Garths, Mrs. Bulstrode, and the other permanent residents of the town who, guaranteeing the enduring life of Middlemarch itself, also provide the moral norms of the book. The novel's action, excluding the Finale, stops before the Reform Bill becomes a fact; and the characters who threaten Middlemarch's values are changed (Dorothea and Will), defeated (Lydgate), killed (Casaubon), or condemned (Rosamond). Away from Middlemarch, they may influence a wider world or merely dwell in lonely exile.

It is possible that what I have described as structural ambivalence is in fact accounted for by Eliot who, unlike Austen and Brontë, calls her book not after her principal character but after a place; *Middlemarch* is not the story of Dorothea or anyone else in particular but attempts, more expansively, to be *A Study of Provincial Life.* Eliot's fiction, in other words, is deliberately unheroic, even antiheroic. Great visions are annihilated and glorious plans revealed as inglorious illusions because realism compels us to recognize what heroism would deny: the necessity, utility, and even virtue of ordinary lives and small, self-mocking visions. Still, the particular sense of reality which the book as a whole engenders, the bitter recognition of wasted powers provoked by Dorothea's and Lydgate's fates, derives from a persisting memory of heroism. This evocation of rebellion against the accepted and the commonplace is an attitude that realism can suspend but not dissolve.

The image of Dorothea presented at the book's beginning is, to borrow a phrase from Simone de Beauvoir, transcendent. To turn to her from Celia, Mary Garth, and Mrs. Garth is to leave women who are themselves both innately conservative and a cause of conservatism in others, who either have no energies—like Celia—or who ruthlessly suppress them—like Mrs. Garth—women whose stasis impels others to return to the fold, and approach one for whom radical upheaval, both personal and social, seems possible. Like Jane Eyre, Dorothea seeks a wider world, hoping to find a transforming ritual in marriage, if nowhere else. In her original view, union with Mr. Casaubon seems to promise that "a fuller life was opening before her: she was a neophyte about to enter on a higher grade of initiation. She was going to have room for the energies which stirred uneasily under the dimness and pressure of her own ignorance and the petty peremptoriness of the world's habits" (chap. 5, p. 32). With her ardent nature, her intelligence, her desire not simply to be good but to discover what might be good in order to use the fruits of this discovery to change the world, Dorothea is a new character to nineteenth-century fiction. Even today, women readers in particular feel in the book's opening chapters the promise of a new spiritual substance, possibly even an entirely new creation. We wait for the author's imagination to divine a world whose existence we have long suspected, although its reality has been perpetually denied.

But, however much we may wish it otherwise, *Middlemarch* gives very little evidence that George Eliot wished to be the god in some new machine. From Prelude to Finale, and for eighty-six chapters in between, she tells us instead that in the early part of the nineteenth century in England, a woman whose "passionate ideal nature demanded an epic life" (Prelude, p. 3), whose inner "flame . . . soared after some illimitable satisfaction, some object which would never justify weariness, which would reconcile self-despair with the rapturous consciousness of life beyond self" (Prelude, p. 3) would be defeated or, at best, deflected. George Eliot is writing not the ultimate comedy of a new incarnation but rather the record of its failure. Faced with a world which lacked "coherent social faith and order" (Prelude, p. 3), George Eliot either would not or could not choose to create an alternative universe in her fiction. Instead, she records the dislocation which is "offspring of a certain spiritual grandeur ill-matched with the meanness of opportunity," (Prelude, p. 3), the isolation of the cygnet who "never finds the living stream in fellowship with its own oary-footed kind" (Prelude, p. 4).

This failure could be tragic, and Dorothea a tragic hero rather than a heroine, but only if her aspirations at the book's beginning were taken entirely seriously by her creator. And they are not. Throughout the book, George Eliot tempers her sympathy for Dorothea's situation with rejection of her longings as self-deluding and indeed pretentious. Nor is this attitude of sorrowful amusement consequent upon Dorothea's marrying Casaubon; it precedes the marriage and accompanies the presentation of Dorothea as the sort of woman who would marry Casaubon. Dorothea is short-sighted, a physical defect that here also has psychic implications.[10] Moreover, George Eliot—or her narrative surrogate in the book—continually addresses the elder Miss Brooke as "poor Dorothea" and ranges herself regretfully but unequivocally with Celia in her assessment of Dorothea's character. In chapter 7, for example, the narrator asserts that "Miss Brooke was certainly very naive with all her alleged cleverness. Celia, whose mind had never been thought too powerful, saw the emptiness of other people's pretensions much more readily" (chap. 7, p. 47). Although the pretensions referred to here apparently belong to Casaubon, it is equally possible that they belong to Dorothea as well, for the immediately preceding sentence states that Dorothea "had not reached that point of renunciation at which she would have been satisfied with having a wise husband: she wished, poor child, to be wise herself" (chap. 7, p. 47).

If the possibility that Dorothea's quest for knowledge is at best misguided were raised only here, the passage would hardly be worth noting. But George Eliot repeatedly insists on the futility and even foolishness of any desire to find an outlet for energy in the acquisition of wisdom defined narrowly as education and dissociates Dorothea from Casaubon by saying that "it would be a great mistake to suppose that Dorothea would have cared about any share in Casaubon's learning as mere accomplishment" (chap. 10, p. 63). On the contrary, she seems to be saying that Dorothea's desire for knowledge is a confused expression of her true longing for a combined moral and intellectual guidance, an analogue to the force which the Catholic faith provided for Saint Theresa. Unable to find her "ideal of life" in the "walled-in maze" which constitutes the usual occupations open to a woman of the leisured class, Dorothea sees knowledge as offering the only way out of the labyrinth. But the radical implications of this vision are moderated from its inception since both Dorothea and her creator see this knowledge in terms of a "union which . . . would . . . give her the freedom of voluntary submission to a guide who would take her along the grandest path" (chap. 3, p. 21). This union is not a transcendent link-

ing of the mind with abstract principles systematically combining wisdom and morality but an all-too-human, unheroic
marriage, first to Casaubon, then to Will Ladislaw.

Dorothea wants to lead "a grand life here—now—in England" (chap. 3, p. 21), but neither she nor George Eliot can
see a way to realize this desire directly. "Since the time was
gone by for guiding visions and spiritual directors, since
prayer heightened yearning but not instruction" (chap. 10,
p. 64), and more interestingly, since George Eliot does not
even consider the possibility of educational reform as a way
out of Dorothea's dilemma, marriage becomes the educating
institution. In marrying Casaubon, Dorothea is mistaken
about the contents of necessary knowledge, but not about the
form through which such knowledge should come to her.

When Dorothea says that "people may really have in them
some vocation which is not quite plain to themselves" (chap.
9, p. 60), she is speaking to Casaubon about Will. We, however, may hear her words as unwittingly or ironically self-
referential and as revealing, as well, George Eliot's bafflement
with certain aspects of Dorothea's character. For Dorothea is,
no less than Will, a character in search of a vocation, a form
in which her spiritual and social energies can be harmonized
and through wihch they can be directed in order to affect the
world at large. Since, however, like Brontë's Jane, she is one
to whom "permanent rebellion, the disorder of a life without
some loving reverent resolve" (chap. 20, p. 144) is impossible,
her search for a vocation is similarly truncated. In contrast to
Will, who has not only time but space in which to try on different roles, Dorothea has no arena of her own. And where
Will can attempt and reject a number of vocations, before
finding his niche as a member of Parliament, Dorothea cannot. Unlike Will, Dorothea has only two alternatives: she can
marry or she can remain a spinster. But even this choice is
more apparent than real. Dorothea *must* marry. For unmarried and unendowed with the strength for permanent rebellion, she cannot begin to find for herself the wisdom she de-

sires. She can devise plans for cottages, but their fireplaces may well interfere with their stairways. And even were her plans correct, she cannot build the cottages in any case, having neither the money nor, more important, the courage to do so on her own. Her wish for freedom, like Jane Eyre's, is always checked by her equally strong desire to submit. If we ignore this definition of Dorothea's character, the ending of *Middlemarch* must be incomprehensible.

Jane Eyre marries Mr. Rochester so that she may finally be loved, and love in *Jane Eyre* fuses a controlled eroticism with an unassailable, indeed a fortresslike security. Dorothea Brooke Casaubon's marriage to Mr. Ladislaw is also a love match. Our sense that this is so, that Dorothea and Will are happy in each other, provides a point of rest, an apparently comic resolution for the otherwise rather grim and unresolved plot. Sexuality, however, does not provide the key to Will's significance, though the truth of this statement may indicate a gap in Eliot's perceptions. Far from being an erotic radical, a post-Brontëan Rochester or a pre-Lawrencian Mellors saving Dorothea by his phallic force, Will is merely a social reformer who is given a vocation commensurate with his romantic liberalism; at the book's conclusion he becomes a member of Parliament and "an ardent public man" (Finale, p. 610). Taking over Dorothea's adjective, Will becomes an acceptable—because male—version of Dorothea herself.

The puzzle in Dorothea's second marriage is not that she "chooses" Will, but that she "chooses" marriage, and in doing so must sacrifice the opportunity given Will to find her own path and forge her energies into a new mold. This problem, of course, belongs more to Dorothea's creator than to Dorothea, and George Eliot acknowledges that "many who knew her [Dorothea] thought it a pity that so substantive and rare a creature should have been absorbed into the life of another, and be only known in a certain circle as a wife and mother" (Finale, p. 611). Admitting that Dorothea is a character who might have been fulfilled in a wider world than the one her author finally provides, George Eliot declares that no one who objected to Dorothea's final disposition "stated exactly what else that was in her power she ought rather to have done" (Finale, p. 611). George Eliot simply could not find this new and bigger world; the religious power which inspired Antigone and Saint Theresa to perform their heroic deeds alone is as unavailable to women in *Middlemarch* as it was in *Jane Eyre*. To fill this vacuum George Eliot found it necessary to impose tradition, widened only to the extent of allowing Mary Garth to write a book and Dorothea to go to London. Eliot does not explore the possibility of a world born not in reality's mirror but in the artist's will. She might have achieved this vision by holding the mirror to reflect not only the world both she and Dorothea knew and left behind but also the world she herself forced into existence when she stopped being Mary Ann Evans and became George Eliot instead. In *Middlemarch* George Eliot refuses this option and accepts a safety which she does not entirely celebrate but rather tinges with regret.

When we draw away from Dorothea to look instead at Rosamond, the reasons for George Eliot's ambivalent attitude toward Dorothea's energy become clear. Rosamond is as much Dorothea's shadow, the dark underside of her virtue, as Bertha Mason was Jane Eyre's or Frank Churchill was Emma's. At first glance it might appear that Rosamond is simply the typical nineteenth-century heroine, exposed to the persistent hostility of George Eliot's vision. This view, while not entirely incorrect, is insufficiently complex, for it fails to take note of precisely that facet of Rosamond's character which is most interesting: the strength of her will. Like Jay Gatsby, Rosamond would spring from her own Platonic image of herself. Formed, like him, out of mixed romanticism and vulgarity, her recklessness is greater than Dorothea's because it is not tempered by either the cooling winds of self-effacement or the broadening channels of social concern. What Rosamond wants is simply her own way out of Middlemarch. But her way, like Dorothea's, is defined throughout the book in society's terms—though Rosamond's society is, to be sure, more limited because more narrowly class- and money-conscious than Dorothea's. And, like Dorothea, Rosamond cannot get her way, cannot gain both the freedom from Middlemarch's constrictions and the material perquisites she feels are due her, without a husband.

George Eliot shares John Stuart Mill's powerful awareness of the strength and potential destructiveness of Rosamond's kind of energy. And, as is the case with her handling of Dorothea, Eliot can find nothing to do with the force that propels Rosamond, no place to lodge it safely once the possibility of wifely submission is denied. For behind Rosamond lurks the even more frightening spectre of Madame Laure, whose actions, concretizing the passionate power of women's rage against male authority and social forms, serve the same function as Bertha Mason's attacks on her brother and husband in *Jane Eyre*. As Harriet Smith's flight from the gypsies in *Emma* both marks the boundaries of Austen's world and reveals what she fears lurks beyond Highbury's hedges, so Madame Laure, too, serves as a symbolic marker; she is less a character than an image of atrocity. Madame Laure is a French actress whom Lydgate meets while he is studying in Paris. He observes her performing in a play where her part requires her to stab her lover, a role taken by her real-life husband. One night, during a performance, her foot slips, and, instead of acting a part, she enacts a crime. Tried for murder, she is acquitted; and Lydgate, persuaded of her innocence, courts her, trying to persuade her to marry him. To his horror, he learns that truth defies his idealistic visions: Madame Laure, in fact, is guilty as charged. " '*I meant to do it,*' " she declares. Offered justifying reasons, her husband's brutality, perhaps, or her own passionate aversion—she denies them. She acted only because " 'he wearied me; he was too fond: he would live in Paris, and not in my country; that was not agreeable to me. . . . You are a good young man,' " she tells Lydgate, " 'but I do not like husbands. I will never have another' " (chap. 15, p. 114).

Madame Laure is revealed as a woman who is willing literally to kill for freedom and who, moreover, has no regrets and
shows no remorse. This scene illuminates Lydgate, showing us
what he can't yet see—that he would do well to stay unmarried—revealing those "spots of commonness [that] lay in the
complexion of his prejudices" and prevented his "intellectual
ardour" from penetrating "his feeling and judgment about
furniture, or women" (chap. 15, p. 111). Madame Laure also
reflects something of Rosamond, a spiritual rather than a
physical murderer. Less obviously, however, the actress reflects
Dorothea, too; Mr. Casaubon's knowledge that Dorothea has
penetrated his intellectual disguise deals his ego a mortal
blow. Madame Laure thus serves as a clarifying image, making
us fully aware of the potential deadliness of marital relationships and of the source of this deadliness in unbridled female
anger and frustration.

George Eliot's conservatism is both the logical conclusion to
the problem that female energy poses in her work and, less
happily, the result of the failure of her imagination to create
even the sorts of alternatives Mill envisions in "The Subjection of Women." Middlemarch and its environs are a closed
world whose survival depends on the continuing life of values
cherished by the author. Her fidelity to these values, however,
prevents George Eliot from arriving at a radical solution—or,
indeed, any solution—to the problems of female energy the
book considers. Like *Emma* and *Jane Eyre, Middlemarch*
struggles to contain the energy, to force the new wine back
into the old bottles, and overtly condemns women who cannot
be so imprisoned as hostile to the community and values that
are generally endorsed. By underscoring the violence of Madame Laure's desire, the ruthlessness of her power, George
Eliot reveals what she fears will be the consequence if she
leaves her female characters unfettered.[11]

We can only wonder—and perhaps regret—that the ideal
of female freedom was not pursued further and in another
direction: that neither George Eliot, Jane Austen, nor Char-

lotte Brontë created a woman who knew before the fact that she neither liked nor needed husbands, if these sentiments required her either to submit to or destroy them. Had these authors been able to erect a system of values by which such a woman could live, they might have succeeded in breathing life again into Saint Theresa's desiccated image. Emma's history as head of Hartfield, the tale of Jane Eyre as a political revolutionary, the story of Dorothea as a social force: these books do not exist. The fictions Austen, Brontë, and Eliot did write expose the insufficiency of conventional comedy as a vehicle for expressing heroic women's impulses or conveying their satisfactions. The land of happily ever after is emotionally stagnant and psychically limiting, since the novel must acknowledge marriage as a social fact as well as a literary gesture. Authors who would make their women happy in marriage must either challenge the social meaning of marriage or reduce heroic women to the smaller, more limited role of heroine, thereby also diminishing their male consorts. We are used to thinking of Rochester as castrated, of Mr. Casaubon as impotent, and of both Mr. Knightley and Will Ladislaw as somehow lacking in sexual vitality. This diminution of male energies restores parity between the male and female characters (although it is significant that we tend to notice such reduction more in men than in women), even as it expresses a kind of vengeance that the authors exercise on behalf of their women characters against their male counterparts.

I will venture two concluding observations. First, "happy" marriage in nineteenth-century fictions focusing on socially rebellious and intellectually aggressive women, far from signaling triumph and symbolizing command as it can for male characters, serves as the agency which guarantees women's continuing assent to their own subordination. And second, comedy's requirements will subvert rather than express the claims of female heroism so long as we conceive of comedy as requiring a single gesture which insures the continuation of the species at the same time as it guarantees the present society's survival. Psyche, you will remember, gave birth to a daughter and moved from an earthly to a heavenly realm; Emma Knightley, Jane Rochester, and Dorothea Ladislaw all have sons and remain worldly beings. This conjunction is no accident: the sex of their offspring serves to suggest the abatement of their power. Trapped between their husbands and their sons, Emma, Jane, and Dorothea are reduced to fit the narrow dimensions of their final role: no longer the hero's, but the heroine's.

Chapter 4

"'Weddings be funerals'"

Sexuality, Maternity, and Selfhood in
Jude the Obscure, The Awakening,
and *The Portrait of a Lady*

"'Weddings be funerals 'a' b'lieve nowadays. Fifty-five years ago, come Fall, since my man and I married! Times have changed since then!'"

> Thomas Hardy, *Jude the Obscure*

Seen from the standpoint of the matriarchal world, every marriage is a rape of Kore, the virginal bloom, by Hades, the ravishing, earthly aspect of the hostile male. From this point of view every marriage is an exposure on the mountain's summit in mortal loneliness, and a waiting for the male monster, to whom the bride is surrendered. . . . Marriage as the marriage of death is a central archetype of the feminine mysteries.

> Erich Neumann, "The Psychic Development of the Feminine"

Eros, then . . . is the brother of death and not the principle that will save us from it.

> James Hillman, *The Dream and the Underworld*

In comedy, formal closure typically reciprocates narrative resolution. Happiness displaces discord. Virtue conquers vice. Separation merges into union. The flux of time gives way to the permanence of ever after. Unresolved problems arising out of growth and change are pushed to the periphery, where they offer only an oblique challenge to the values mediated by the form's conventions. In such narratives, an endless chain of generation binds the originally restless hero. Soothed, gentled, tamed, transformed, she becomes a heroine, a wife.

The impulse toward this transformation still persists. In fiction, as in life, the wedding march continues. During the last decades of the nineteenth century, however, the conflict-ridden relationship between marriage and female heroism begins to shift increasingly from the edge to the center of the plot. Imbalances between an implied transcendence and the mundane world, tensions between eternal ritual and social contract, irresolutions previously glimpsed out of the corner of the eye are now confronted directly. Works typical of this era do not yet offer a fully realized alternative form expressive of a changed vision of psyche, society, and the relationship between them. Nonetheless, because they expose the incongruities among formal, social, and psychological structures, they reformulate the problematic areas for life, art, and female heroism.

The catharsis accomplished by comedy's reliance on weddings is analogous to that accomplished by tragedy's reliance on religion. Both conclusions suggest that human conflict is resolvable only in terms of some enduring reality of generation or judgment. Insofar as these states are perceived as permanent, impervious to change, they also inevitably distort a heroism predicated on the need for personal or social alterations. Since rituals of incorporation and exclusion—weddings and funerals—are used to represent the twin poles of worldly continuation and personal defeat (even if for the sake of some more generalized social or metaphysical victory), it is appropriate that works which oppose cosmic certainties and concentrate instead on human processes conflate positive and negative imagery and seek, even in their endings, a kind of formal openness. In the works we now turn to—*Jude the Obscure* (1896), *The Awakening* (1899), and *The Portrait of a Lady* (1881; 1907–8)[1]—marriage remains the central ritual, the place where personal and communal interests merge or struggle. But, in these fictions, the meaning of marriage as both

private act and public drama is anatomized rather than celebrated; its value as an existential emblem is severely qualified
by the misery of its particular examples; its imagery is consistently funereal.

In discussing the structured processes of social action, Victor
Turner hypothesizes a "moment" in all ritualized movement
"when those being moved in accordance with a cultural script
[are] liberated from normative demands," a moment when, in
consequence, "almost anything may happen."[2] Such moments,
he continues, characterize those "forms of symbolic action,
those genres of free-time activity, in which all previous standards and models are subjected to criticism, and fresh new
ways of describing and interpreting socio-cultural experience
are formulated."[3] These symbolic structures are distinguished
from the preceding stabilized frameworks by both their formal requirements and their effect on an audience:

the "serious" genres of symbolic action—ritual, myth, tragedy, and
comedy . . . are deeply implicated in the cyclical repetitive views of
social process, while those genres which have flourished since the Industrial Revolution . . . though less serious in the eyes of the com-
monality . . . have had greater potential for changing the ways men
[sic] relate to one another and the content of their relationships. . . .
Because they are outside the arenas of direct industrial production
. . . to be either their agents or their audience is an optional activity—the absence of obligation or constraint from external norms imparts to them a pleasurable quality which enables them all the more
readily to be absorbed by individual consciousnesses. Pleasure thus
becomes a serious matter in the context of innovative change.[4]

The basic elements of the particular late-Victorian plot we
shall now consider are not much changed from the narratives
we have already examined: the main character is still a young
woman whose more than usual interest rests on her sense of
her own uniqueness and importance (supported by the judgment of the author and of other characters in the text), and
on her need to choose between conventionally acceptable and
psychically fulfilling alternatives. Yet, because the attitude
taken toward the plot's central ritual is altered, its architec-

ture and its meaning are entirely changed. Although marriage once again represents the traditionally sanctioned choice, the emphasis is now on the illegitimacy of this claim—on the deficiencies of the institution, specifically its inability to connect two equally developed subjects, and its consequent failure to serve as a bridge, for women in particular, between the self and a reciprocating community. Isabel Archer's painful observation that " 'the world's very small' " (chap. 55, p. 481) illustrates George Eliot's reflection that "there is no creature whose inward being is so strong that it is not greatly determined by what lies outside it. . . . The medium in which . . . ardent deeds took shape is for ever gone" (Finale, p. 612). In *Middlemarch* Eliot granted this knowledge only to her narrator; in *The Portrait of a Lady,* James bestows it on his character, who revises her opinion and decides, after all, that the world is vast. As the structural relation between participants and plot alters, the old fixed ending disappears; the plot's capacity to generate a sense of finality and containment dissipates.

The relationship between narrative and audience shifts, as Turner indicates, in response to these internal variations. Northrop Frye in marking this passage suggests that the aesthetic satisfactions provided by such works as *Emma, Jane Eyre,* and *Middlemarch* can be understood in terms of "the incorporation of an individual very like the reader into the society aspired to by both, a society ushered in with a happy rustle of bridal gowns and bank notes."[5] In a more general account of the rhetorical and psychic strategies of particular narrative structures, Kenneth Burke points out that in the total experience of a literary work, there is always a potential tension between "the psychology of the *hero* [and] the psychology of the audience."[6] Literary form along with structuring details of the narrative, reflects patterns of human desire. Formal paradigms inevitably implicate the reader in the text:

[A] work has form in so far as one part of it leads a reader to anticipate another part, and to be gratified by the sequence. . . . Given
certain things, certain things must follow, the premises forcing the
conclusion. . . . The audience from its acquaintance with the premises, feels the rightness of the conclusion. . . . The arrows of our
desire are turned in a certain direction, and the plot follows the direction of the arrows.[7]

Late nineteenth-century fictions no longer possess this direc-
tionality. Cherished values in these works are up for general
questioning, and none is entirely endorsed.[8] A wider world is
postulated as possible for Sue Bridehead, Isabel Archer, and
Edna Pontellier than for their fictive predecessors; economic
viability and social acceptability are considered separable from
a woman's marital status. In the case of *The Portrait of a
Lady,* speculation beyond the book's conclusion seems called
for; Isabel's life continues, although James's novel ends. If access to this wider world is still not fully realized, the potentiality for heroism is at least no longer undercut by suprahuman moral, metaphysical, or formal authorities. Even in *Jude
the Obscure,* in some ways the most conservative of the texts
under consideration, Sue's ultimate reliance on traditional
Christian morality is depicted as wrong and outmoded precisely because God's ordinances contradict human needs.
Where external forms no longer constitute an absolute imperative, action comes to be seen as grounded in and emerging
from psychological necessities. An inner war confirms the earlier opposition between the protohero and social restraints.
The ambivalence which is perhaps Sue's, Isabel's, and Edna's
most striking characteristic has, significantly, a single common
source and consequence: originating in a profound sexual dis-
ease, it hedges these women in and creates a barrier between
their own theoretical formulations and their capacity for
action.

Hardy's, James's, and Chopin's women initially manifest a
by now familiar sense of alienation, that first requisite for all
rebellion, whether successful and heroic or not. Sue Bridehead

tells Jude that " 'the social moulds civilization fits us into have no more relation to our actual shapes than the conventional shapes of the constellations have to the real star-patterns' " (pt. fourth, chap. 1, p. 211). Isabel Archer informs Caspar Goodwood:

"If there's a thing in the world I'm fond of . . . it's my personal independence. . . . I am not bound to be timid and conventional. . . . I try to judge things for myself; to judge wrong, I think, is more honourable than not to judge at all. I don't wish to be a mere sheep in the flock; I wish to choose my fate."

(Chap. 16, p. 141)

Similarly, Edna Pontellier "even as a child . . . lived her own small life within herself. At a very early period she had apprehended instinctively the dual life—that outward existence which conforms, the inward life which questions" (chap. 7, p. 15). Embodying this inner life, defying society's strictures, choosing one's fate has, in *The Awakening*, two requisites: election—" 'many gifts—absolute gifts—which have not been acquired by one's own effort' "—and bravery—" 'the courageous soul . . . the brave soul . . . the soul that dares and defies' " (chap. 21, p. 63).

These figures, like the others we have examined, stand on the border between one way of life and another, between one set of claims and another. Located in a recognizable social world, they challenge the boundary between that world and the self, as well as the wall that separates one definition of self from another, that divides an authentic being from one condemned to living death. If marriage in *Jude the Obscure, The Awakening,* and *The Portrait of a Lady* retains some of its traditional power as a conventionalizing social institution, it is seen as wielding this power insofar as it destroys women's autonomy and warps female sexuality. Acquiescing to marriage signifies, in each of these books, submitting to at least a spiritual death.

The motif of the deadly marriage is not newly created by Hardy, James, or Chopin. It is a staple of female heroic plots, as Psyche's original relationship to Amor, Clarissa's to both Solames and Lovelace, Hester's to Chillingworth, Dorothea's to Casaubon, and Jane's to St. John Rivers clearly demonstrate. In all these cases, however, the blighted marriage is seen as a mistake common to a developmental stage. Marking an end to maidenhood and female innocence, it is a prelude to future, more enlightened and harmonious unions with man, society, or God. Chopin, James, and Hardy break with their predecessors in suggesting that the iconography of marriage is generically funereal, a blank wall not a transitional passage. The badness of a particular union is thus neither accident nor idiosyncrasy, but a constant, arising out of the basic terms of the relationship. If one might say that *Clarissa, Jane Eyre,* and *Middlemarch* were "about" the desire for reformed husbands, *Jude the Obscure, The Portrait of a Lady,* and *The Awakening* are about the inadequacies of such a wish in the face of the institutional realities of marriage.

Sue Bridehead, for example, observes " 'how hopelessly vulgar an institution legal marriage is—a sort of trap to catch a man' " (pt. fifth, chap. 3, p. 276). Hardy's narrator similarly reflects that "the fundamental error of [the] matrimonial union [is] that of having based a permanent contract on a temporary feeling which had no necessary connection with affinities that alone render a lifelong comradeship tolerable" (pt. first, chap. 11, p. 75). Isabel Archer's bleak account of the dark, constricted vistas of her married life is another representation of marriage as a gloomy labyrinth:

She had taken all the first steps in the purest confidence, and then she had suddenly found the infinite vista of a multiplied life to be a dark, narrow alley with a dead wall at the end. Instead of leading to the high places of happiness . . . it led rather downward and earthward, into realms of restriction and depression where the sound of other lives . . . was heard as from above, and where it served to deepen the feeling of failure. It was her deep distrust of her husband—this was what darkened the world. . . . [T]he shadows had begun to gather . . . as if Osmond deliberately . . . put the lights out one by one.

(Chap. 42, p. 349)

Osmond's residence, which Isabel first perceives as "a seat of ease . . . luxury . . . and refinements frankly proclaimed" (chap. 22, p. 193) is bared as in truth "the house of darkness, the house of dumbness, the house of suffocation. Osmond's beautiful mind gave it neither light nor air" (chap. 42, p. 353). It is, in short, a tomb. And Edna Pontellier, in *The Awakening*, sees even "happy" marriages as stultified, fossilized, depressing rather than exalting. The spectacle of the Ratignolles' "domestic harmony . . . gave her no regret, no longing. It was not a condition of life which fitted her, and she could see in it but an appalling and hopeless ennui. She was moved by a kind of commiseration for Madame Ratignolle,—a pity for that colourless existence which never uplifted its possessor beyond the region of blind contentment" (chap. 18, p. 56).

Because the emblem of marriage is empowered by fertility, it necessarily presumes sexuality on the part of the participants. The ambivalence with which female sexuality has historically been regarded in Western culture is now so commonly acknowledged as to require no further documentation. What is of particular relevance here is the way in which *The Awakening, The Portrait of a Lady,* and *Jude the Obscure* represent the sterility of marriage as precisely correlated with its repression of the wife's libidinal desires. In Sue Bridehead's view, the marital relationship is perversely and explicitly antisexual. She tells Jude,

"If the marriage ceremony consisted in an oath and signed contract between the parties to cease loving from that day forward, in consideration of personal possession being given, and to avoid each other's society as much as possible in public, there would be more loving couples than there are now."

(Part fifth, chap. 1, p. 264)

Edna Pontellier similarly, if somewhat less flamboyantly, defines her state:

She grew fond of her husband, realizing with unaccountable satisfaction that no trace of passion or excessive and fictitious warmth colored her affection, thereby threatening its dissolution.

(Chap. 7, pp. 19–20)

Isabel Archer repeatedly rejects Caspar Goodwood, whose "kiss was like white lightning, a flash that spread, and spread again, and stayed." Acknowledging that "while she took it, she felt each thing in his hard manhood . . . justified of its intense identity and made one with this act of possessing" (chap. 55, p. 482), she nonetheless returns to Rome. Osmond's proposal, on the other hand, is accepted because Isabel discovers within herself "a terror in having to begin to spend" that "force" stored within her "like a large sum stored in a bank," that "something within herself, deep down, that she supposed to be inspired and trustful passion (chap. 29, p. 258). Making pointed use of the standard equation of economic and sexual language, James reveals that Isabel, in accepting Osmond, need not commit herself to the fearful prospect of spending her stored hoard; instead, marriage commits her to forced savings.

The narrative patterns of *The Portrait of a Lady, The Awakening,* and *Jude the Obscure,* emphasizing and reinterpreting the motif of the deathly marriage, focus on the bafflement of Isabel, Edna, and Sue. Relating an acknowledged, if still largely potential, female sexuality to other equally compelling psychological needs for autonomy and power, and setting all such needs in conflict with the antilibidinous compulsions of marriage, Hardy, James, and Chopin simultaneously provide further demonstration of the bonds restraining female heroism and set the stage for a new typology for female heroic plots.[9] If Edna, Sue, and Isabel do not themselves cross into the promised land, theirs is the vision which finally makes such passage possible to future generations of characters and readers.

Sue's, Edna's and Isabel's interminable vacillations, their hesitations, even their seemingly perverse suppression of their own sexuality do not remain purely internal flaws. In each case, the character's psyche is unbalanced by the need to respond to real and unavoidable external phenomena. In a social world—fictional or real—containing actively heterosexual adult women but lacking birth control, the consequences of enacted sexuality are predictable: children. But although indulged sexuality produces children, children inhibit, even destroy, sexuality. Children fix responsibility, yet sexuality for women, as for men, is inherently promiscuous. Furthermore, as long as the family is regarded as a necessarily patriarchal institution, children's need for family protection contradicts their mothers' needs for self-expression. Sue Bridehead terms marriage " 'only a sordid contract,' " where " 'material convenience in householding, rating, and taxing' " is on a par with " 'the inheritance of land and money by children, making it necessary that the male parent should be known' " (pt. fourth, chap. 2, p. 215). It is no accident that the device Hardy employs to return Sue to the world of conventional forms involves the murder of her illegitimate offspring by Jude's legitimate heir. Similarly, in the penultimate scene of *The Awakening*, Edna Pontellier witnesses the birth of Adèle Ratignolle's child "with an inward agony, with a flaming outspoken revolt against the ways of Nature" (chap. 38, p. 109). Dr. Mandelet, accompanying Edna's departure from the scene, calls the failure to recognize the simultaneous linkage and incongruity between sexuality and maternity one of youth's illusions. Nature provides passion merely as " 'a decoy to secure mothers for the race' " (chap. 38, p. 110). Avoiding this "decoy" means, for Edna, choosing death—first privately, in marriage to Léonce, then publicly, in the waters of the Gulf. Children provide the final impulse. Edna's sons "appeared before her like antagonists who had overcome her; who had overpowered and sought to drag her into the soul's slavery for the rest of her days. But she knew a way to elude them" (chap. 30, p. 113): she drowns herself. Even for Isabel, who has no living children of her own, the bond that commits her both initially and finally to Osmond is maternal. The implications of the facts that the child that binds her is a stepchild, and a daughter rather than a son, shall be considered later; at this point it is sufficient to note that Pansy, like Father Time in *Jude the Obscure*, serves first to sever the sexual relationship between her parents, Gilbert Osmond and Serena Merle. Pansy's existence compels Madame Merle to seek a wife for Osmond not in order to satisfy anyone's adult sexual or emotional needs but rather to secure a wealthy mother for her child. A wealthy mother is necessary to provide a dowry, so that Pansy may marry well and participate in the system's perpetuation. Isabel's sexual reluctance qualifies her for the role Madame Merle calls on her to play.

Each of these women is classically doubly bound, a participant in a situation defined by a set of competing, mutually contradictory injunctions.[10] In these cases, the charges run as follows: Marry in order to legitimize sexuality versus marry in order to destroy sexuality versus do not marry in order to indulge sexuality. Be sexual in order to produce children versus produce children in order to divert sexuality versus do not produce children in order to retain sexuality. Additionally, so the theory of the double bind requires, there must be another negative injunction preventing the subjects from escaping from the field; here the society we see revealed in each fiction is presumed to convey the totality of possible communities. And finally, according to Gregory Bateson, who first described and analyzed such circumstances, "the complete set of ingredients is no longer necessary when the victim has learned to perceive [the] universe in double bind patterns."[11] When this state occurs, no one in the situation is conscious of the contradictions, and the victim is certifiably schizophrenic.

Although none of the novels under discussion seems intended as a case history, I think it is fair to infer that the authors' collective refusal to push their characters into clear and permanent psychosis may be read as indicating their desire to endow these women with a high degree of psychic strength.[12] Nonetheless, as the motif of the deathly marriage moves to the forefront in the narratives we are now discussing, irrationality and despair, the "madness" which has characterized isolated moments in earlier narratives correspondingly expands.[13] This psychic chaos is, to be sure, a neurotic symptom. But, grounded in the total cultural contexts of the narratives, such neurosis is if not a "healthy" response, at least one based on a realistic evaluation of the surrounding circumstances. Sue, Isabel, and Edna are not simply mired in contradictions; they become increasingly aware of the relationship between their own psychic dilemmas and a corresponding set of competing cultural imperatives. A period of breakdown and confusion, required to some extent by *all* heroic narratives, is a necessary precursor of any future cultural synthesis.

As heroes, then, these characters take on two separate but interrelated tasks. First, each consciously confronts the ideological and psychological antisexuality which surrounds and sanctions marriage in the nineteenth century in order, as it were, to force fictional narratives to take account of these factors in using marriage as a narrative gesture. Second, each comprehends the incongruent relationship among marriage, sexuality, and maternity in a world where, because children are conceived as the paradoxical representation of contradictory forces—the sexuality required for reproduction and the antisexuality required by marriage—their continued "safe" existence requires a denial of their natural, impulsive origins.

The magnitude of these psychic labors makes them worthy of more than the language of symptomatology. To say this is not to deny what might be called the objective neuroses of these characters but to suggest that an emphasis on the struggle to comprehend internal ambivalence and social maladjustment is necessary to balance the account and provide an understanding of the characters' legitimate appeal. Such appeal is manifest in the concern inspired in others within the respective texts and the anxiety their stories continue to provoke in readers. Even at the dismal conclusion of Hardy's novel, Jude remembers Sue as " 'a woman-poet, a woman-seer, a woman whose soul shone like a diamond' " (pt. sixth, chap. 3, p. 356). Chopin characterizes Edna as a woman "different

from the crowd," a person "beginning to recognize her relations as an individual to the world within and about her"
(chap. 6, pp. 14–15). And James defends the naive, untested
Isabel against charges he apparently anticipates his readers
making: "She would be an easy victim of scientific criticism
if she were not intended to awaken on the reader's part an
impulse more tender and more purely expectant" (chap. 6,
p. 54).

In the light of these evaluations, the claim, for example,
that "Edna's central problem . . . is that her libidinal appetite has been fixated at the oral level"[14] or that "the portrait
of Sue Bridehead . . . remains one of the most impressive in
all fiction of a neurotic and sexually maladjusted woman"[15]
is not so much incorrect as unnecessarily restrictive.[16] Separating the psyche from its wider social and narrative contexts,
such assessments create an unnecessary distance from the substance of the fictions and sever the connection between the
reader and the text.

Without sentimentalizing neurosis or glamorizing martyrdom, we can see the characters' psychic incapacity in positive
terms. Considered as impersonal and representative, the generalized response of consciousness to objectively verified circumstances, the characters' fates revise our response to past relationships at the same time as they serve future possibilities.
Even if Hardy, James, and Chopin do not yet succeed in creating new alternatives for their central female figures, authors
and characters together push the imagination forward because
they render retreat impossible. What is once known can never
be unknown.

Isabel Archer, for example, chooses Gilbert Osmond in
terms which recapitulate those governing Jane Eyre's final
choice of Mr. Rochester:

He was poor and lonely and yet . . . somehow he was noble—that
was what had interested her and seemed to give her opportunity. . . .
She . . . felt at the same time that he was helpless and ineffectual,
but the feeling had taken the form of a tenderness which was the very

flower of respect. . . . It was in all this she had found her occasion.
She would launch his boat for him; she would be his providence; it
would be a good thing to love him. And she had loved him . . . a
good deal for what she found in him, but a good deal also for what
she brought him . . . a kind of maternal strain—the happiness of a
woman who felt that she was a contributor, that she came with charged
hands.

(P. 351)

Despite the difference between Rochester's and Osmond's
characters, the collapse of Isabel's marriage, because it exposes
the contradiction at the heart of romance, still tends retroac-
tively to undermine the foundation of Jane's relationship to
Rochester. Where one party subsumes the other and makes or
is made another's project, "love" must be a deadly struggle for
the power to submerge.

Structure not personality determines this effect. Edna Pontellier's friends are thus quite right when they declare "that
Mr. Pontellier was the best husband in the world" (chap. 4,
p. 9). But he is "best" in a society where Edna's sun tan makes
her "a valuable piece of personal property which has suffered
some damage" (chap. 1, p. 4). The struggle to work through
this contradiction, to attain a wider degree of autonomy
within the framework of heterosexual relations, sets particular devastation against future possibility, temporary sterility
against potential growth. As Chopin remarks early in *The
Awakening*:

The beginning of things, of a world especially, is necessarily vague,
tangled, and exceedingly disturbing. How few of us ever emerge from
such beginnings! How many souls perish in its tumult!

(Chap. 6, p. 15)

The souls that perish are, of course, weak in some way,
flawed, inadequate to the task confronting them. But, we need
not see them—and we do not respond to them—as only thus
diminished. For any effort to define the self against the norms
of the quotidian world may generate a force that is felt as
potentially heroic insofar as this opposition is endowed with

existential or social significance and accepted as legitimate either within the fiction or by its audience. The pressure exerted by such efforts defines a boundary, forcing both sides to clarify their attitudes; it also makes conscious what was formerly inaccessible, repressed. Because articulated structures emerge out of a previously undifferentiated mass, future developments will necessarily have a clearer focus. The very fluidity of the circumstances, however, tends to invalidate previously normalizing standards and criteria for judgment. The characters, groping to realize a vision that is nowhere recognized, fall between categories and frequently puzzle even themselves.

Nowhere is this perplexity more apparent than in the characterization of Sue Bridehead. There is, I think, no way to resolve the contradictions in Sue's nature. Ethereal but sensual; one who exhorts free love but refuses to commit herself to it; a champion of what she calls " 'Greek joyousness' " who chooses an extreme, unnecessary, and futile form of Christian self-mortification and penitential sacrifice; Sue is more tantalizing if no less obscure than Jude himself. On the one hand, she writes to Phillotson, " 'No poor woman has ever wished more than I that Eve had not fallen, so that . . . some harmless mode of vegetation might have peopled Paradise' " (pt. fourth, chap. 3, p. 231). On the other, she denounces the allegorization of The Song of Solomon as " 'humbug' " that attempts " 'to plaster over with ecclesiastical abstractions such ecstatic, natural, human love' " (pt. third, chap. 4, p. 157). She aligns herself with " 'some of the most passionately erotic poets' " (pt. third, chap. 4, p. 154), but tells Jude that " 'My nature is not so passionate as yours! . . . My liking for you . . . is a delight in being with you . . . and I don't want to go further and risk it by—an attempt to intensify it!' " (pt. fourth, chap. 5, pp. 246–47) and requests, somewhat puzzlingly, that he " 'kiss me like a lover, incorporeally' " (pt. fifth, chap. 4, p. 288). Refusing to marry Jude, Sue says she stands for natural love, not crabbed scruples; she seems to Jude like " 'one of the women of some grand old civilization, whom I used to read about in my . . . classical days, rather than a denizen of a mere Christian country' " (pt. fifth, chap. 3, p. 276). Yet, in the end, feeling her actions to have violated those moral canons whose existence and claim she had earlier denied, she is chastened and attempts to atone: " 'We ought to be continually sacrificing ourselves on the altar of duty! . . . I well deserved the scourging I have got! I wish something would take the evil right out of me, and all my monstrous errors, and all my sinful ways!' " (pt. sixth, chap. 3, p. 351). Jude sees Sue's loyalties as hopelessly torn between her desire to love and her fear of sex, between her boldness and her conventionality. In seeking to model her relationships with men on their relationships among themselves, Sue hopes to gain friendship by evading sex. She wants a union based " 'on walking tours, reading tours, and things of that sort—like two men almost' " (pt. third, chap. 4, p. 153). Jude sees this desire for parity as demonstrating chiefly Sue's "epicene tenderness" (pt. third, chap. 4, p. 158), her "strange ways and curious unconsciousness of gender" (pt. third, chap. 4, p. 154). The narrator refers with commendable restraint to "the state of that mystery, her heart" (pt. fourth, chap. 5, p. 246).

We can speculate about the sort of psychic background that might produce such bafflement, but we can never plumb its depths, because Hardy doesn't provide us with enough information. It is only by looking at the effects that desire—her own for Jude; Jude's, Phillotson's, and the unnamed undergraduate's for Sue—has on Sue that we can begin to understand what causes her fears and perhaps justifies her ambivalence. In the world of Hardy's fiction, sexuality contaminates Sue's imagined intimacy because, compelling marriage, it becomes an agent of bondage rather than an expression of freedom. By entering into a sexual relationship outside of marriage, Sue hopes to make private ideology conquer social convention. She pits " 'Nature's intention, Nature's law . . .

that we should be joyful in what instincts she afforded us' " (pt. sixth, chap. 2, p. 345) against " 'that dreadful contract to feel in a particular way in a matter whose essence is its voluntariness' " (pt. fourth, chap. 2, p. 218) and loses. Her dilemma thus transcends the internal, the psychological, even the personal. It expresses instead an external conflict Hardy observes between the abstract forces of nature and society. Impulse and convention war in Sue because Hardy sees them generally at war. Sue's predicament merely localizes and specifies Jude's earlier "perception of the flaw in the terrestrial scheme, by which what was good for God's birds was bad for God's gardeners" (pt. first, chap. 2, p. 21).

For Sue this conflict centers on the production of children. Hardy shows how reproduction, as both a natural and a social event, alters the context in which instinctive behavior must be considered. As British sociologist Ann Oakley points out:

> Childbirth stands uncomfortably at the junction of the two worlds of nature and culture. A biological event, it is accomplished by social beings—women—who consequently possess a uniquely dual character. . . . Childbirth is a constant reminder of the association between women's "nature" and nature "herself": it must become a social act, since society is threatened by the disorder of what is beyond its jurisdiction. The cultural need to socialize childbirth impinges on the free agency of women. . . . Thus, just how reproduction has been socially constructed is of prime importance to any consideration of women's position.[17]

Hardy works out the consequences of Sue's capitulation to a world of sexuality by showing what happens to Sue's children, the outward and visible forms of her inward and spiritual condition. Sue's fate as a sexual and social being cannot be separated from the fate of these offspring. The children's fates, in turn, cannot be separated from their economic and social circumstances. These circumstances, finally, are indissolubly bound up with their parents' marital status. Because Sue, fearing to lose her psychic autonomy and control over her sexual capacities, will not marry Jude, the children that result from the sexuality she does express are compromised. Emblems of

Sue's sexual experience, they are, from society's point of view, not free but only illegitimate.

When Little Father Time (Jude's son and the product of his lawful union with Arabella) first appears on the scene, Jude attempts to frame a new context for his care:

"The beggarly question of parentage—what is it, after all? What does it matter, when you come to think of it whether a child is yours by blood or not? All the little ones of our time are collectively the children of us adults of the time, and entitled to our general care. That excessive regard of parents for their own children, and their dislike of other people's, is, like class-feeling, patriotism, save-your-own-soul-ism, and other virtues, a mean exclusiveness at bottom."

(Part fifth, chap. 2, p. 280)

Earlier, Mr. Phillotson had tried to see a way in which spontaneous sexual unions could nonetheless proivde care for future generations. To his friend Gillingham's objections that " 'if people did as you want to do, there'd be a general domestic disintegration. The family would no longer be a social unit' " (pt. fourth, chap. 4, p. 238), Phillotson replies that he doesn't " 'see why the woman and the children should not be the unit without the man' " (pt. fourth, chap. 4, p. 238). Hardy fears, however, that "matriarchy" cannot be guaranteed; Arabella doesn't want her son. Where blood's claims fail, only law can compel; but law, by definition, can operate only in relation to a larger system of artificial constructs. Divorce is part of this system no less than marriage. What might have been construed as Jude's and Sue's free relationship to any child is utilized instead to show the invincibility of legal ties. And the promise of Sue and Jude's free relationship to each other is betrayed by Father Time's unliftable depression. Sue bases her hope on the possibility of making a virtue out of joy; Father Time believes, on the contrary, that " 'all laughing comes from misapprehension' " (pt. fifth, chap. 3, p. 281). And Father Time becomes inevitably the agent of Sue's capitulation.

Sue's former belief that cosmic forces are indifferent to hu-

man life and that, in consequence, it falls to individuals to
make their fates as best they can, is utterly annihilated by the
deaths of her children:

> "We must conform! . . . All the ancient wrath of the Power above
> us has been vented upon us . . . and we must submit. There is no
> choice. . . . It is no use fighting against God! . . . I have no more
> fighting strength left; no more enterprise. I am beaten, beaten!"
>
> (Part sixth, chap. 3, p. 348)

The closed circle of Sue's defeat is represented by her return
to Phillotson and her remarriage to him. "Chastened, world-
weary, remorseful," she is literally shrunken, "smaller in outline than . . . formerly" (pt. sixth, chap. 5, pp. 375–76). This
image of reduction describes more than Sue's physique, for
Sue is left with a reduced self, ground down in the battle between the social and the impulsive requisites for reproduction.
Hardy may wish us to judge Sue wrong for giving in to conventional morality. Yet, he has arranged the plot so as to make
her convictions psychologically plausible and socially if not
metaphysically accurate. The death of the children, an event
at which Hardy has connived no less than Father Time, finally
makes it impossible for Sue to maintain her posture of defiance: " 'Arabella's child killing mine was a judgment—the
right slaying the wrong' " (pt. sixth, chap. 3, p. 356).

Marriage remains funereal: ' 'The flowers in the bride's
hand are sadly like the garland which decked the heifers of
sacrifice in old times' " (pt. fifth, chap. 4, p. 293); Sue has been
" 'cowed into submission.' " But Hardy's adherence to this
view is not compensated by a balancing commitment to any
alternative option or strategy for escape. The book's structure,
like the characters' fates, is a dead end. The old forms mori-
bund, efforts to discover or create new ones prove deadly.

Although Hardy does not completely turn his back on Sue,
his imagination is drawn to catastrophe more than to promise,
and his ultimate evaluation of Sue sees her reason derailed by
a combination of her afflictions and her sex. Sue's heroism,
which resided in her capacity to recognize the contradiction

between the desire for affiliation and the enforced unity of marriage, is destroyed. But, through her agency, the contradiction remains exposed.

Kate Chopin uses Edna Pontellier to explore a similarly unresolvable conundrum in *The Awakening*. Like Sue, Edna has both a perfectly "good" but boring and somewhat overbearing husband and a lover who excites her but with whom she cannot live. And like *Jude the Obscure*, *The Awakening* explicitly connects the imposition of limits on female sexual indulgence with the special relationship between women's sexuality and, not parenthood, but specifically maternity. In comparison with the former novel, however, *The Awakening* is much richer, for it describes both the formal limitations curtailing Edna's sexually based vision and an alternative structure capable of providing a new measure of female emotional fulfillment and economic autonomy.

Chopin's title provides the image which controls Edna's psychic life throughout the book. The plot demonstrates how the process of Edna's waking into an awareness of her body's life alters the psychic and social structures that orient her in the world: "She was seeing with different eyes and making the acquaintance of new conditions in herself that colored and changed her environment" (chap. 14, p. 41). Unfortunately, this alteration serves merely to move her from the anesthetized world of the comic heroine, unsatisfactory despite—or because of—"her husband's kindness and . . . uniform devotion (chap. 3, p. 8), into the equally unsatisfactory world of the fairy tale or romance.[18] For Edna's involvement with Robert, like her more disturbing if less complex relationship with the rakish Alcée Arobin, is rooted in childhood's infatuations with remote, fantastic figures. Edna believes that the warmth aroused by these men—a cavalry officer, a tragic actor, and a young man already engaged to someone else—could never blaze in reality; her marriage to Léonce signals her acceptance of the chilly deadliness of life.

Chopin embodies Edna's ambivalent feelings towards both her own denied sensuality and the sanctioned structures of repression in an extremely rich, almost dreamlike fragment of memory brought to the surface of consciousness by Edna's encounter with Robert in the summer by the sea. In this fragment, Edna feels her way back to her early childhood in Kentucky. She remembers " 'a meadow . . . as big as the ocean' " and a " 'very little girl walking through the grass, which was higher than her waist. She threw out her arms as if swimming when she walked, beating the tall grass as one strikes out in the water' " (chap. 7, p. 17). Edna surmises that the early encounter took place on a Sunday morning when she ran " 'from the Presbyterian service, read in a spirit of gloom by my father that chills me yet to think of' " (chap. 7, p. 18). This part of the memory is echoed in the main body of the fiction when Edna flees the church service to which Robert has taken her and finds refuge in Madame Antoine's providentially provided house. There she goes to sleep and wakens to discover Robert waiting for her. The final significant motif in this highly charged recollection emerges in Edna's description of herself as wearing a sunbonnet that " 'obstructed the view' " so that she " 'could see only the stretch of green before me, and . . . felt as if I must walk on forever, without coming to the end of it' " (chap. 7, pp. 17–18). Edna's struggle throughout *The Awakening* concerns her efforts to cast off this obstruction, metaphorically associated also with parasols and all manner of restrictive or "protective" clothing, in order to stand fully exposed to the sun's light and to the revelation of her consciousness. Léonce first voices his objections to what he experiences as a change in Edna and hostility towards himself by telling her she is " 'burnt beyond recognition,' " by which he means that she is "a valuable piece of personal property which has suffered some damage" (chap. 1, p. 4). The motif of Edna's awakening is associated with a return to her earliest childhood in order to bring the sunlight of adult awareness to bear on a mode of existence which her Presbyterian upbring-

ing has forced into repression.[19] The mysterious and somewhat sinister "lady in Black," counting her rosary and haunt-
ing the equally shadowy pair of young lovers—"the lovers,
shoulder to shoulder creeping; the lady in black gaining
steadily upon them" (chap. 12, p. 34)—suggests similar tensions existed even in the much less repressed life Edna shared
with the Creoles on Grand Isle.

Edna's inability to cast her awakening into social terms is
directly related to her seduction by the childish forms already
established to contain her sensual impulses. This failure rests
partly with her and partly with Robert—her inspiration, her
collaborator, but a man whose arrested capabilities are finally
as shocked by his encounter with Edna as hers are by her involvement with him. Both regard their own person and the
other as characters in a predetermined fairy tale. She, like the
young and mortal Psyche, is the sleeping princess; he, like
Amor, is the charming prince.[20] When Edna awakens to find
Robert after her flight from church, she remarks, " 'How many
years have I slept? . . . The whole island seems changed. A
new race of beings must have sprung up, leaving only you and
me as past relics. How many ages ago did . . . our people
from Grand Isle disappear from the earth?' " Robert responds
in kind: " 'You have slept precisely one hundred years. I was
left here to guard your slumbers' " (chap. 13, p. 238).

If this structure liberates in some ways, it confines in others.
Edna's existence as the princess requires Robert to be the
prince. When, unwilling to take on the burdens of this role,
Robert flees to Mexico (perhaps in a similar indulgence of romantic possibility denied by the obligations of the adult
world), Edna feels stranded. Tortured "with the biting conviction that she had lost that which her impassioned, newly
awakened being demanded" (chap. 15, p. 46), she feels that
Robert's absence leaves "a void and wilderness behind her"
(chap. 16, p. 47). Meaning has leached from the world. "The
street, the children, the fruit vender, the flowers growing there
under her eyes, were all part and parcel of an alien world

which had suddenly become antagonistic" (chap. 16, p. 54). Whatever options this period of isolation provides for Edna, it leaves her need for a combined intimacy and sensuousness unsatisfied. It is only when Robert returns, prepared to do what the fairy tale requires and marry Edna, that she realizes this plot suffers from the same restrictiveness as the one in which she is already involved in her life with Léonce. When Robert reveals his " 'wild dream' " of Edna's becoming his wife, his recollection of " 'men who had set their wives free' " (chap. 36, p. 106), Edna is indignant:

> "You have been a very, very foolish boy, wasting your time dreaming of impossible things when you speak of Mr. Pontellier setting me free! I am no longer one of Mr. Pontellier's possessions to dispose of or not. I give myself where I choose. If he were to say, 'Here, Robert, take her and be happy; she is yours,' I should laugh at you both."
>
> (Chap. 36, pp. 106-7)

Without Robert, though, what might Edna do? It is in considering this point that Chopin's novel is most interesting. For, unlike almost every other female protohero we have previously considered, Edna might indeed do something: paint. She might use her art both to express and to support her newly discovered self. Further, should she elect this role, she need not endure utter isolation but might, rather, affiliate herself with another woman—Mademoiselle Reisz, a pianist who, "by her divine art, seemed to reach Edna's spirit and set it free" (chap. 26, p. 78). Mademoiselle Reisz recognizes Edna as a kindred spirit: " 'You are the only one worth playing for' " (chap. 10, p. 27). Electing herself Edna's mentor, she makes music that moves Edna to the same experience she had when Robert's lessons took effect and she first swam out to sea.

> The very first chords which Mademoiselle Reisz struck upon the piano sent a keen tremor down Mrs. Pontellier's spinal column. . . . Perhaps it was the first time she was ready, perhaps the first time her being was tempered to take an impress of the abiding truth.
>
> She waited for the material pictures which she thought would gather and blaze before her imagination. She waited in vain. She saw no pictures of solitude, of hope, of longing, or of despair. But the

very passions themselves were aroused within her soul, swaying it, lashing it, as the waves beat upon her splendid body.

(Chap. 9, p. 27)

When the Pontelliers return to New Orleans and Robert flees to Mexico, Edna feels at a crossroads in her own life. Resolving "never to take another step backward" (chap. 9, p. 57), she breaks the unspoken contract that had previously existed between herself and her husband, an exchange of his "courtesy" for her "tacit submissiveness" (chap. 19, p. 57). "Casting aside that fictitious self which we assume like a garment with which to appear before the world" (chap. 19, p. 57) Edna contemplates possible alternative futures, one of which involves "working with great energy and interest" and a sense that, although nothing she now produces "satisfie[s] her in the least degree" (chap. 19, p. 57), she might with hard work and concentration improve her efforts and succeed. Chopin uses Edna's painting not to set her apart as a dweller in the sacred realm of art but, more mundanely, as a way of providing her with enough money to enable her to live independent of her husband and, indeed, of any man:

"I am beginning to sell my sketches. Laidpore [a prominent art dealer] is more and more pleased with my work; he says it grows in force and individuality. . . . I feel that I have gained in ease and confidence. . . . I can live in the tiny house for little or nothing. . . . I know I shall like it, like the feeling of freedom and independence." . . . Conditions would some way adjust themselves, she felt; but whatever came, she had resolved never again to belong to another than herself.

(Chap. 26, pp. 79–80)

Art, then, serves Edna as vocation and livelihood, a means of securing both spiritual and economic independence. Its function is related to, but distinct from, the promise offered by further involvement with Robert.

Chopin uses distinctive images to contrast the two possibilities. Edna's relationship with Robert is continuously linked with water, with the moon and the ocean, with a blurring of boundaries, with seduction and a loss of self, with the surrender of consciousness, and ultimately, of course, with death. Chopin first conjures the sea in the encounter promised by Robert's swimming lessons as "seductive; never ceasing, whispering, clamoring, murmuring, inviting the soul to wander for a spell in abysses of solitude; to lose itself in mazes of inward contemplation" (chap. 6, p. 15). Edna's first solitary swim takes place when "the night sat lightly upon the sea and the land" and "the white light of the moon had fallen upon the world like the mystery and the softness of sleep" (chap. 10, p. 28). In swimming, Edna gathers "an impression of space and solitude" conveyed by "the vast expanse of water, meeting and melting with the moonlit sky" (chap. 10, p. 29). As she swims, she seems "to be reaching out for the unlimited in which to lose herself" (chap. 10, p. 29). Unused to such experience and quickly exhausted by it, Edna glimpses a "quick vision of death" (chap. 10, p. 29) and struggles back to shore.

The possibility of art, at least insofar as it is associated with Mademoiselle Reisz, is marked, both imagistically and literally, by a complete avoidance of the sort of unconscious merging Robert holds out to Edna. Mademoiselle Reisz herself is characterized by an almost grotesque avoidance of water, a "natural aversion . . . sometimes believed to accompany the artistic temperament" (chap. 16, p. 48). As Robert tempts Edna down into the darkness of the water, Mademoiselle Reisz summons Edna in the opposite direction, toward the sun and the sky. Her apartments are always directly under the roof; her windows are "nearly always open," admitting into the room "all the light and air that there was" (chap. 21, p. 61). She greets Edna with the exclamation " 'Ah! here comes the sunlight' " (chap. 26, p. 78). When Edna talks to her of her own artistic longings, Mademoiselle Reisz warns that more is involved than either talent or application: " 'to succeed, the artist must possess the courageous soul. . . . The brave soul. The soul that dares and defies' " (chap. 21, p. 63). The artist, likened to " 'the bird that would soar above the level plain of tradition and prejudice, must have strong wings' " (chap. 27,

p. 82). Lacking these, " 'it is a sad spectacle to see the weak-lings bruised, exhausted, fluttering back to earth' " (chap. 27, p. 82).

Edna, then, is a bird in flight, testing her wings, trying her strength. Leaving her husband's house, she takes up residence in the small, aptly named "pigeon house," a self-selected nest just big enough for one. In rejecting her social position as her husband's wife, Edna has cast off the responsibilities such a position entails. Having "descended in the social scale," she has a "corresponding sense of having risen in the spiritual" (chap. 32, p. 93).

> Every step which she took toward relieving herself from obligations added to her strength and expansion as an individual. She began to look with her own eyes; to see and to apprehend the deeper under-currents of life. No longer was she content to "feed upon opinion" when her own soul had invited her.
>
> (Chap. 32, p. 93)

But however much Edna values her newly found independence, she lacks the strength to maintain it. It is not Léonce Pontellier who stands in her way. He, on the contrary, adjusts the appearances of his life to disguise the reality of Edna's. When Edna leaves home, for example, he issues an announcement that his house is being remodeled and sends in a team of architects and builders to render the dwelling uninhabitable in Edna's absence. Although he seems unable to tolerate the idea of an absolute break with his wife and is quite prepared to have her declared ill or mentally unstable as a final camouflage, these maneuvers are ultimately unnecessary.[21] Instead, Chopin shows how Edna is baffled by conflicts which have little to do with either Léonce's presence or his attitudes. Internally divided, Edna is torn between her desire to soar as an independent woman, her flight guided by the example of Mademoiselle Reisz, and her wish to lose this identity in a passionate sexual union with Robert. She can fly or she can swim, but she cannot do both. Thus, when she paints, chance memories of Robert intrude and distract her: "A subtle cur-

rent of desire passed through her body weakening her hold
upon the brushes and making her eyes burn" (chap. 19, p. 58).
In an attempt to combine the two modes of being—the imaginative, artistic, and independent and the corporeal, sensuous,
merging—Edna gives a dinner party to celebrate her last night
in her husband's house. Life becomes art: gorgeous, splendid,
softly lit, and burning. Edna is the artwork's living center:

> The golden shimmer of Edna's satin gown spread in rich folds on
> either side of her. There was a soft fall of lace encircling her shoulders.
> It was the color of her skin, without the glow, the myriad living tints
> that one may sometimes discover in vibrant flesh. There was some-
> thing in her attitude, in her whole appearance when she leaned her
> head against the high-backed chair and spread her arms, which sug-
> gested the regal woman, the one who rules, who looks on, who stands
> alone.
>
> (Chap. 30, p. 88)

But even this triumphant moment is spoiled by Edna's incapacity to endure the solitude her queenliness and aesthetic
creativity require:

> As she sat there amid her guests, she felt the old ennui overtaking
> her; the hopelessness which so often assailed her, which came upon
> her like an obsession, like something extraneous, independent of
> volition. It was something which announced itself; a chill breath that
> seemed to issue from some vast cavern wherein discords wailed. There
> came over her the acute longing which always summoned into her
> spiritual vision the presence of the beloved one, overpowering her at
> once with a sense of the unattainable.
>
> (Chap. 30, p. 88)

When Edna finally discovers that even with Robert, the
structures of sexual relationships ill fit the evanescence of desire, the implications of this revelation are devastating. Edna's
love for Robert makes her wish to see him as unique and herself as faithful. But the attraction between herself and Alcée
Arobin forces her to acknowledge that sensuality, once roused,
is inherently promiscuous. Edna has also misjudged Robert,
who reveals himself to be as conventional as Léonce. Robert's
love for Edna includes a wish to marry her, and he cannot

understand that marriage is, at best, irrelevant to the qualities Edna most values in their relationship. If merging with Robert means marriage, marriage—to Edna—means death. The wish to merge is only a screen for the wish to die. Isolation and sexual abstinence is the only viable alternative, but Edna cannot endure a solitary life. She is not strong enough to live under the austere tutelage of Mademoiselle Reisz. She cannot submit her newly discovered feelings to the discipline of work, or alter their forms or functions by the application of imaginative vision. By the end of the book she knows that " 'to-day it is Arobin; tomorrow it will be someone else. It makes no difference to me' " (chap. 39, p. 113). There is "no human being whom she wanted near her except Robert; and she even realized that the day would come when he, too, and the thought of him would melt out of her existence, leaving her alone" (chap. 39, p. 113). Edna finds this knowledge too much to bear. If she cannot give in to Robert's wish for marriage, neither can she carry on without him.

At the same time that she acknowledges her spiritual solitude, Edna must also admit that she is not literally alone. Her presence at the Ratignolles' home when Madame Ratignolle is giving birth compels her "with an inward agony, with a flaming, outspoken revolt against the ways of Nature" (chap. 37, p. 109) always to " 'think of the children. . . . Remember them!' " (chap. 37, p. 109). Like Hardy's Sue, Edna is trapped in the awareness that succumbing to sexual desire moves one from the private realm of feeling to the public realm of production and that children can demand the mother's life, even if they cannot claim the woman's soul. As Edna walks down to the waters of the Gulf, the children appear before her "like antagonists who had overcome her; who had overpowered and sought to drag her into the soul's slavery for the rest of her days. But she knew a way to elude them" (chap. 39, p. 113). Suicide: a way indeed.

Edna's hope that individual consciousness could be combined with sensual union is unfulfilled. The sun is not " 'warm enough to have warmed the very depths of the ocean' " (chap. 39, p. 112). The flight from the controlling norms—morality, marriage, maternity—that began on a Sunday in childhood when, running from church, she found herself in a grassy meadow, blue-green like the sea, ends with Edna's vision of a "bird with a broken wing . . . reeling, fluttering, circling disabled down, down to the water" (chap. 39, p. 113). Adèle Ratignolle's plea that Edna " 'think of the children' " (chap. 37, p. 109) is countered, but not conquered, by the memory of Mademoiselle Reisz's derisive summation: " 'And you call yourself an artist! What pretensions, Madame! The artist must possess the courageous soul that dares and defies' " (chap. 39, p. 114). The moment at which Edna stands "for the first time in her life . . . naked in the open air, at the mercy of the sun" (chap. 39, p. 113) is ironically, bitterly, the moment that precedes her death. Like Sue, Edna is aware of the contradictions that have destroyed her life. Unlike Sue, however, Edna is given a literal death rather than a return to a zombie's existence within the forms approved by society. Her death is more defiant than Sue's life but not therefore more triumphant: "It was too late, the shore was far behind her, and her strength was gone" (chap. 39, p. 114).

Edna Pontellier dies yielding to the seductive whispers of the sea, accepting its invitation "to wander in abysses of solitude" (chap. 39, p. 113); Isabel Archer encounters, but ultimately resists, a similar enticement. Near the end of *The Portrait of a Lady*, Isabel leaves Rome to return to her starting point at Gardencourt. Fleeing Osmond, disobeying his commands in order to see her cousin Ralph one last time, Isabel discovers that she "[envies] Ralph his dying" (chap. 33, p. 457). On her journey from Rome she has "moments . . . which were almost as good as being dead. She sat in her corner, so motionless, so passive, simply with the sense of being carried, so detached from hope and regret, that she recalled to herself one of those Etruscan figures couched upon the receptacle of their ashes" (chap. 33, pp. 457–58). In the book's last scene, Caspar Goodwood, encouraged by Henrietta Stackpole, seeks Isabel out in order once again to ask her to marry him. Knowing Isabel's marriage to Osmond has failed, aware that she is miserable, Caspar (whose function here is analogous to Jude's in *Jude the Obscure* and Robert's in *The Awakening*) offers himself as refuge:

"You're the most unhappy of women, and your husband's the deadliest of fiends . . . [Y]ou're afraid to go back. You're perfectly alone; you don't know where to turn. . . . Now it is therefore that I want you to think of *me*. . . . Here I stand; I'm as firm as a rock."
(Chap. 55, pp. 480–81)

Isabel feels herself almost overwhelmed by the strength of his plea. The image of the sea arises at this point and carries the same significance for James as it does for Chopin; it appeals as a place where burdens will be lifted because struggles will at last be ended, turned over to a force external to and larger than oneself:[22]

The world . . . seemed to open out, all round her, to take the form of a mighty sea, where she floated in fathomless waters. She had wanted help, and here was help; it had come in a rushing torrent. . . . [S]he believed just then that to let him take her in his arms would be the next best thing to . . . dying. This belief, for a moment, was a kind of rapture, in which she felt herself sink and sink. In the movement she seemed to beat with her feet, in order to catch herself, to feel something to rest on.
(Chap. 55, p. 481)

James's protagonist, unlike Chopin's, recovers from this temptation, acknowledges the ocean as a psychological rather than a literal phenomenon, and finds the strength to stand her ground:

The confusion, the noise of waters, all the rest of it were in her own swimming head. In an instant she became aware of this. . . . [S]he had heard of those wrecked and under water following a train of images before they sink. But when darkness returned she was free. . . . [S]he . . . darted from the spot. . . . In an extraordinarily short time . . . she had moved through the darkness . . . and

reached the door. She had not known where to turn; but she knew
now.

(Chap. 55, pp. 481–82)

This knowledge intensifies Isabel's earlier sense that, even in
her deepest misery, she "saw herself . . . in the attitude of a
woman who had her life to live. . . . Deep in her soul—
deeper than any appetite for renunciation—was the sense that
life would be her business for a long time to come. . . . It
was a proof of strength—it was a proof she should some day
be happy again" (chap. 53, p. 458).

At first glance, the resoluteness of this language hardly
seems matched by the facts of Isabel's decision. Her return to
Rome, presumably to take up life again with Osmond, might
seem to align Isabel with Sue, who also completes her tale by
turning back to an unsatisfactory husband, rather than offering a previously unexplored, unimagined option for plot or
psyche. If we allow our final estimate of Isabel's position to be
informed by her reemergent determination, the renewed resistance to engulfment signified by her refusal of Caspar's proposition, then we must reevaluate the meaning of Isabel's decision. She feels undefeated, and if Ralph is right when he says
" 'You'll grow very young again' " (chap. 54, p. 471), the patterns of the plot itself should legitimize this feeling.

If we compare certain significant elements in James's,
Hardy's, and Chopin's plots, we observe several important distinctions. First, Isabel is rich. This wealth is a mixed blessing,
and it is traditional to see it as more of a hindrance to Isabel's
freedom than a guarantee of her independence. But Isabel is
not, unlike Clarissa Harlowe, simply the victim of an inheritance that designates her as a desirable object, a rich territory
to be annexed and plundered; Isabel's wealth remains her own,
to control and dispense as she sees fit. Most important, this
capacity survives her marriage.[23] Although James doesn't explicitly evoke contemporary statute law, if he did not mean us
to understand that Isabel's fiscal authority persists, Osmond's
concern with her continued presence and, even more, his de-

sire to make Isabel feel responsible for Pansy's fate would make no sense. If the money were Osmond's by right of marriage, then he could provide or withhold Pansy's dowry as he wished. Isabel's absence would affect neither his own material position nor his ambitions for his daughter. Since Isabel is not Pansy's mother, her defection could cast no moral blot on Pansy's character, but would alter only her economic position, the price Pansy can command, through Isabel's interest, on the marriage market. Countess Gemini, for one, cannot believe that Isabel's generosity will outlast her enlightenment. " 'Don't-tell me now that you'll give her a *dot*,' " she exclaims (chap. 51, p. 447).

Isabel's true relationship to Pansy is much more complex than Osmond or his sister can conceive. Nonetheless, it is important to underscore the internal evidence suggesting there is a contingent relationship between Osmond and Isabel's money and, therefore, Isabel can wield an enormous amount of real power in any struggle between herself and her husband. Isabel's marriage to Osmond is originally predicated on her fear of the amount of power her fortune guarantees:

"A large fortune means freedom, and I'm afraid of that. It's such a fine thing, and one should make such a good use of it. If one shouldn't one would be ashamed. And one must keep thinking; it's a constant effort. I'm not sure it's not a greater happiness to be powerless."

(Chap. 21, p. 190)

Her feeling for Osmond is colored by "a kind of maternal strain—the happiness of a woman who felt that she was a contributor, that she came with charged hands" (chap. 42, p. 351). Madame Merle's hidden motive in bringing Isabel to Osmond, her wish to use the match as a means of securing her own daughter's future, is perfectly complemented by the displaced maternalism revealed in Isabel's feelings for both Osmond and Pansy, and by her sense of being weighed down by wealth:

At bottom her money had been a burden, had been on her mind, which was filled with the desire to transfer the weight of it to some other conscience, to some more prepared receptacle. Unless she should have given it to a hospital there would have been nothing better she could do with it; and there was no charitable institution in which she had been as much interested as in Gilbert Osmond.

(Chap. 42, p. 351)

By the end of the book Isabel knows that Osmond did not repay this interest. And we cannot understand the meaning of her return to Rome unless we factor the effect of this knowledge into our assessment. The adoring, naive, charmingly adolescent Isabel we saw at the beginning of the book has developed into a woman who is profoundly mistrustful of her husband. Her mistrust is grounded not only in the reality of her husband's actions and character, but in her own, previously obscured, relationships to material and social circumstances. Learning the truth about Osmond means also learning the truth about Madame Merle and Pansy, as well as the facts of the bargain between Ralph and his father that originally secured Isabel's legacy. At last possessed of these secrets, Isabel defies Osmond and leaves Rome. Having returned to England and said good-bye to Ralph, Isabel starts out again from Gardencourt, ready for a new beginning as a fully grown woman. She has again renounced Caspar's proffered sexuality, but this renunciation, significantly, does not promise to end either her life or our interest in it. Ralph succumbs; Caspar subsides; Isabel prevails.

Thus, the concluding action of the book, which looks so much like retreat, repetition, diminution, is the opening turn of a new, so far unwritten fiction. However we imagine this fiction evolving, it is premised on the end of that notional, theoretic, romantic world that Isabel—like Sue and Edna—hoped originally to inhabit. Illusions vanish and with them, a world of heroism based on suffering, on the desire to keep the flag flying long after the fortress has surrendered, also disappears. " 'I'm not at all helpless,' " Isabel tells Henrietta. And, she continues, " 'I shall never make another promise' " (chap. 48, p. 410). Knowing the previously hidden "truth of things, their mutual relations, their meaning, and . . . their horror" (chap. 53, p. 457), Isabel is prepared, finally, to live.

The terms of this new life include not only a revised relationship to her money and her husband but also, perhaps even more significant, an altered position vis-à-vis Madame Merle and Pansy. It is as though an attempt to imagine new possibilities for female heroism necessarily involves the invention of a line of female characters to act as initiators and descendants. Heroes need workers to prepare the ground for them, prophets to predict their coming, and disciples to follow in the broken ground. The absence of female precursors, the inadequacy of maternal figures, has been striking in the narratives we have considered in earlier chapters, as has the perhaps more startling attempt to use male characters in this role. Madame Merle, glittering, seductive, worldly, traitorous, serves Isabel first as a necessary mentor—an ideal and guide. The original relationship between the two women resembles that which Chopin establishes between Edna and Mademoiselle Reisz. In both instances, the older women are depicted as singling out the younger women as uniquely worthy of their attention. Madame Merle, like Mademoiselle Reisz, seems to offer new possibilities for a ready-made, independent female life. Edna is always aware of the price such power entails, of the mixture of respect and reservation that isolates Mademoiselle Reisz, even as it also supports her, but Isabel's initial response to Madame Merle is much less guarded:

[Isabel] had always passed for a person of resources and had taken a certain pride in being one; but she wandered . . . round the . . . talents, accomplishments, aptitudes of Madame Merle. She found herself desiring to emulate them, and in twenty such ways this lady presented herself as a model.

(Chap. 19, p. 163)

Madame Merle is a vision of what Isabel desires for herself: To be "so cultivated and civilised, so wise and so easy, and still make so light of it—that was really to be a great lady" (chap. 19, p. 164). Whatever ironies this description involves are invisible to Isabel at the time of this assessment. Indeed, it is hardly an exaggeration to say that Isabel falls in love with Osmond only because she first falls in love with her own idealization, in the image of Madame Merle. After Isabel's marriage, as her vision is sharpened by familiarity with Osmond, her idea of Madame Merle alters correspondingly. Madame Merle is hard: "Her will was mistress of her life. . . . Madame Merle had suppressed enthusiasm; she fell in love . . . with nothing; she lived entirely by reason and by wisdom" (chap. 40, p. 330). Isabel, too, is hardened: She becomes "aware more than before of the advantage of being like that—of having made one's self a firm surface, a sort of corselet of silver" (chap. 40, p. 331). If Madame Merle betrays Isabel, she also teaches her a necessary lesson.

James does not merely take away with one hand what he had offered with the other. Madame Merle being toppled, Countess Gemini steps temporarily into her vacant place. This woman, Osmond's sister, openly promiscuous and by the conventional world's standards more than a little sleazy, offers Isabel enlightenment untainted by hidden motives or subterranean self-interest. By revealing that Osmond and Madame Merle had been lovers and that Madame Merle is Pansy's mother, Countess Gemini clarifies Isabel's most important relations—to her husband, her stepchild, and her erstwhile friend. Empowered by her knowledge, Isabel encounters Madame Merle for the last time. Without a word, the woman who had used her power as a guide perversely—in order to lead Isabel deeper into the labyrinth and feed her to the Minotaur—is vanquished. Her position and Isabel's have been reversed:

Madame Merle had guessed in the space of an instant that everything was at an end between them, and in the space of another instant she had guessed the reason why. The person who stood there was not the same one she had seen hitherto, but was a very different person—a person who knew her secret. This discovery was tremendous, and from the moment she made it the most accomplished of women faltered and lost her courage. . . . The tide of her confidence ebbed, and she was able only just to glide into port. . . .

Isabel saw it all distinctly. . . . That Madame Merle had lost her pluck and saw before her the phantom of exposure—this in itself was a revenge, this in itself was almost the promise of a brighter day. And for a moment . . . Isabel enjoyed that knowledge. . . . What remained was the cleverest woman in the world standing there . . . knowing as little what to think as the meanest.

(Chap. 52, pp. 450–51)

Madame Merle decamps for exile in America. Isabel is left with Pansy.

Isabel's conquest over Madame Merle affects her relationship with Osmond's daughter at least as much as her connection with Osmond himself. Pansy's innocence is so radical as to amount almost to a parody of Isabel's; her regard for Isabel is an exaggerated version of Isabel's idealization of Madame Merle. Pansy's faith coerces Isabel, forcing her to jeopardize her own most obvious interests for the sake of Pansy's; "not to neglect Pansy, not under any provocation to neglect her—this she had made an article of religion" (chap. 40, p. 334). But all Isabel's care and concern seems insufficient to prevent the girl from being " 'ground in the very mill of the conventional' " (chap. 54, p. 470). When Osmond shows himself willing to sacrifice Pansy's very life rather than permit her to choose her own future, Isabel seems powerless to frustrate his intent. The revelation of Madame Merle's maternity, followed by her presumably permanent departure from the scene, affects the vectors of the plot by altering the field of activity for remaining participants. Osmond's innate laziness and conventionality can no longer be overcome by Madame Merle's indomitable will. His desire for stasis, however, must reckon with the force of Isabel's knowledge of his own falseness and his daughter's illegitimacy. And Isabel's claim on Pansy is finally no less than Pansy's claim on Isabel. The promise of an older woman to support a younger one is at last validated by the elder's knowledge and power.

In resisting Caspar, Isabel denies herself to sexuality. As

long as sexuality is linked with death, however, this denial amounts to a renewed commitment to life. James honors this commitment by providing Isabel with a new role. At the end, Isabel has become again the virgin hunter her maiden name suggests, the sort of benevolent, protective, powerful female figure we have not seen before.[24] The sons of Jude Fawley and Léonce Pontellier are the social agents primarily responsible for the collapse of Sue's and Edna's visions, hopes, and aspirations. The daughter figure Pansy is used in a contrary way, to redefine Isabel's maternal role, to entice her energies away from the deadly destructiveness represented by male authorities, so that they can be trained instead on the tender, living bond between two generations of women. Pansy Merle, Osmond's bastard, makes Isabel Archer a new and legitimate mother.

The Road to Olympus

Women Heroes and Modern Texts

Chapter 5

Psyche's Ascent

A New Earth, A New Heaven

Literature . . . is common ground. Let us trespass freely and fearlessly and find our own way for ourselves. It is thus that . . . literature will survive if commoners and outsiders like ourselves make that country our own country, if we teach ourselves how to read and how to write, how to preserve, and how to create.

Virginia Woolf, *A Room of One's Own,*
as quoted by Tillie Olsen in *Silences*

For those of us (few yet in number, for the way is punishing) . . . kin and descendants who begin to emerge into more flowered and rewarded use of our selves . . . and by our achievement bearing witness to what was (and still is) being lost, silenced.

Tillie Olsen, from the dedication to *Silences*

Time and history have not miraculously conspired to bring change to Psyche's life. In life, in art, domestic walls continue to define the dwelling place of countless women. In cities and in suburbs, Amor's cave survives. This structure, however, no longer guarantees contentment. Though heroines abide there, affirming, as Jane Eyre did, the happiness within, few hold their security inviolate, seek not to know the true identity of those they live with, or accept unquestioningly the sovereign laws of patriarchy. Once lit in the novel, Psyche's lamp reveals the stark harshness of the system that has so long confined her. Clarissa Harlowe's tragedy, the devolution of

Emma Woodhouse and Dorothea Brooke, Hester Prynne's and Sue Bridehead's forced capitulations eliminate romantic shadows.

Authors, however, even in our century, still fear Psyche's dagger, revile her as dangerous to children and opposed to male—hence all—freedom, celebrate the female spirit as ornamental, self-effacing. The fear that animates such portraits is so distorting that their authority has largely disappeared. If the sex of Dickens's Mrs. Jellyby is not incidental, it is also true that as a caricature of the meddling philanthropist, she has her male parallel in Mr. Gradgrind. Roth's Mrs. Portnoy and Mailer's Mrs. Rojack are, on the other hand, merely—and gratuitously—insulting. Stereotypes dependent on existing reflexes of approval or of outrage, they are unable to compel belief or even to inspire concern for their effects on others. Described only as hideous and ludicrous, they have no history, no motives, no cause beyond themselves. Portnoy mourns his impotence; Rojack murders to avenge it; rather than leave the cave with Psyche, they will sit in it and stink. Such a posture seems preposterous unless, of course, the books are read as satires on themselves, parodying the horror they seek to arouse.

The defeats of Hardy's Sue, Chopin's Edna, Richardson's Clarissa approach the tragic because they result inevitably from unfair circumstances and inescapable contradictions. Their creators make us see that they, like their failed heroes, had no alternatives available. Reading, we feel their regret. A work like *Love Story,* in contrast, makes a narcissistic mockery of such presumed inevitability. The death of its heroine is no tragedy. Not even pitiable, it is merely pathetic, a device designed to consolidate patriarchal bonds frayed by an unseemly and too passionate commitment to a woman. If Segal seems a simple target, consider Hemingway instead. *The Sun Also Rises* and *For Whom the Bell Tolls,* works undeniably more complicated and more powerful than *Love Story,* are similarly exploitative of feminine weakness; both appropriate female sexuality, both exult when women die. Hemingway's memorials, like Segal's, are monuments to authorial sentimentality; the tears shed at graveside are reptilian. While Nick is disillusioned at the end of *The Great Gatsby*, Gatsby himself is killed by his own incurable delusions, a romanticism literally fatal. Daisy doesn't need to push him into the swimming pool; he jumps. Fitzgerald's novel reveals Nick's illusions as, like Gatsby's, pure nostalgia: a longing for a mythology that has vanished, unable any longer to control the present.[1]

Attempting to inscribe her own myth in its place, Psyche's saga enters its ascendant phase. Stepping out into the larger world beyond the heroine's confining plot, Psyche attempts to imbue society, as well as art, with the values she has learned to honor in the course of her long oppression. She struggles to find a new sustaining structure, a fictive form that will express affiliation without simultaneously imposing hierarchy, that will render life not an endless battle but a celebration. The fictions examined in the next three chapters, whether or not they rely on modernism's pyrotechnics, contrive to escape the fixed endings of their forebears. Their conclusions are open, indeterminate. Their heroes (and others—from Mary Datchet in Virginia Woolf's *Night and Day* to Clara Maugham in Margaret Drabble's more recent *Jerusalem the Golden*) live by will and strain; they fear what will happen if they lose their nerve, as they see before them a future of endless conjunctions, endless dissolutions, endless interest in the process of their own growth and survival. Their creators invite us to imagine their stories evolving after the narrative's last page has concluded. Shifting the burden of continuation from themselves to the reader, these authors forge the bond between reader and hero. While denying knowledge, they inspire hope. Their narratives merge with our lives and model them.

Having given heroes new things to do, as well as provided new shapes for the plots in which they figure, such novels suggest that the forces represented by these characters are the nodal points of an entirely new kind of social order, an alternative to the repetitions and rigidities of patriarchy. Women enter the public worlds their fictions portray. They take on jobs previously reserved to men and command respect—and money—for their labors. Rhoda Nunn, the hero of George Gissing's *The Odd Women,* not only saves women from the horrors of factory life, but offers them a social status they could otherwise attain only through marriage. Marie Rogers, in Agnes Smedley's *Daughter of Earth,* works at a dizzying number and variety of jobs, educates herself, and becomes politicized; she finds a lineal descendant in Marge Piercy's Vida: worker, terrorist, and hero.

What is most interesting about these fictions is not that they have given women a variety of new tasks but that they have conceived of work in a new way. Heroic labor is not a job, narrowly defined, but rather a means of restructuring society and its representations. If forced to choose between the vote and an independent income, Virginia Woolf declares in *A Room of One's Own,* she would unhesitatingly choose the income. Money provides independence, allows choices. Lacking money or the access to it, the woman hero's life is obviously restricted. Edith Kelly's *Weeds,* Meridel LeSeuer's *The Girls,* Tillie Olsen's *I Stand Here Ironing* and *Tell Me A Riddle* emphasize the hardness of this fact in the same way that *Daughter of Earth* and *The Dollmaker* do. Money, however, is not fetishized. Capital permits freedom; it is not freedom's substitute. The values of the marketplace need not be material. Work redeems Psyche because it liberates her soul.

Cooperation and affiliation are possible in public life as well as in the home, not because women are magically endowed with these potentialities by virtue of biology, but because Western culture generally and historically has invested these ideals in women and compelled us to learn their worth at home. Pledging herself to a world-wide political revolt, Marie Rogers seeks to make society at large into the family she should have had, but didn't. Novels as ideologically diverse as *The Odd Women, Gaudy Night,* and *The Golden Notebook* productively exploit the woman hero's capacity to redesign the marketplace. Form and function are indeed inseparable. Mary Barfoot's typing school is as radical an invention in *The Odd Women* as Sayers's Shrewsbury College is in *Gaudy Night*. Institutions designed to give women access to society's means of production, they preserve and teach the old lessons—nurturance, sympathy, tolerance, compassion—whose wisdom women have learned in the duties and the deprivations of the private house. Serving human needs, not propagating abstract ideologies, they expand, cohere, survive, while Marie's marriage, for instance, predicated on the power of a fixed ideological commitment, shatters.

As effort, life is labor; as invention, art. In either case, toil and creation are communal acts. Reversing the pattern established for male artist-heroes, the art of women heroes is neither self-referential nor self-reverential. It does not serve to show the hero's "greatness," to yield up honors and rewards, to make the world kneel at the hero's feet. In *To the Lighthouse,* Lily Briscoe's painting is destined to be rolled up, forgotten on some attic floor. Lily's love for Mrs. Ramsay allows Lily to sympathize with Mr. Ramsay and send him, at last, to the lighthouse with his children. Lily's legacy from Mrs. Ramsay, this love in turn grants Lily her own vision and allows her to capture it in art. It is not the painting itself that matters to Woolf or to Lily; their focus is, instead, on intensity and integrity of feeling, on love's evolution and its permutations, on the relationship of consciousness and action. Its purpose served, the artifact itself has no importance. Harriet Vane's projected novel is similarly shaped—not by detached artistry, but by the complex reflections and perceptions prompted by the mysteries at Shrewsbury, by the vulnerability of a man she believed invincible, by the steadfastness of a female community in the face of an attack. The dolls that Gertie Nevels makes are carved from wood that might have been material for a masterpiece, by hands that might have shaped one. If we mourn the loss of Gertie's monumental sculpture, we should not mourn the loss of Gertie's art. As creators, all these women are heroic artists because they incorporate their own lives—and the lives of others—into their aesthetic. They allow their art to take its form from the lives they live and admit the needs such lives impose.

It is not the work by itself—whatever its nature—that ultimately matters but the reciprocity among work, emotional experience and communal flexibility. Joining the private to the public realm, the art of women heroes serves best when its artistry draws no attention to itself. When art becomes invisible, life itself becomes the carefully wrought achievement we habitually think available to art alone. Creators in common, what these women share through creativity is themselves. The fictional narration of the artist's life becomes the artifact of heroism that informs the society surrounding it. Telling her story, Janie, in Zora Neale Hurston's *Their Eyes Were Watching God,* transforms not just her single chosen listener, Pheoby Watson, but through Pheoby, all of Eatonville. Sula, who gives her name to Toni Morrison's novel, intertwines her life with her friend Nel's. When Sula dies, Nel realizes the meaning of the life now lost; she assumes Sula's freedom and accepts Sula's identity as a burden and a promise that must be continued. Through "talking story," Brave Orchid knits herself and her daughter—the narrator of Maxine Hong Kingston's fictive memoir—into the story of Fa Mu Lan, the woman warrior of the book's title. The narrator, in turn, "talks story" to us. Her life is as mythicized as the warrior's; its text is itself a myth designed to reveal the truth about our lives.

Biology is no longer the only guarantee of inheritance and stability. Mother, daughter, friend, and lover—Psyche, as the maker of her own mythology, becomes, at last, again a god. Using both physical and mental powers to change the sense and substance of reality itself, the woman hero incarnates, as she did in the beginning, a new world, its deity is no longer patterned after patriarchy's male ideal. Clarissa Dalloway's parties become the equivalent of, and finally the replacement for, a world at war, Clarissa being the earthly embodiment of a divinity imagined as a serene and universal lover, warming all humanity in her embrace, rather than as a dying figure tortured and writhing in agony on a cross. The woman hero is fierce, as Fa Mu Lan is fierce, or Clarissa is fierce when refusing to yield to Peter Walsh's knife or to his efforts to re-form her character; like Brave Orchid and her daughter, she is a dragon. Her unions are a whirling dance, insubstantial as fire, like the embrace of the old couple in Fa Mu Lan's story. Like Clarissa, "drenched in fire," she moves among the party's guests, meeting and mingling, honoring life, asking nothing more than to help "one day follow another." Glimpsed behind the walls of the apartment where the narrator dwells in Doris Lessing's *The Memoirs of a Survivor,* she is the unseen presence, the Rightful Inhabitant of the unnameable space where myth is born. From the ruins of our civilization—patriarchy's world—she summons us to come with her and promises humanity its own rebirth.

Chapter 6

Love and Work

Reciprocity and Power in *The Odd Women,*
Daughter of Earth, and *Gaudy Night*

Those who are condemned to stagnation are often pronounced happy on the pretext that happiness consists in being at rest. This notion we reject.

Simone de Beauvoir, *The Second Sex*

> *The world waits*
> *For help. Beloved, let us work so well,*
> *Our work shall still be better for our love*
> *And still our love be sweeter for our work.*

Elizabeth Barrett Browning, *Aurora Leigh*

The stone walls that activism runs into have buried foundations. Any reader who has pushed in a practical way against the legal or economic or other institutional barriers blocking change . . . knows how sturdy these concrete societal barriers are, and how fiercely defended. But what must be recognized is that these external problems are insoluble unless we grapple at the same time with internal problems, of feeling and understanding, that are at least equally formidable.

Dorothy Dinnerstein, *The Mermaid and the Minotaur*

Clarissa and Hester; Emma, Jane, and Dorothea; Edna, Sue, and Isabel: these are the would-be heroes we have so far seen. Their heroism has been largely blunted, their energies redirected or defeated. Their collective right to claim heroic status is emergent only, dependent on challenge offered rather than success achieved. Of the figures just named, Isabel alone, if we see her as returning not *to* Osmond but *for* Pansy—that is, as a powerful, experienced adult not a naive, romantic child—has been allowed to refine her heroic sense of self and enact her honor. Her independent female presence in the world survives as a force of opposition to patriarchal egotism; *The Portrait of a Lady* is unique among the books examined in preceding chapters in offering us a being liberated—both psychically and economically—from a ritualized bondage to authority, one whose final actions are an attempt to pass this liberation on to her chosen female descendant. But, even though the heroism of the remaining seven characters is variously vanquished, deflected, or encapsulated in conventionalizing institutions, this constriction is insufficient to negate their original creative force. On the contrary, their initial opposition to both social norms and formal categories survives as a permanent, if as yet unrealized, counterforce to their final, more or less sad, fates. Once the legitimacy of the protoheroes' claims is even partially acknowledged, the traditional generic and emotional closures—tragedy's deathly ennoblement or comedy's static happiness—are revealed as irresolute, incompletely cathartic. Too much has been sacrificed, not enough redeemed. As the plots considered have focused increasingly on the motif of the deathly marriage, on the ways in which weddings and funerals are mutually supportive rather than contrasting social rituals, female principals have served as vehicles for forcing consciousness of this alliance and thus preventing a return to the old neatness and simplicity.

What has been missing until the turn of the twentieth century is a clear sense of alternatives, a development of new structures upon the ruins of the old ones. If the protoheroes have made us aware of the inadequacies of traditional formulae and the irreconcilable contradictions between abstract meaning and concrete circumstances, these characters—or, more properly, their creators—have been able to discern only the vaguest outlines of a new set of options. The shift from

protoheroism to heroism itself depends precisely on such discovery, on the emergence of new structures from the ashes of
the wedding-funeral. The protoheroes' task has been to test
and finally to overwhelm the boundaries of the old frameworks and social paradigms. In doing so, they have pushed
down the defining walls and liberated the impulses that the
old inventions both shaped and contained. These impulses are
free now to seek some new form, some positive gesture beyond
muted submission or futile revolt, some way to socialize the
need for power by combining power's needs with love's.

How is it possible to express this interpenetration, to make
autonomy less lonely and love less embattled? These are the
questions we must now face. A paradigm cannot be countered
by either negativity or chaos, but only by an alternative offering. We have reached a crisis in human relations represented
by the struggle of a female character against conventions
which are not only personally repressive but socially stultifying. Such a critical moment marks, as Victor Turner tells us,
"a threshold between . . . phases of the social process . . .
and dares the representatives of order to grapple with it. It
cannot be ignored or wished away."[1] At these moments, the
actual members of society—as well as the symbolic representatives they send forth into art—must force the opposing tendencies toward anarchy or stagnation to yield up a new crystallization of desire. As Turner suggests, "human social groups
. . . find their openness to the future in the . . . contest of
their paradigms."[2]

The first successful possibility to be offered to the aspiring
female hero as a way of release from the paralyzing conflicts
of the old order is quite simple—so simple, in fact, that it is
easy to overlook its formal and social implications. It is, then,
simply: work. In the three fictions we shall now consider—
George Gissing's *The Odd Women* (1893), Agnes Smedley's
Daughter of Earth (1929), and Dorothy L. Sayers' *Gaudy
Night* (1936)[3]—work has a multiple function. As labor that is

economically compensated, it becomes a realm of objective, collective activity and thus mediates the conflict, still present in each book, between love or the need for intimacy and human contact, on the one side, and autonomy or the need for some externalized expression of the self, on the other. In addition, the working world, as a communal structure, offers a formal replacement within the novels' plots for the devitalized systems of domesticity.

Turning first to the earliest example, *The Odd Women*, we find Gissing putting economic fact to spiritual use. The fact, fixed in the demography of late-Victorian England, specifies that middle-class women far outnumber middle-class men. For this reason alone, marriage can no longer be relied on to provide the sole medium for absorbing women's lives. Women who cannot marry, because there aren't sufficient men to go around, and who have no patrimony to support their independence must seek outside employment. Gissing's fiction documents much more than this particular social crisis. The book maintains its contemporary interest because of the author's perception that a particular verifiable phenomenon can be made to serve spiritual ends.[4]

Near the end of the first half of *The Odd Women*, for example, Mary Barfoot, one of the book's principal female characters, delivers a speech to a small group of young women who are students at a clerical school she runs with her friend and companion, Rhoda Nunn. The title of this speech is "Woman as an Invader"; its subject is the need for women, individually and collectively, to have work for which they are specifically trained and for which they will be paid a decent wage. Although it is difficult for us today to see typing as a radical activity, Miss Barfoot's exhortation appears, within the context of nineteenth-century social and aesthetic possibilities, as nothing less than a call to revolution, a demand that women seize control of a new technology and use it to secure their freedom. Supporting this position against the attack of an anonymous unemployed male clerk who accuses working women of taking needed jobs from men, Gissing's narrator observes that "in the miserable disorder of our social state, one grievance had to be weighed against another, and Miss Barfoot held that there was much more to be urged on behalf of women who had invaded what had been exclusively the men's sphere, than on behalf of the men who began to complain of this invasion" (chap. 13, p. 135).

Such analysis validates and organizes Mary's lecture, which sees women's entry into a new sphere of activity as vitally related to a new synthesis of the relationship between gender and role. Previously, the terms "womanly" and "womanish" were seen as synonymous; and a " 'womanly occupation means, practically, an occupation that a man disdains' " (chap. 13, p. 135). Miss Barfoot, however, speaking as " 'a troublesome, aggressive, revolutionary person,' " attacks this terminological conflation and favors instead a new order of definition and possibility.

> "It must be something new, something free from the reproach of womanliness. I don't care whether we crowd out the men or not. I don't care *what* results, if only women are made strong and self-reliant and nobly independent! The world must look to its concerns. Most likely we shall have a revolution in the social order greater than any that yet seems possible. Let it come, and let *us* help its coming. When I think of the contemptible wretchedness of women enslaved by custom, by their weakness, by their desires, I am ready to cry, Let the world perish in tumult rather than things go on this way."
>
> (Chap. 13, pp. 135–36)

Although Mary's speech acknowledges " 'the economic aspects of the question,' " she refuses to confine herself to this narrow material framework and emphasizes instead what we might call the intellectual, and beyond that, the psychological—even spiritual—function of work. " 'To put the truth in a few words,' " she says, " 'I am not chiefly anxious that you should *earn money*, but that women in general shall become *rational and responsible human beings*' " (chap. 13, p. 135). Earlier, in a discussion with her cousin, Everard Barfoot, Mary asserts that work makes a woman " 'wholly . . . different from what she would otherwise have been. Instead of a moping, mawkish creature, with—in most instances—a very unhealthy mind, she is a complete human being. She stands on equality with the man. He can't despise her as he now does' " (chap. 10, p. 99). Women, even rich ones, are " 'to be brought up to a calling in life, just as men are' " (chap. 10, p. 98) in order to annihilate forever " 'a class of females vulgarized by the necessity of finding daily amusement' " (chap. 10, p. 99). Mary Barfoot is prophesying a new creed, articulating a new faith which gives both primacy and power to its female practitioners:

"It's better to be a woman in our day. With us is all the joy of advance, the glory of conquering. Men have only material progress to think about. But we — we are winning souls, propagating a new religion, purifying the earth."

(Chap. 10, p. 99)

Gissing offers salvation by work quite self-consciously as a replacement for what he sees as the old ideal—practically outmoded as well as inherently unrealistic—of salvation by marriage. In the marriage exchange, women who lack independent means must offer themselves " 'to the first decent man who offers them five or six hundred [pounds] a year . . . and make good, faithful wives, in mere gratitude to the man who saved them from—horrors' " (chap. 12, p. 119). Even where the economic balance of this exchange favors the woman, the social scale tips toward authority for the man. Everard Barfoot, a relatively poor man with a somewhat shady character and a profession he refuses to practice, might nonetheless woo "with fair chance in a . . . wealthy family, where . . . daughters . . . waited . . . for the men of brains who should appreciate them" (chap. 16, p. 142). There is no question here of love; Barfoot marries Agnes Brissenden primarily because "he needed a larger income" and "wanted to travel in a . . . satisfactory way" (chap. 14, p. 142).

Economic calculation and an inability to strengthen herself for the rigors of independence also informs Monica Madden's disastrous marriage to Edmund Widdowson. A pretty girl, brought up "without rational training" (chap. 11, p. 107), Monica weds as an escape from the fatality of factory work or genteel starvation with her sisters. Although her prospective husband "had a stiff dry way, and . . . she did not think it possible to regard him with warm feelings; yet . . . as things went in the marriage war, she might esteem herself a most fortunate young woman . . . she felt no love . . . but between the prospect of a marriage of esteem and that of no marriage at all there was little room for hesitation" (chap. 7, p. 68). Rejecting the choice provided by Mary and Rhoda, Monica seals her fate. She must join her life to another's because " 'she's fit for nothing else. . . . We mustn't look for any kind of heroism in Monica' " (chap. 11, p. 107). Rejected heroism, in this book as in the others considered in this chapter, is a clearly articulated position; its perpetual result is frustration, followed by either a bitter acceptance of conventional constraints or an aborted, ambiguous rebellion culminating in death. In this instance, Monica, unable to endure imprisonment, takes the second route.

Daughter of Earth, too, subverts the seductions of traditional love by first appealing to the need for economic independence, then instituting a larger structure to suffuse this independence with communal meaning. The rhythm of Smedley's novel is marked by a series of reflections on the disasters that arise because marriage both fosters and exploits female dependency. Like Jane Eyre, Marie Rogers tells her own story; but where Jane sees herself as uniquely isolated and hopes to force society to include her within its protective walls, Marie sees herself as part of a class—the poor—and a caste—the female—that are permanently alienated within conventional society. These excluding categories must be systematically destroyed and their inhabitants integrated into a world built along new lines. The revolutionary language of Mary Barfoot's speech is realized in the much broader political analysis

of *Daughter of Earth*. The latter novel offers, in conventionally political terms, a more radical indictment of patriarchal
values and a correspondingly subversive version of alternative
modalities.

Daughter of Earth renders the oceanic flood of heterosexuality that swept away Edna Pontellier and threatened the integrity of Isabel Archer as the tears of women, clear representations of strangulated rage, barrenness, and impotence. An
ascending spiral in contrast to the concealed circularity of
Jane Eyre and the draining whirlpool of *The Awakening*,
Daughter of Earth begins with Marie contemplating the infinite, poised on the shore of a sea without limit or horizon,
watching as "a bird with outspread wings, takes its way over
the depths" (p. 7). Where Edna's dying vision included an
associative glimpse of a wounded, drowning bird, Marie begins by citing ascendance: "I belong to those who do not die
for the sake of beauty. . . . For we are of the earth and our
struggle is the struggle of the earth" (part 1, p. 8). Standing "at
the end of one life and . . . the threshold of another" (part 1,
p. 8), Marie ponders the nature of her journey and the distance she has traveled. The ocean of her vision opens away
from a delta of women's tears, fed by their entrapment, poisoned at the source, pitiful. At her back, Marie feels the presence of her mother damping down the fires of her life, imagination, love, a Niobe weeping for her own wasted existence
even more than for her child's. Her tears are Marie's bitter
legacy, dissolving romance's veil and revealing the harsh outlines of an asymmetrical system of subordination and defeat.
In memory her mother stands perpetually immobilized, a
muted figure "in her loose faded calico wrapper, her hands
clasped before her, her head bowed" (part 1, p. 37). She cries
"very softly"; but these soft tears, Marie reflects, "embittered
my life!" (part 1, p. 37).

A series of similar memories—the causes and products of
such tears—flows from this core and reinforces its centrality.
A woman who was raped and therefore unmarriageable ap-

pears as "rich," not "at all unhappy that no one would marry her!" (p. 36) Far from appearing miserable, "her lovely face was dignified and calm. Calmer than my mother's" (p. 36). In contrast, Marie invokes this emblematic recollection of a woman for whom she worked:

> She had been a laundry girl . . . but once married, her husband said no wife of his could work! He forced her out of her active, independent life into a three-room house where most of the work was done by me after school.
>
> (Part 2, p. 72)

Her· husband opposes her wish to return to work: " 'What! . . . have people sayin' I can't support my wife!' " (part 2, p. 72). Pregnancy dooms rebellion. The wife grovels, asserting feeling as a mask for degradation: " 'Damn it, kid, you know I love you!' she begged through her tears—for now she could not go back to work even if she wished" (part 2, p. 73).

These appalling words run through the book, a subterranean litany rehearsing the source of Marie's "hatred of marriage" and her "disgust for women who are wives" (part 2, p. 73). Marie hears the woman's pathetic plea as summarizing "the true position of the husband and wife in the marriage relationship" (part 2, p. 73). Later, this scene merges with another memory of a young married couple.

> She stopped work when she married, and sat at home all day long waiting for her husband to return. They lived a purely sex existence. In two or three months eruptions began to show upon her mouth and on her face — the entire house knew what the disease was. She was heavy with child also, but syphilis within marriage is respectable.
>
> (Part 6, p. 201)

When this woman was beaten, "no one dared interfere—she was the man's wife" (p. 201). Again Marie responds as she had earlier: "The weeping of women who are wives—what is more bitter?" (part 6, p. 201).

Fueled by this bitterness, Marie can initially produce only its dark negation, a shadowy, hate-filled counter image: the prostitute as foil to the wife, the woman whose overt trading on her sexuality exposes the economic contract that marriage paradoxically exploits and denies. If Marie's mother dies as a wife, an inevitable victim of "poverty and unhappiness" (part 5, p. 138); her Aunt Helen, her mother's sister, survives as a whore working in a profession that "seemed as honorable as that of any married woman—she made her living in the same way as they made theirs, except that she made a better living and had more rights over her body and soul. No man dared mistreat her. . . . She was pledged to obey no man. . . . Such a life seemed preferable to marriage" (part 5, p. 142). Separating the strands of sexuality, love, and reproduction which bound the fates of the characters examined in preceding chapters, Marie initially endorses an equally rigid and unspontaneous contract. In prostitution, as in marriage, nothing is freely given; nothing is produced; love's territory is reduced to a little island of sensation. Dignity is maintained, but at the price of solitude and sterility:

> In my hatred of marriage, I thought that I would rather be a prostitute than a married woman. I could then protect, feed, and respect myself, and maintain some right over my own body. Prostitutes did not have children . . . men did not dare beat them; they did not have to obey. The "respectability" of married women seemed to rest in their acceptance of servitude and inferiority.
>
> (Part 6, p. 189)

Two factors mitigate the authority of this vision, reducing, not the power of its defiance or the accuracy of its charge, but its viability as a permanent alternative. First, the stance required cannot be sustained, our last glimpse of Aunt Helen reveals her as an aging woman whose declining power to attract men makes her both desperate and despairing. And second, although this posture separates sexuality from love and reproduction at the same time as it joins sexuality to work and psychic autonomy; prostitution, as a formal gesture, is limited by its incapacity to respond to a human need for relatedness, for intimacy, and for continuity beyond the boundaries and lifetime of the individual. Marie is tormented by a set of competing needs and initially irreconcilable demands. On the one side is her belief that Helen's life is led in "decency and self-respect," that "such a life seemed preferable to marriage" (part 5, p. 142), and that "love, tenderness and duty belonged to women and weaklings in general" (part 5, p. 142). If love is weakness, the strong are defined by their knowledge of this fact, and the heroic by their resistance to love's call. On the other side is the fact she must admit, however shamefully, that she, too, knows a "desire for love, tenderness and companionship . . . existed beneath my rough and defiant manner" (part 6, p. 188). Wracked by this contradiction, Marie is torn by "a merciless war being waged within [her] own spirit, a war between [her] need . . . of love, and the perverted idea of love and sex that had been ground into [her] being from [her] first breath" (part 6, p. 202). Smedley's struggle, like Gissing's, involves the effort to terminate this intrapsychic as well as social warfare by devising a structure which allows love as an image of human relationship rather than mortal combat.

The radical politics of *Daughter of Earth* arise from this context of personal contradiction. Searching for a relationship which is " 'understanding, tolerance, freedom—all combined' " (part 7, p. 372), Marie is drawn to revolution as Gissing's odd women are drawn to the vision that inspires Mary Barfoot's typing school. Discrediting existing institutional structures— governmental, educational, and religious, as well as domestic—Marie seeks to lose her loneliness in communal enterprise. In the movement for Indian emancipation from British imperialist rule and, in particular, in its embodiment in the person of exiled leader Sardar Ranjit Singh, Marie finds a channel for her energies, a charge capable of transforming her anguish and her bitterness.

Not a lover, but a teacher, Sardarji offers himself impersonally to Marie's need "for someone to love, for someone to take the place of a father" (part 7, p. 263). The pain of his calling is familiar to Marie, but his message excepts itself from her cynical indictment that people, like "wolves, attack and

destroy one of their kind that is defeated, lamed or wounded"
(part 7, p. 254). Instead, the Indian's words make Marie aware
of "a call to struggle for a new world" (p. 263). Sardarji makes
Marie the offer St. John Rivers made to Jane Eyre: " 'Since
you have no family, why don't you study to come to us?' "
(part 7, p. 267). But, unlike Jane, Marie can accept the offer
because, in contrast to St. John's, it speaks to what the author
has established as the deepest needs of her woman character's
nature. Living with this teacher and his students "as if they
were my father and brothers," she says, "I came to love them"
(part 7, p. 267). Transformed by a desire that makes no threats
but only promises, Marie finds her powers expanded, her capacities extended:

My mind, for months sick and crippled, now became like steel, and
my body as tough as a weed. All the belief and passion of my being
was now concentrated in this work. All hesitancy and fear . . .
gradually left me. Together with my comrades, I was speaking and
writing, and I felt that I was molding the native earth of America.
(Part 7, p. 358)

Fusing political ideology with private feeling she proclaims
that " 'love is not only a personal thing. . . . It is like
thought—it sweeps in every direction and affects the actions of
people' " (part 7, p. 374).

Gaudy Night continues the pattern established by *The Odd
Women* and *Daughter of Earth*. Sayers, like Gissing and Smedley, redefines love by anchoring it in work and in community.
Overtly a mystery story, *Gaudy Night* records the attempt of
Harriet D. Vane, herself a writer of mysteries who has occasionally also functioned as a detective, to discover the identity
of the person who is threatening both the community and the
individual lives of the women of Shrewsbury College, Oxford.
Harriet, we learn, is a former Shrewsbury student who upon
graduation moved to London, had a love affair, and left her
lover when it became apparent that his expectations for their
relationship and hers were incompatible. Her lover was mur-

dered, and although his uncle was the murderer and money the motive, Harriet—as the apparently castoff mistress—seemed at first the likely culprit. When she literally was put on trial for her life, England's richest and most handsome amateur detective, Lord Peter Wimsey, intervened, discovered the identity of the true murderer, and, in the process, fell in love with Harriet. In the five years that have elapsed between this murder and the time of *Gaudy Night*, Harriet has been writing her books and trying to decide whether or not to marry Peter, a man who will neither force himself upon her nor simply disappear.

At the beginning of the novel, Harriet returns to Shrewsbury for an alumnae reunion, the "gaudy night" of the title. Full of ambivalence about her own life and occupation, she views both in relationship to the pure world of scholarship—"the promise of permanence in a Heraclitean universe" (chap. 2, p. 24)—that Shrewsbury trained her to enjoy and possibly to inherit. She knows that she must at last decide what to do about Peter specifically, and—by implication—about love in general, and also about sexuality—another kind of gaudy night. Typically, mysteries focus on crimes and their solution, on the detective's powers of deduction, not on the detective. In this novel, however, the emphasis is reversed. There is in fact no crime, but only a great deal of mischief and suspicion; and Harriet's ultimate capacity to unmask the mischief-maker is tied to her ability to understand herself. *Gaudy Night* is a detective fiction; a novel of manners; and, like *Daughter of Earth*, an exercise in psychological biography.

Harriet's life is, at the outset, neatly if painfully divided into thesis and antithesis: work and love, London and Oxford. The effort of synthesis requires Sayers to send her hero back to school. In order to discover who is disrupting the life of the college, Harriet must identify the sources of her own inner uncertainty about the relationship of female achievement to the surrounding world. By doing so, she objectifies her internal dilemmas, gains the same relationship to them as to any other problem, and finally deals with them as she would with similar encountered difficulties. Sayers's decision to represent the book's resolution—Harriet's new marriage of possibilities—as a process of reeducation is, I think, her most interesting single stroke of plotting. Existing uneasily within the larger patriarchal structure of the university, Shrewsbury is a woman's college, run by women for women. Either it is *alma mater*—the fostering mother, the soul's mother, a force capable of "stretching out reconciling hands to past and present" (chap. 1, p. 7)— or, like other institutions we have examined, it is only a prison, a trap, "the iron hand of the past gripping at one's entrails" (chap. 1, p. 10). Finding a way out of these fixed polarities is Harriet's heroic quest.

Shrewsbury's first attraction is its apparent stasis, its withdrawal from the world's clamor, its seeming "promise of permanence." Yet, this frozen image reflects Harriet's projective needs far more than its own rather more complex realities. For all its visible modesty and insularity, for all of Miss Lydgate's muddleheadedness about the sorting out of proof sheets and Miss Hillyard's bitter and unpopular defensiveness regarding the significance of constitutional law, the college is no mere aggregate of eccentricity. Still less is it an unbound collection of individual egos, each an "Artemis, moon-goddess, virgin-huntress, whose arrows are plagues and death" (p. 220), a caricature of the power that makes strong women feared and fearful. Instead, its values are proclaimed, appropriately, wryly, on a sign hung on a bathroom door: *"Some* CONSIDERATION FOR OTHERS IS NECESSARY IN COMMUNITY LIFE" (chap. 1, p. 12).

The fierce integrity of the college's patron, Mary Countess of Shrewsbury—"a holy terror; uncontrollable by her menfolk, undaunted by the Tower, contemptuously silent before the Privy Council, an obstinate recusant, a staunch friend and implacable enemy and a lady with a turn for invective remarkable even in an age when few mouths suffered from mealiness. . . . the epitome of every alarming quality which

a learned woman is popularly credited with developing"
(chap. 3, p. 47)—is honored through having found its proper
niche. Diffused throughout the group, the Countess's vehe-
ment spirit reveals its positive face. Even the undergradu-
ates—shouting at dinner, sunbathing in underwear, seemingly
oblivious to the institutional and social struggles responsible
for their own privileged positions—find themselves compelled
to manifest public-spirited values, to assume responsibility for
one another. Harriet learns to marvel "at the untiring con-
scientiousness of administrative women. Nobody's interests
ever seemed to be overlooked or forgotten, and an endless
goodwill made up for a perennial scarcity of funds" (chap. 3,
p. 40). When Peter identifies the malefactor impugning these
values and assaulting their practitioners, he observes that
" 'the one thing which frustrated the whole attack from first
to last was the remarkable solidarity and public spirit displayed by your college as a body. I think that was the last obstacle that X expected to encounter in a community of women' "
(p. 360).

Returning Harriet to this place, Sayers, like Gissing and
Smedley, suggests that the war between autonomy and intimacy can be concluded only when the adult hero understands
her need to infuse her work with the spirit of community.[5]
Work here is not grounded in merely individual labor and
private activity, but grows from the complex affiliation of a
necessarily private, struggling soul and an accepting, reciprocating social structure.

That whole wildly heterogeneous, that even slightly absurd collection
of chattering women fused into a corporate unity with one another
with every man and woman to whom integrity of mind meant more
than material gain. . . . How could one feel fettered, being the free-
man of so great a city, or humiliated, where all enjoyed equal citizen-
ship? . . . In the glamour of one Gaudy night, one could realize that
one was a citizen of no mean city. . . . [H]er foundations were set
upon the holy hills and her spires touched heaven.

(Chap. 2, pp. 28–29)

To Gissing's vision of a community of working women as a kind of religious order and Smedley's definition of a radical cadre as an ideally—or truly—familial group, Sayers adds the relationship between Harriet and Shrewsbury as a reworking of the primary intimate bond between a mother and her child. The "normal" ambivalence in this relationship indicated by such post-Freudian theorists as Dorothy Dinnerstein in *The Mermaid and the Minotaur* and Nancy Chodorow in *The Reproduction of Mothering* typically causes children to develop simultaneous and incompatible feelings of overwhelming love for the nurturing provided by the mothering figure and an equally powerful rage against the dependency this nurturance seems to require. Split off from the original maternal figure, these conflicting attitudes persist into adult life and can be recognized in the feelings that attach themselves to figures who seem to represent the mother, usually adult women who occupy positions of authority and who consequently raise questions concerning the function and significance of female power in the larger, more general spheres of society and culture.[6] If the antagonism between love and work arises from a tension between incompatible needs for self-suppression in one realm and self-expression in the other, these antipathies can be resolved only by postulating a single field sufficient to contain both the questing self and the communal structure. For Sayers this synthesis requires what is implied in every other book we have so far examined: first, the reconstruction of the bonds between parent (whether real or symbolic) and child, specifically between mother and daughter, so that the claims of the mother will not be synonymous with those of the socially conventional feminine; and, second, the consequent capacity of the female hero to exist not as a "singular anomaly," but as a person possessing a legitimate inheritance from a spiritual if not a biological mother, an inheritance that, as it no longer implies a balance of infantile dependency and fearful tyranny, can be passed on as a useful model.

To Gissing's and Smedley's understanding of the need to reinvest the energies that remain unabsorbed and unsupported by family life in its narrow traditional definitions, Sayers adds the critical illumination that the limitations and isolation of the family have depended on the constricted role allowed the mother. As long as the mother is conceived as standing for qualities inherently opposed to those required for achievement in the larger world, as long as she either stands aloof from this world or becomes its victim, heroism must necessarily divorce itself from the human virtues of her sphere as well as from its rigidities and confinements. By redefining what it is to be a mother, Sayers suggests that maternity requires neither self-immolation nor domestic dictatorship, both being annexed to the primacy of entrenched authority and hierarchical power. In ending the conflict between the prerogatives of love and the commands of enterprise, Sayers shows how female heroism can bridge the gap between the self whose rebellion exposes the inadequacies of social forms and the enduring need for some structure larger than the self that can accept rebellion, respond to it, and thus perpetuate, rather than defeat or deflect, the self's animating impulses. The effort that *Gaudy Night* shares with the other books considered in this chapter, as well as with much general feminist theory, is to demonstrate the essential interpenetration of private and public realms, of personal and political structures, of love and work.

In this connection, Sayers's Shrewsbury emerges as a quite remarkable and affectionate portrait of a functioning female community held together by neither sentiment nor victimization, but rather by an abiding adherence to " 'the doctrine that loyalty to the abstract truth must over-ride all personal considerations' " (chap. 22, p. 360). If Peter Wimsey finally exposes the identity of the person who has been threatening the life of this community, it is the community itself which, in the unity of its response, has done the most to baffle the aggressor.

"Nothing but the very great loyalty of the Senior Common Room to the College and the respect of the students for the Senior Common

Room stand between you and a most unpleasant publicity. . . .
[T]his particular kind of loyalty forms at once the psychological ex-
cuse for the attack and the only possible defence against it."

(Chap. 22, p. 360)

Shrewsbury is no monolith, no reductive and oversimplified
site of girlish innocence and ingenuousness. Still less is it

> that still centre where the spinning world
> Sleeps on its axis, to the heart of rest

(Chap. 11, p. 189)

memorialized in the opening of Harriet's unfinished sonnet.
Indeed, it is Harriet's inability to get beyond this vision of
Shrewsbury as a cloister immune from the world's complexi-
ties, its struggles, and its tensions, that inhibits her capacity
to finish her poem, to move beyond the conventional forms
limiting the fiction she is writing, or to get on with her life.

What Harriet finally discovers at Shrewsbury is the possibility of delight that is neither rigid nor exclusionary. The
dons and their particular predicament validate Harriet's fidelity to her own work rather than demand that she sacrifice her
calling for theirs. The literary scholar, Miss Lydgate, shows
"no signs of being ashamed of Miss Vane" (chap. 1, pp. 18–19),
remarking instead: " 'I think it's so nice that our students go
out and do such varied and interesting things, provided they
do them well. And I must say, most of our students do do
exceedingly good work along their own lines' " (p. 38). In a
conversation with another alumna, Catherine Bendick, née
Freemantle, "very brilliant, very smart, very lively and the out-
standing scholar of her year" (chap. 3, p. 42), now married to
a farmer—wedded to his cause as well as his person—and obviously victimized by both endogenous and economic depression, Harriet begins to articulate her own emerging values.
Responding to the charge that working "the land . . . was a
service harsh and austere indeed, but a finer thing than spinning words on paper," Harriet agrees, yet establishes her own
reservations:

"A ploughshare is a nobler object than a razor. But if your natural talent is for barbering, wouldn't it be better to *be* a barber, and a good barber — and use the profits (if you like) to speed the plough? However grand the job may be, is it *your* job?"

(Chap. 3, p. 43)

Harriet's exasperated question is, of course, directed at herself as well as her companion. For Sayers, like Plato, judges reality in terms of ideal standards and invents a world where praxis can be made to reflect theory. Like Plato's, Sayers's ideal universe assumes that everyone must work and that an individual must first discover the job that satisfies her capacities and then execute that job in the best way possible, subordinating personal (or interpersonal) claims to the disinterested standards of performance. Work's significance is not abstracted from the worker, but emeregs from the harmony between individual and function. Harriet repeatedly discovers that, within very broad limits, it is not what people do that matters, but rather how well suited they are to do excellently the work that they have chosen. Acknowledging that certain jobs are more important to society than others, more necessary, or charged with higher status, does not mean that virtue automatically resides in their direction. Rather, both failure and crime in *Gaudy Night* originate from the same source. Both result from choosing inappropriately (on insufficient grounds, contrary to the evidence) or with the wrong motives.[7]

The particular triumph of Sayers's fictive vision, the territory newly claimed by Harriet's heroism, lies in its commitment to a process of continuous development and change, as well as on the possibility of combining what were previously considered opposing categories.[8] But the struggle to find a vehicle which can merge feeling and intellect is central to each of the fictions examined in this chapter. And, in all three, heterosexual love functions as a potential threat to this ideal fusion. Where *The Odd Women* and *Daughter of Earth* find no way through the impasse of desire, *Gaudy Night* successfully redefines the terms by which men and women are intimately intertwined.

In Gissing's text, the crusade to give women work and so catapult them into economic and spiritual independence is tested against both Rhoda's aborted relationship to Barfoot and Monica Madden's marriage to her suitor, Edmund Widdowson. As Harriet Vane initially suspects the dons' detachment from the world's emotions, so Monica withdraws her allegiance from Rhoda's prodigious energy. Where Monica's sister, Virginia, sees in Rhoda " 'the most wonderful person. . . . quite like a *man* in energy and resources' " (p. 30), Monica "saw the characteristics which made Virginia enthusiastic, but feared rather than admired them" (p. 36). Predictably, then, this youngest Miss Madden marries. A man much older than Monica, Widdowson shares traits with husbands we have seen before. Like Edward Phillotson, he is a loving but sexually repulsive spouse, and, like Léonce Pontellier, he is a "good husband," which is to say, one who defines his role according to his smugly self-serving understanding of its terms. Inevitably, the marriage is disastrous, as Gissing, like Hardy and Chopin, uses the marital relationship as an image of sexual repression and human bondage. Yet, predictable as this segment of the plot seems at this point, it is saved from utter redundancy by its relationship to Rhoda and her occupations. When Monica rebels against the constrictions of her life with Widdowson, she appeals to an existence larger than any she has ever actually known. Claiming her right to liberty and to friends of her own choosing, she asserts:

"I don't think . . . there's much real difference between men and women. That is, there wouldn't be, if women had fair treatment. . . . A woman ought to go about just as freely as a man. . . . When I have done my work at home I think I ought to be every bit as free as you are. . . . And I'm sure, Edmund, that love needs freedom if it is to remain love in truth."

(Chap. 16, pp. 163–64)

Gissing makes clear that even this limited and compromised rebellion is fueled by Monica's acquaintance with the values embraced by Rhoda and Mary:

Monica held with remarkable firmness to . . . her steadfast yet quite rational assertion of the right to live a life of her own apart from that imposed upon her by the duties of wedlock. A great deal of this spirit and the utterance it found was traceable to her association with the women whom Widdowson so deeply suspected; prior to her sojourn in Rutland Street she could not even have made clear to herself the demands which she now very clearly formulated. Believing that she had learnt nothing from them, and till late instinctively opposing the doctrines held by Miss Barfoot and Rhoda, Monica in truth owed the sole bit of real education she had ever received to those few weeks of attendance in Great Portland Street.

(Chap. 16, pp. 167–68)

However skeptical Gissing seems to be about the rewards of marriage—even the "happy" marriage of the Micklethwaites is stifling and unproductive, characterized by "repose" and "drowsiness" (chap. 17, p. 176)—he seems compelled to make its prospects somehow tempting to Rhoda. Partly, I think, Gissing takes this course as a way of both humanizing Rhoda's general character and asserting her sexual potential, although finally these energies are redirected and absorbed into a single-sex community. Rhoda's entanglement with Barfoot, which is, from one point of view, gratuitous, is from another, necessary: Gissing wants to establish clearly that Rhoda's existence among the "odd women" is determined not by a deficiency in her nature or by an unhealthy repression but by choice. From someone who seemed "to liken herself to the suggestion of her name by the excessive plainness with which she had arranged her hair" (chap. 8, p. 78), a woman who strikes Barfoot "as a male acquaintance might have done" (chap. 10, p. 101), she alters under his attentive gaze, revealing her "chestnut-brown eyes, with long lashes; the intellectual lips . . . the big, strong chin; the shapely neck—why, after all, it was a kind of beauty" (chap. 10, p. 101).

For Barfoot, as for Widdowson, heterosexual love signifies the very opposite of those communal values that bind women to each other in a network of mutual support; it means, instead, the desire of one party to dominate the other, to define the roles which both will play in their relationship to one another. Initially intrigued by Rhoda's resistance, enjoying the spectacle of "her freedom asserting itself" (chap. 13, p. 130), Everard's attitude quickly reverts to an almost reflexive desire to overpower her. In love though he may be, his main wish is "to amuse and flatter himself by merely inspiring her with passion. . . . To obtain her consent to marriage would mean nothing at all; it would afford him no satisfaction. But so to play upon her emotions that the proud, intellectual, earnest woman was willing to defy society for his sake—ah! that would be an end worth achieving" (chap. 17, pp. 176–77). A bit later he openly admits to Rhoda that

"love revives the barbarian; it wouldn't mean much if it didn't. In this one respect . . . no man, however civilized, would wish the woman he loves to be his equal. Marriage by capture can't quite be done away with. . . . Just because I am stronger than you, and have stronger passions, I take that advantage — try to overcome, as I may, the womanly resistance which is one of your charms."

(Chap. 17, p. 182)

As the veneer of liberalism and genial tolerance gets stripped away, Barfoot is revealed as increasingly intransigent.

Loving her . . . he could be satisfied with nothing short of unconditional surrender. Delighting in her independence of mind, he still desired to see her in complete subjugation to him, to inspire her with unreflecting passion.

(Chap. 25, p. 261)

What was implicit in the early scenes between Jane Eyre and Mr. Rochester is explicit here, but Gissing invents no bigamous marriage to save Rhoda from entombment in a relationship in which all permanent power belongs to the male partner. And, unlike Henry James, Gissing refuses the temptation of making marriage the vehicle whereby the woman hero learns to measure and perhaps escape her domestic preserve. Instead, as though building on the completed plots of his predecessors, Gissing forces Rhoda to consider the reality of Barfoot's proposals, the illusoriness of the choices he puts before her—to marry him or to live with him "freely" outside of marriage—and, in full consciousness of her own capacity to act, to reject him and live her life alone, though not, therefore, in solitude.

Although it does not culminate in marriage, as it almost certainly would have in earlier fiction, the passionate interlude with a man (Barfoot) continues to serve to take the woman (Rhoda) on an inward journey, compelling her to confront, even honor, her own sensuous and physical nature. Finally, powerfully acquainted with the irrational side of her own being, victor over those forces that resist or evade the pull of ideology, her position as a leader among women is doubly re-formed by the book's end. At first, Barfoot's attentions primarily flatter Rhoda's vanity: "Secretly she deemed it a hard thing never to have known the common triumph of her sex. And, moreover, it took away from the merit of her position as a leader and encourager of women living independently. There might be some who said, or thought, that she made a virtue of necessity" (chap. 14, p. 147). Then she, like he, is roused by the admixture of passionate feeling and her own participation in the struggle for control:

If she rejected his proposal for a free union, was he prepared to marry her in legal form? Yes; she had enough power over him for that. But. . . . more likely than not his love of her depended upon the belief that in her he had found a woman capable of regarding life from his own point of view.

(Chap. 25, p. 254)

Rhoda's jealousy over Barfoot's possible involvement with Monica merely provides another occasion for her to attempt to demand his surrender: "Even if it were proved in the clearest way that she ought to have believed him she would make no submission. If he loved her he must woo once more" (chap. 27, p. 287).

Finally, however, *The Odd Women* offers Rhoda no alternative other than withdrawal. The other choices—marriage or free love—offer no resolution, no fulfillment, but only the promise of bitter sniping and perpetual border skirmishes; capitulation to Barfoot's embraces would serve only to mark the interludes between the acts of war. Everard goes on to marry someone else, Agnes Brissenden, a rich young woman, "placid . . . never aggressive," whose posture is not "in declared revolt against the order of things, religious, ethical, or social" (chap. 30, p. 319). Although Rhoda's choice is for a single, and presumably a celibate life, her psychic exertions have served a purpose. If she has not been annexed by masculine authority, her involvement with Everard illuminates her renewed commitment to the community over which she and Mary Barfoot will continue to preside.

Where earlier she had held herself aloof from sympathy with a young woman, Bella Royston, who had left the protection offered by herself and Mary, "disgraced herself" (chap. 13, p. 128) with a man, and then sought to return to female society, she now feels her kinship with "the average woman." She can now understand "those poor of spirit, the flesh prevailing" (chap. 27, p. 291). If woman's traditional enemy is a too easy pity—a sympathy that threatens to slide the sympathizer over into the position of the victim—an unyielding rigidity born of an unwillingness or inability to test oneself against one's own capacity to feel tempestuously is equally dehumanizing. It is with the weight of justice on her side that Mary Barfoot regards Rhoda's rejection of Miss Royston as naive and dangerous:

"You have hardened your heart with theory. Guard yourself, Rhoda: To work for women one must keep one's womanhood. You are becoming — you are wandering as far from the true way — oh, much further than Bella did!"

(Chap. 13, p. 132)

The movement that begins here in the quarrel between the two women finds its way to closure through the course of Rhoda's relationship to Barfoot. Rejecting him, Rhoda nonetheless recognizes what it was that led the unfortunate Bella astray: "Passion had a new significance; her conception of life was larger, more liberal; she made no vows to crush the natural instincts" (chap. 27, p. 291).

Baptism by sexuality serves wonderfully in *The Odd Women* not to divert the hero's attention or dilute her primary resolve, but rather to return her to her chosen course revitalized and with a deeper understanding of the processes harnessed by her own commitment.[9] Rhoda returns from her seaside excursion resolved not to abandon her enterprise in response to masculine desire, but determined instead to remain "the same proud and independent woman, responsible only to herself, fulfilling the nobler laws of her existence" (chap. 27, p. 291). Everard is forced on this occasion to acknowledge her courage, her dignity, and the significance of her struggle.

Rhoda seems victorious at the end of *The Odd Women*. Secure in self-possession, she presides unreservedly over the battlefield of the world. Her command, like Isabel Archer's, is acknowledged by the author's offer of a girl child, a surrogate daughter, whose life will be hers to help shape and nourish. The child here belongs to Monica, who has died after giving birth, defeated by the accumulated strains of domestic life with Widdowson and by her own incapacity to will herself into any other sort of existence. Abandoned by her father, the baby is given over to Monica's sisters, Alice and Virginia. This pair, inspired by Rhoda's call to work, has found new energies for life and the possibilities of earning economic independence. But the sense of triumph that this schematic outline might suggest is mitigated by Gissing's portrayal of the grimness of the struggle, of the price exacted by such conquest. Although the novel's final words are Rhoda's, they are not the closing phrase of some grand Wagnerian ode. Muted, tender, she nurses Monica's child in her arms and empathetically acknowledges, if not its fate, at least the stern requirements of its circumstances: " 'Poor little child' " (chap. 31, p. 336).

Daughter of Earth parallels *The Odd Women* in recording

the painful process of successful struggle rather than the joyful celebration of glorious ascendance. For Marie as for Rhoda, the energies liberated by communal life are threatened and almost overwhelmed by the intrusions of personal, sexual commitment.[10] Unlike Rhoda, Marie marries, and not once, but twice. The first marriage is as predictable a failure as Isabel's and Osmond's, or Monica's and Widdowson's; that is, its dissolution follows on an incomplete understanding of the actual terms on which the union was originally founded, as well as on the incompatibility between the requirements of one party and the nature of the other. Marie chooses her first husband, Knut, because she seeks companionship; she wants no children and thinks that this negative wish will free her from the need of sexual contact as well. For Knut, however, companionship implies sexuality; and although he is more than commonly tolerant of Marie's reservations, their intercourse, which Marie sees as his activity, makes her pregnant. She has an abortion; he urges her to deny her pain; she leaves him. The story differs with her second husband, Anand. In this instance, Smedley breaks new ground because here, at last, Marie thinks she has found a human relationship which can be freely sexual, which can even allow for the possibility of children because it springs from shared values, from "understanding, tolerance, freedom—all combined" (part 7, p. 372). Yet this connection, also, fails horribly.

Chronicling the collapse of the marriage between Marie and Anand, Smedley provides a harrowing portrait of the battle between psychological and theoretical configurations and investigates the causes and consequences of psychic resistance to rational reform. Marie's legitimate preoccupation with the way social inequities are replicated in the structures of domestic life appears to justify her refusal of intimacy as the only choice consistent with dignity and freedom. Yet the privations of her earliest emotional life persist in adulthood as an unpaid debt. A question, an uncertainty, hollows out her core. On the one hand, she regards love as a force which compels women's complicity in their own victimization: "Love and tenderness meant only pain and suffering and defeat. I would not let it ruin me as it ruined others!" (part 5, p. 155); on the other, she admits "the desire for love and the need for tenderness between man and woman. Somewhere there was loneliness, uncertainty, sadness" (part 6, p. 219). Wondering if human beings could "be tender and still not weak" and if there could "really be love free from dangers and subjection for a woman" (part 6, p. 185), she hardens herself against her own perplexity, guards herself against the feelings "that menace the freedom of women," protects herself from the knowledge that "one builds fortifications only where there is weakness" (part 5, p. 156). "Ashamed of the desire for love . . . and companionship that existed beneath [her] rough and defiant manner" (part 6, p. 188), Marie's most private, internal life is a battlefield commandeered by competing wants and impulses: "There was a merciless war being waged within my own spirit, a war between my need and desire for love, and the perverted idea of love and sex that had been ground into my being from my first breath" (part 6, p. 202). Such defensiveness, however necessary, is a crippling, deforming posture; "A young tree cannot grow tall and straight and beautiful if its roots are always watered with acids" (part 3, p. 97).

Smedley's rendering of Marie's predicament connects cultural analysis and intrapsychic anatomy. Marie's particular mistrust of marriage springs from her passionate rejection of the socially sanctioned female role, the role she saw her mother play in relation to both her father and herself. In Marie's childhood, Mrs. Rogers, alternately beaten down by her husband and rebelling more or less futilely and passively against him—silence and tears her only weapons—acts out the intolerable frustrations of her position in the only way she can, in her mistreatment of her daughter. Because Marie is doubly weak, as a child and a female, she is fair game for hostility allowed no other outlet. Marie's earliest memory of her mother is one of unappeasable anger: Marie is being beaten for lighting fires in a homemade fireplace constructed against the back wall of the family's cabin. Protecting the house from incineration is not the issue here; Mrs. Rogers' motivations are more highly charged, but not directly accessible:

My beautiful fires, my glorious fires that she stamped out when she found them . . . it was like stamping out something within me. . . . Why she whipped me so often I do not know. I doubt if she knew. But she said that I built fires and that I lied.

(Part 1, pp. 10–11)

Retrospectively, Marie understands a "spiritual link between fire and the instinct of love" (part 1, p. 10), and it may be possible that despite Marie's denials, Smedley would have us see that Marie's mother also understood this connection. In either case, smothering Marie's fires represses her needs to express, give, and receive love; and Marie's mother, as the agent of this repression, is felt as the first enforcer of social limitations. Furthermore, in punishing Marie for setting fires, Mrs. Rogers links her daughter's pyrotechnics with the act of lying which can be seen as a representation of all imaginative expression. But, for Marie, imaginative truth is the only way to validate the existence of aspirations denied by the economic and emotional impoverishment of her daily life.

Marie is caught in a double bind, though a different one than that which pinched the characters viewed in the last chapter. Where what cannot be granted is forbidden even to be envisioned, where fidelity to social truth betrays psychological necessity, Marie learns that it is only by *really* telling lies, by not revealing what she knows but instead telling her mother "only the things I thought she wanted to hear" (part 1, p. 12) that she can avoid punishment. If Marie's mother is the arbiter of social convention, Marie's long struggle to tell the truth about life as she actually experiences it and explode the "silence" that enshrouds female identity is fused eternally with the struggle to achieve an authentic heroism.

Daughter of Earth, unlike either *Gaudy Night* or *The Odd Women,* does not conjure up the hope of a living, powerful community of women; in Marie's world, women are, collectively, always at least potential victims, and their very impotence makes them doubly threatening—as warning and as traitor—to one of their own kind who seeks for some alternative. Private alliances exist—between Marie and her Aunt Helen, between Mrs. Rogers and her sister, between Marie and her sister-in-law, and finally even between Marie and her mother; but because Smedley seems to share Marie's skepticism about the range of power that can rise from women's unions, these personal rapprochements fail utterly to make a mark on the larger world. Mrs. Rogers's repressiveness is rooted in a simultaneous desire to preserve her daughter for life in the world as it actually is and to punish her for the life imposed by these actualities.

> My mother . . . never believed in imaginin' things. . . . Yet . . . I wonder . . . her eyes were wistful. Perhaps she did not dare let herself see the clouds and dark forests, or the ripening berries on the mountain-side . . . the workers cannot afford to take their eyes off the earth.
>
> (Part 2, pp. 63–64)

What yokes women to each other in *Daughter of Earth* is simply "a bond of misery that was never broken" (part 3, p. 114).

This compromised bond is most powerfully evoked when Marie returns home to see her mother through the last stages of a fatal illness. Suffering intensely, Mrs. Rogers begs Marie for solace, but the doctor has specifically forbidden any more of the bicarbonate of soda that has previously offered her only release from pain. In violation of the doctor's stricture, Marie grants her mother's wish and in doing so becomes, literally, her mother's murderer. The point here is not legalistic or judicial, but emotional; a helping hand offered out of pity becomes a weapon of ultimate destruction. Sympathy brings death—as Psyche was warned when she journeyed to the underworld; its seductions must therefore be rejected.

This meaning is underscored later in the book when Marie

refuses to return home again in answer to her father's request that she help her brothers, Dan and George. Marie's resistance in this instance is seen as correct; at home she can do nothing to assist her brothers, but can only add her destruction to their own. Yet the price of Marie's strength is an equal measure of crippling guilt. What cannot be felt positively does not disappear, but makes its presence felt as anguish, rage, depression:

I resented everything, hating myself most of all for having been born a woman . . . hated my brothers and sister because they existed and loaded me with a responsibility I refused to carry; hated my father and mother for bringing me into a world when I didn't ask to come.
(Part 5, p. 143)

When George dies, digging ditches, a victim of the city of Omaha's need for a new sewer, Marie weeps once and then lies silent, "trying to forget the years that had passed . . . trying to forget the words of Dan telling how George had been killed. . . . I did not want to remember . . . I would rather that . . . memory were dead" (part 6, p. 246)

Wish, however, cannot kill memory. What is denied release on the surface of life impresses itself overwhelmingly upon the psyche and emerges, willy-nilly, in bafflement and blindness. Marie's rejection of her role as the "good" daughter, the "good" sister, the "good" woman, partly frees her, but partly cloaks her in permanent ambivalence. Admitting that in her deepest self she, too, has a maternal aspect, she seeks an outlet for her stifled desire to nurture and protect.

I was a mother nature. . . . This was not only the basis for my intellectual work, but it was the basis of my personal relationships. It seems to me now that had this part of my nature been permitted to develop instead of being poisoned, I would have loved life more than I do now . . . and I would have been very happy and very creative. . . .

But as it was . . . I searched for peace, for harmony, and found none; for there was no peace in my heart.
(Part 7, p. 364)

Marie's power as an agent of subversion is checked by her sense, however irrational, that others have unfairly paid for her escape.

> Once again I began building a wall against the past. To think of my
> father or to think of Helen brought misery . . . My mind built a
> wall of forgetfulness. . . . Perhaps my spirit brooded . . . perhaps
> it was the memory of him and of my brothers that troubled me when
> I awoke from dreams to lie staring into the darkness of my little room.
>   (Part 7, p. 259)

At the book's conclusion, when Marie's hope of happy marriage to Anand has been wrecked, when she is once again reduced from a comrade to a woman, this never deeply submerged layer of unresolved material pushes again to the surface of Marie's mind in another series of despairing dreams peopled with transformed but oddly undisguised figures from her past. In one she sees the firelight shining on "the face of Death . . . and Death was a gigantic woman with the face of my dead mother" (part 7, p. 400). This figure tempts Marie to salute her with a kiss, abandon the struggle, merge her lot with the common lot of women, and so rest.

Resisting this lure throughout the book forces Marie away from the reductions of her mother's prison and out into the larger world of her father. If her mother represents submission to social authority, her male parent offers the hope of vision, the attraction of a dream. Prior even to her remembrance of her mother's beating is an earlier "feeling of love and secrecy" (part 1, p. 8), a sense of her "father holding me close to his huge body in sleep" (part 1, p. 8). Whether this sense of warmth, safety, and security is memory or dream, Marie can't tell; but the feeling persists and is attached always to her father's physical presence, to the sensations of being cuddled and enveloped, to her father's dream of a better life than any he has lived. Where maternal influences have betrayed the imagination by stifling it, Marie's paternal legacy is equally warped in the opposite direction. For John Rogers, unable to force his dreams into being, unable to alter the world which reads his poverty as an indication of his personal incapacity, drifts from one scheme to another. Maddened by his circumstances, he is unequipped to understand their causes and focuses misguidedly on doomed efforts to make money. His energies are devoured by projects which render him always his bosses' dupe.

As a native American himself, with hopes of becoming an employer, he tried to identify himself with the sheriff and the officials of the camp against the strikers, who were foreigners. Still he was unclear; he had men working for him and yet he was an ignorant working man himself, and however hard he worked he seemed to remain miserably poor. He was too unknowing to understand how or why it all happened.

(Part 3, p. 119)

Unable to grasp the nature of the system by which those who control him maintain their power, he feels the effects of his own incapacity in his continued failure. His hopes thwarted, his dreams delusions, he withdraws increasingly into an embittered, alcoholic haze. Yet he survives in Marie's character as the force impelling her to honor hope, as the motive behind her search for a way to unite her single experience of love and tenderness with a new world sheltered by a masculine embrace. This complex web of prohibition and appeal is focused finally in Marie's marriage to Anand. Both partners in this relationship agree intellectually that the blame for the deformities and compromises of their past histories rests with the world, and that the capacities of individuals to bring a new world into being are linked with their ability to form new terms for personal relationships. *Daughter of Earth* supports this hope, but Smedley also painfully details the past's tenacity, its subterranean influence, its persistence as a fatal legacy that cannot be disowned at will. Marie's connection to Anand is not the future's new beginning, but the past's dead end, an Edenic idyll disrupted by the old satanic snake, heterosexuality, which is destructive because it is enmeshed in a larger network of patriarchal assumptions.

This force is personified in the figure of a man, Juan Diaz. Appearing first in the book as a participant in the Indian movement, he is, by the end, revealed as a traitor to the cause, a probable double agent who despises Marie because he thinks that, as a woman, she has no place in political life. In an effort to gain information, he preys on Marie's psychological susceptibility to his particular sexual qualities. In their single, profoundly ambiguous sexual connection—it is unclear in Marie's account whether Juan Diaz has raped or seduced her, whether she is his victim or his partner—Smedley renders the negative underside of the positive sexual and political dynamic that maintained Marie's union with Anand. The cynicism, despair, intense and sinister physicality of Juan Diaz attract Marie precisely because he reminds her of her father as he stands illuminated in the firelight, flames glinting off his belt buckle. Like her father, he uses his sexual potency as a weapon to destroy the woman who yields to him.

Marie's unresolved ambivalence about the significance of her own sexual energies is coupled with Anand's and the other Indians' equally unresolved feelings on the same subject. Marie's capacities to act as either an independent political agent or a free partner to her husband are nullified. The point here is not just that Marie is politically compromised through her connection to a traitor, but the way in which her right to an independent, asexual political stand is undercut by the intertwining of political and sexual motifs. Despite overwhelming evidence that Marie is not herself a traitor—she has, in fact, served a term in prison because of her fidelity—Anand feels personally betrayed and belittled because knowledge of Marie's past sexual history now permeates the group in which he has pledged to live his political life. When Marie declares her willingness to reveal publicly her version of the story, Anand is horrified.

"You would stand before a body of men and tell such things! Don't you know that not one of those men would believe you or would

respect you even if they believed, even if you were in the right and
Juan Diaz in the wrong? For he is a man and you a woman."

(Part 7, p. 388)

Because he shares this belief, Anand's capacity to act is limited
by Marie's sexual past.

"I have suffered . . . through you! . . . Now that I know you have
lied, how do I know but that you have lied about everyone else . . .
that perhaps all the other men are my countrymen also. . . . that I
am sitting in their presence each day, and any time I take an independent stand, one of them may arise and try to break me because of
you!"

(Part 7, pp. 388–89)

Despite their mutual declarations that their union is a free
one, Anand and Marie are driven apart. Anand's jealousy, not
just of Juan Diaz, but, through him, of all her past encounters, however meaningless, suggests to Marie that men's "primitive attitude toward woman as a purely physical being" (part 7,
p. 378) transcends their cultural differences or their stated
ideologies. And yet, because she, too "was poisoned with the
belief that sex expression was sin" (part 7, p. 378), because both
are unable fully to admit, much less remedy, what has come
between them, they must part. Marie announces her decision:

"There is no trust or understanding between us — and without these
there is no love. We are both too miserable. I cannot go further."

(Part 7, p. 405)

On the last page of *Daughter of Earth,* Marie is alone; pre-
paring to flee her house, her marriage, her country; apparently
an image of defeat. But the book curls back upon itself. The
events that conclude *Daughter of Earth* precede the analysis
Marie provides when she recounts her story. The exhaustion
of existence yields to the enterprise of autobiography. If the
separate strands of personal and political life are not yet knit
into a single harmonious pattern, the entirety of *Daughter of
Earth* provides a searing study of the difficulties and necessities
inherent in the struggle. In showing how ideological commit-

ment alone is insufficient to neutralize the tyranny of experience over our psychic lives, the book also refuses to allow
Marie to abandon her vision to either suicide or social conformity. Smedley renders Marie as indeed a hero, a woman
who understands what holds her back at the same time as she
continues to struggle to move forward.

The final importance of *Gaudy Night* derives from Sayers's
capacity to bring together the strains that remain discordant
at the ends of both *Daughter of Earth* and *The Odd Women*
in order to show how ideological and psychological needs can
interact in the interests of a living synthesis. At the end of her
story, Harriet Vane has resolved at last to marry Peter Wimsey.
Although this conclusion might, at first, seem a reversion to
the happy ending of conventional comedy, its function differs
because its premise, the nature of the love between the parties,
is not founded on the power struggle that marred Rhoda and
Barfoot's relationship nor on the chaos of unresolved attitudes
and guilts that destroyed Marie and Anand. Instead, as Harriet's experiences at Shrewsbury have altered and freed her,
Peter's initiation into love with Harriet has correspondingly
altered him. Harriet discovers the sources of her own strength
when they are fostered and nurtured by the women dons of
Shrewsbury; Peter symmetrically reveals his vulnerability, the
nexus of personal fears and attachments carefully masked
throughout his long courtship. Peter's sexual jealousy, his
sense of his own advancing years, his ambivalence about his
relationship to his family's aristocratic lineage, his need to disguise his work as an elaborate game which serves no ends but
the needs of wit, the tenderness of his own need for Harriet—
all are revealed as the novel progresses. Harriet's power for
good or ill over Peter's destiny becomes ascendant. Discovering
that "for the first time in their acquaintance [she] had the
upper hand and could rub his aristocratic nose in the dirt if
she wanted to" (chap. 9, p. 159), Harriet discovers, surprisingly,
delightfully, that she doesn't want to.

If love is a recognition of mutual vulnerability, it is not in consequence a crippled, static, or, still less, a retrogressive state. It is instead a new category of relationship, founded in reciprocity, resting in the admission of one's own need, for the sake of gaining access to another's authenticity. When Harriet reads the conclusion that Peter has wrought to the sonnet she started, the sonnet whose subject was her yearning for Oxford as a place of rest outside the claims of personal feeling, she suffers an unalterable illumination.

> He did not want to forget, or to be quiet, or to be spared things, or to stay put. All he wanted was some kind of central stability, and he was apparently ready to take anything that came along, so long as it stimulated him to keep that precarious balance. . . . In the five years or so that she had known him, Harriet had seen him strip off his protection, layer by layer, till there was uncommonly little left but the naked truth.
>
> That, then, was what he wanted her for. For some reason . . . she had the power to force him outside his defences. . . . Perhaps the sight of her struggles had warned him of what might happen to him, if he remained in a trap of his own making.
>
> (Chap. 18, pp. 304-5)

Harriet's division between love and work, the choice that Peter seems willing to allow her, is illusory. Her efforts to keep "the bitter, tormenting brain on one side of the wall and the languorous sweet body on the other, and never let them meet" (chap. 21, p. 350) has resulted in work which, while good enough of its kind, is now no longer satisfactory. The world of highlight and shadow, of recessed psychological motivations and subtly nuanced gestures is open to Harriet; her knowledge of its existence renders a fiction which excludes them as mechanical, a kind of jigsaw puzzle, a game which no longer pleases her, no matter the skill it takes to play. Peter does not force this discovery upon Harriet; rather, Harriet's deepening understanding of the difficult possibilities her own experience has made available to her, and her awareness of Peter's participation in that experience, widens Harriet's life and enlarges her work as well. Love and work no longer compete with one another in mutually exhausting tension. Instead both participate in making a new rhythm, a counterpoint where the burden is carried by both voices.

The solution of the mystery at Shrewsbury reveals that a woman is, in truth, the villain of the piece, though not one nurtured by the college. She is Annie Wilson, the widow of an aspiring graduate student, a man who suppressed evidence in order to prove an untenable thesis. Annie has vowed revenge against the person who originally exposed the falsification, Miss deVine, now a member of Shrewsbury's faculty. In Annie's eyes, Miss deVine and all those other women who are like her share sole responsibility for the destruction of a man's career and for his ultimate suicide as well. When Annie attacks Miss deVine, Harriet, and the other members of the Shrewsbury community, she does so in the name of the old ideology of love, a love that demands the suppression of one partner's interest ostensibly for the sake of the other's advancement, a relationship that requires abandoning the capacity to judge, that removes the participating parties from the common standards of the world, that renders both, in their disguised vanity and egotism, a little less than human. The conclusion of *Gaudy Night* annihilates this position; Annie and her views have been exposed as corrupt, destructive, and finally insane. The compassion that is threatening in *Daughter of Earth* and necessary but somewhat sad in *The Odd Women* pervades the network of principle and mutuality illuminating Shrewsbury. Where logic might righteously have sent Annie off to prison, sympathy sends her instead for psychiatric help. And Shrewsbury is no longer threatened by its desire to include what it can of this traditionally female, formerly incapacitating, feeling.

We do not know at the end of *Gaudy Night* what the outcome of Harriet and Peter's marriage will be. The world that the couple moves into is the open, complicated universe of mutability and alteration, rather than the closed universe of traditional comedy, in which the ending guarantees happiness by denying growth. Anyone in this new world may err, misstep, mistake; these acts will not be seen as caused by God or fate or the machinations of authorial invention, but rather as the result of human capacity which human effort might continue to reorder. This emphasis on rationality rather than morality, this replacement of fate with responsibility, this sense that the ending of the book is not the ending of the story serves to separate *Gaudy Night* from the kind of traditional comedy that disguises stagnation with the promise of happiness ever after and thus presents an acceptable alternative to that final, stagnant emotion for which women, in the past, have always had to pay so dearly.

Chapter 7

Makers of Art, Makers of Life

Creativity and Community in *Sula, Their Eyes Were Watching God,* and *The Dollmaker*

⅊ *By the rivers of Babylon, there we sat down, yea, we wept, when we remembered Zion. . . .*

How shall we sing the Lord's song in a strange land?

Psalm 137

⅊ *Our liberation consists in refusing to be "the Other" and asserting instead "I am"—without making another "the other." . . . The new sisterhood is saying "us versus non-being."*

Mary Daly, *Beyond God the Father*

Each point of closure marks a new beginning. The last chapter demonstrated how an existing social context, the world of work, can be commandeered by the woman hero and reinvested with energies frustrated in the formal and cultural cul-de-sac of marriage and the family. Used to represent collaboration and communal enterprise, the working world replaces isolated domesticity and stagnation. But where an activity, such as work, puts the performer in line for the world's rewards, its capacity to represent heroism, a gesture in permanent opposition to whatever momentarily exists, is theoretically limited.[1] Heroism is a habit of mind as much as a set of behaviors. In the yin and yang of social change, attitude matters as much as action, feeling as much as form. Imagination must persist, sniffing restlessly round the roots of any objectivity, seeking not so much a place to be as a stance to take toward that place and the universe that binds it.

Interposing wish and will between experience and the culturally prescribed patterns that assign meaning, we grope toward new expressions of our relationships to our surroundings. This ability to wrestle with the angel for the name that truly measures our experience, to make reality mirror what we know first in our dreams, inheres in all of us. It marks us as a species, separates us from everything else in the universe which does not project vision and sensation into the contours of a hypothesized future discernible even in the absence of a material incarnation. But we do not—or cannot—all exercise this talent equally. The carriers of this capacity are our artists, our creators. Heroes because of their power to improvise rather than accept, they write the script we read, compose the tune the rest of us can only beat out in assigned rhythms to the double bar.

To some extent, the subject of this chapter, the portrait of the hero as a female artist and the portrait of the artist as a woman hero, has been implicit in the preceding discussions. Hester Prynne, Edna Pontellier, and Harriet Vane are all explicitly described as artists. Jane Eyre and Marie Rogers tell us their own stories and so are responsible for the designs created in their texts. The narratives containing Clarissa Harlowe, Emma Woodhouse, Dorothea Brooke, Isabel Archer, and Sue Bridehead each record an isolated imagination struggling for legitimacy in a hostile or uncomprehending world. These characters' collective heroism is measured in the fates assigned their artworks, or their powers of personal invention, within the various novels, as well as in the relationship—or absence of relationship—that joins their private imaginings to the structure of society. In its largest sense, the exercise of heroism is always an artistic enterprise in that heroism seeks perpetually to chart new territories on the margins of old maps, to inscribe in life what is first felt only as the soul's desire. The figures we shall be considering in this chapter—Sula Peace,

Janie Crawford, and Gertie Nevels—are separated from their predecessors only in degree and not in kind. Not unique instances, the trio chosen here crystallizes tendencies present in all the narratives we have so far examined, providing us with representative rather than singular examples.

In her introduction to *The Golden Notebook*, Doris Lessing provides a partial paradigm for the characters whose fates and tales will soon be examined. Lessing observes that

> the theme of the artist has been dominant in art for some time — the painter, writer, musician, as exemplar. . . . Those archetypes, the artist and his mirror-image the businessman, have straddled our culture, one shown as a boorish insensitive, the other as a creator all excesses of sensibility and suffering and a towering egotism. . . . Heroes a hundred years ago weren't often artists. They were soldiers and empire builders and explorers and clergymen and politicians — too bad about women who had scarcely succeeded in becoming Florence Nightingale yet. . . . But to use this theme of our time "the artist", "the writer", I decided it would have to be developed by giving the creature a block and discussing the reasons for the block. These would have to be linked with the disparity between . . . overwhelming problems . . . and the tiny individual who was trying to mirror them. But what was intolerable, what really could not be borne any longer, was this monstrously isolated, monstrously narcissistic, pedestalled paragon.[2]

Like Lessing's artist, Sula, Janie, and Gertie each are "blocked"; each blockage occurs at the point at which cultural conventions impinge on the possibilities of free creation. These characters are all denied forms of expression or even access to expression because of the difficulties each encounters, in her culturally contradictory roles of woman and artist, in connecting a private world of need and vision to a public realm. The inhabitants of Morrison's Bottom, Hurston's Eatonville, and Arnow's Kentucky discount the pain required to render repression as morality. Seeking to connect the world of the self to the world of society, Morrison's, Hurston's, and Arnow's heroes boldly outline perceptions and identities that their original circumstances have rendered all but invisible. Whether asserting the necessity of negativity, as Sula does, or battling, like Janie and Gertie, for a new and positive identification of self and society, each denies the model of the "pedestalled paragon," refuses both its isolation and its elevation.

These characters make other points which Lessing's full description either overlooks or denies. In the first place, Lessing's account proceeds from the assumption that the "filter which is a woman's way of looking at life has the same validity as the filter which is a man's way."[3] Applauding the truth of this statement ought not to allow us to confuse validity with identity; and the fact of gender, if not the biology of sex itself, is functionally important in *Sula* (1973), *Their Eyes Were Watching God* (1937), and *The Dollmaker* (1954).[4] In a social world in which the putative privileges of isolation, egotism, and romantic sensibility have been genderized and assigned typically to men, the artist who does not, or cannot, claim these prerogatives by right, whose relationship to authority is seen as inherently questionable rather than assumed, is, within the canon of cultural convention, always "feminized," if not always literally female. Yet even the female artist cannot discard egotism as easily as Lessing's statement suggests; indeed, such a move would be, in some sense, fatal to her capacity to be an artist at all. The ego's nature may be redefined, but ego itself persists, for the artist moves by establishing a world out of the self's creative power. Where there is no self, where society has sought to obliterate its existence or render its status dubious or dangerous, the artist's struggles are not thereby resolved but are, on the contrary, more starkly outlined than would be the case where the rights of the ego are unthinkingly accepted. Sula Peace, Janie Crawford, and Gertie Nevels strive to imprint their visions and their selves upon fixed social habits denying both. In approaching this synthesis, the ego's assertion surmounts Lessing's description of it as necessarily narcissistic and encapsulated.

Still, Lessing's ideal of an egoless artist suggests a legitimate reorientation of the relationship of creativity to both self and production, a revision neither met nor anticipated in typical accounts rendered through the personae of male artists. That is, the ordinary heroism (to be deliberately paradoxical) of the artist-figure focuses on the construction of a masterpiece, a singular, great work. In that sense, the artwork's significance is not tied to its power to effect social change by reflecting new possibilities for human interaction, but to its testimony to the primacy of the artistic self. This is the egotism which Lessing's analysis seeks to discredit. *Sula, Their Eyes Were Watching God,* and *The Dollmaker* extend Lessing's thinking by suggesting that their heroes' importance does not lie in their capacity to make monuments that, whatever their relationship to culture, are primarily self-reflective. Instead, the figures considered in this chapter are creative in that they model not objects, but people and society. Considered abstractly, their efforts seek to replace the static hierarchies of community with a more free-flowing, less role-bound communitas. In altering the organization of society, Sula, Janie, and Gertie are artists whose medium is life itself. Making characters who fuse aesthetic and social impulses, Morrison, Hurston, and Arnow create heroes—women and artists—who begin in an isolation predicated on their gender and become images of that radical involvement Lessing endorses.[5]

Toni Morrison's Sula, caught between aspiration and alienation, is the epitome of ambiguity. Her posture reflects the issue of artistic ego that Lessing framed. Stigmatized from birth as "different,"[6]—marked above her eye by a rose, perhaps, or a tadpole, or something more sinister—"as willing to feel pain as to give pleasure, hers was an experimental life" (part 2, p. 102). It is this quality of uncertainty, this desire to play games with unclear rules and unstated goals, that defines her for her creator and for us. Underscoring this point, Morrison remarks in an interview that "Sula . . . knows all there is to know about herself . . . she examines herself . . . she's perfectly willing to think the unthinkable thing."[7] Like Lessing's artist, Sula is "completely free of ambition, with no affection for money, property or things, no greed, no desire to command attention or compliments—no ego. For that reason she [feels] no compulsion to verify herself—to be consistent with herself" (part 2, p. 103).

A possible exemplar of Lessing's model, Sula demonstrates its contradictions. Lack of ego, literal selflessness, empowers Sula, as Lessing thinks it ought, but also limits her.[8] Her life is a long series of extreme and bizarre behaviors; she can do anything, because she has nothing to protect. Permanently resistant to the mores of the community that bred her, she is regarded by it as pariah, as surely as Puritan Boston looped that label round the neck of Hester Prynne. Unlike Hester, Sula has committed no single, convenient sin; she is simply evil generalized. Seeking to contain her, as Puritanism ultimately contained Hester, the Bottom says that she has done *its* unforgivable thing and slept with white men, but Sula's case differs from Hester's in offering no evidence to support the accusation. Really, anarchy is Sula's sin: anarchy, rage, desperation, and hopelessness. Convinced that half the town needs killing and the other half a "drawn-out disease" (part 2, p. 83), Sula's vision of ultimate acceptance promises apocalypse rather than Hawthorne's vague and rosy future:

"They'll love me all right. It will take time, but they'll love me. . . . After all the old women have lain with the teen-agers; when all the young girls have slept with their drunken uncles; after all the black men fuck all the white ones; when all the white women kiss all the black ones; when the guards have raped all the jailbirds and after all the whores make love to their grannies; after all the faggots get their mothers' trim; when Lindbergh sleeps with Bessie Smith and Norma Shearer makes it with Stepin Fetchit; after all the dogs have fucked all the cats and every weathervane on every barn flies off the roof to mount the hogs . . . then there'll be a little love left over for me."

(Part 2, p. 125)

Out of her "tremendous curiosity and her gift for metaphor" (p. 105), Sula creates this Bosch-like garden of delight, gloriously detailed, exultantly perverse. Lacking "paints, or clay, or . . . the discipline of the dance, or strings" Sula is seen by the narrator as "an artist with no art form," and hence "dangerous" (part 2, p. 105).

Menacing others, endangering herself, Sula's wildness is, of course, also the basis of her strength. Although she acts as a lightning rod for society's doubts about its own complacency, Sula, like all heroes, perpetually risks being cast off by her world as a mere agent of chaos, a gambler risking too much—and calling others to risk too much—in a game rigged to favor the house, the status quo. Of all the figures we have looked at, Sula comes closest to attracting to herself all of this fear and projected negativity. Rejoicing in the status thus conferred, Sula, from the Bottom's point of view, seems initially not compelling, but only malign. Unwilling to atone for her actions, to gray herself in Hester's kindness, utility, and sympathy for others, Sula violates all of the Bottom's norms. And in sending her grandmother away to a county home run by whites, Sula forfeits her humanity, becomes "a roach" (part 2, p. 97). She is, nonetheless, as locked into the Bottom as Hester was locked into Boston. Her neighbors can't utterly dissociate themselves from her any more than the Puritans, in Hawthorne's view, could deny their relationship to Hester. Virtue in both cases depends reactively on vice. When Sula dies, the Bottom discovers that her dark vision has permanently marked the community and can no longer be distanced or disowned. The neat polarities of good and evil the town sought to maintain have become blurred and are replaced by the sense, in one chosen observer, of the necessity of danger, the ethics of outrage, the moral obscurity of life. Sula's mortality may be a function of her art. In death, Sula's life becomes exemplary, useful, another's talisman against the dissolution Sula both battled and endured.

When *Sula*'s narrator asserts that Sula has no art form, she means that Sula has been denied the materials that artists conventionally use to express, but also to mediate, their visions. Instead, Sula's energies are engaged directly by the world around her. But this world is itself an artwork, albeit an un-successful one, and Sula's efforts to recast its mold are not eva-sions but avowals of artistic enterprise. An artifact, an inven-tion, the Bottom exists as Sula finds it through the agencies of history and prior social intervention. It is an archetype of anti-heroism, created by ante-bellum Southern whites in vengeance against the possibility of liberated blackness. The story of the Bottom's founding is a parable of trickery, a betrayal of the questing figure by intractable, illegitimate authority, a jest at the expense of the one who performs the impossible task or solves the insoluble riddle.

A good white farmer promised freedom and a piece of bottom land to his slave if he would perform some very difficult chores. When the slave completed the work, he asked the farmer to keep his end of the bargain. Freedom was easy — the farmer had no objection to that. But he didn't want to give up any land. So he told the slave that he was very sorry that he had to give him valley land. He had hoped to give him a piece of the Bottom.

(Part 1, pp. 4–5)

The Bottom, says the farmer, is the land high up in the hills, the land God looks down on, "the bottom of heaven." Pressing his master for some of this desirable territory, "the nigger got the hilly land, where planting was backbreaking, where the soil slid down and washed away the seeds, and where the wind lingered all through the winter" (part 1, p. 5). The would-be hero has been transformed into a fool; his descendants, laugh-ing at this story, mock at their own lives. But an "adult pain rests somewhere under their head rags and soft felt hats" (part 1, p. 4).

The sense of betrayed ceremonies, of subverted expectations, of contradictions understood but unresolved, marks the Bottom and its inhabitants from the first pages of the book. Blighted from birth, it survives as a cultural structure through a dense webbing of counterrituals, incantations performed to insure the growth of seeds which must fall on barren ground. A vor-tex at the center of this network, Sula's rebellion is thus neither random, purposelessly anarchic, nor artistically unstructured. Her force foils others' sacraments, principally those of three competing figures: Helene Wright, the mother of Sula's only friend and a woman who personifies the denial of reality that produces the neighborhood's wooden conventionality; Shadrack, a soldier who, returning from the First World War shell-shocked and insane, attempts to organize and control the death and violence the world has taught him to acknowledge and even honor; and Eva Peace, Sula's formidable grandmother, a woman supremely larger than life, able, like Shadrack, to manipulate violence, and, like him again, unable to find a viable alternative.

Helene Sabat Wright is the person closest to the Bottom's center. Static and conforming, she is one of a long line of women we have already seen and will see again, a child cut off from her maternal roots. Helene's mother, Rochelle, light-skinned and beautiful, used these supposed advantages to set herself up as a whore at the Sundown House in New Orleans. Raised by her grandmother "under the dolesome eyes of a multicolored Virgin Mary counseling her to be constantly on guard for any sign of her mother's wild blood" (part 1, p. 15), Helene grows up embracing the values of correctness, devoting herself to an asphyxiating domesticity. A woman "who won all social battles with presence and a conviction of the legitimacy of her authority" (part 1, p. 16), she is church-going, God-fearing, and smug: "All in all her life was a satisfactory one. She loved her house and enjoyed manipulating her daughter and her husband. . . . She had indeed come far . . . away from the Sundown House" (part 1, p. 16). Helene passes on to her daughter Nel the same fears that her grandmother passed on to her; she stands for restraint, repression, inhibition: "Any enthusiasms that little Nel showed were calmed by the mother until she drove her daughter's imagination underground" (part 1, p. 16).

The inadequacies of this stance are revealed to us as well as to Nel when mother and daughter return to New Orleans to attend Rochelle's funeral. Boarding a train bound for the darkness of the deep south, Helene and Nel accidentally stray into a car reserved for whites. Caught by the conductor as they retreat into apparent safety behind a door marked COLORED ONLY, Helene's status is breached by a white conductor. No longer Mrs. Wright, she is simply " 'gal.' " Prey, as her mother was prey, to be set out "in the city where the red shutters glowed" (part 1, p. 17), she is subject to all "the old vulnerabilities, all the old fears of being somehow flawed" (part 1, p. 18). Cringing, crawling, asking to be excused for not only her behavior but her very existence, she does not rebel, but begs for mercy. She smiles at her oppressor, revealing her inadequacy to her daughter and to a whole carload full of black men who, like Nel and like Helene herself, are now forced to accept the consequences of a weakness and humiliation they can scarcely admit to consciousness. As the walls of her mother's solidity buckle and collapse, Nel experiences a double illumination. First, she senses that her mother's polite goodness is actually an evil, that the men in the car are "bubbling with a hatred for her mother that . . . had been born with the dazzling smile" (part 1, p. 19). Second, she realizes that Helene's social position is as fraudulent as her moral stance. Imposing façades, they are a custard's skin, permeable, soft, and gelatinous.

The significance of Helene's dethronement must be read in its effects on her daughter and, in turn, on the alignment of Nel's eventual relationship to Sula. Nel reacts to her mother's unmasking with a complex mixture of fear and repulsion—which are predictable responses—and pleasure, which is not. Ashamed and afraid, she is also tantalized and invigorated by her discovery: "She had gone on a real trip, and now she was different. . . . 'I'm me,' she whispered. 'Me.' . . . Each time she said the word *me* there was a gathering in her like power, like joy, like fear" (part 1, pp. 24–25). Her mother's impotence simultaneously produces Nel's new identity and threatens it: "If this tall, proud woman who was very particular about her friends, who slipped into church with unequaled elegance, who could quell a roustabout with a look, if *she* were really custard, then there was a chance that Nel was too" (part 1, p. 19). The shock of this possibility, of birth poised on the brink of death, creates a blankness in Nel, a sense of mysterious forces undermining the world's foundations. The mixture of ridicule and contempt reflected in the soldiers' eyes floods Nel's former margin of safety. The rage Helene suppresses when she smiles spills over into Nel as the waters of a galling bitterness, a force which cannot be diverted by the repeated rituals—the nose pulling, church going, and physical repression—which are all Helene's "goodness" can offer to propitiate society's bloodthirsty gods. The potentiality to take action against her mother's stagnation, and her own, lies cradled in Nel now and waits for Sula to excavate the channels into which it might flow.

Like the soldiers in the colored car, Shadrack is a representative of blackness and maleness in a white world, a world infrequently mentioned but always there, content to use but not reward him. Because Shadrack is even more radically uprooted than Helene from both the inner sources of his own identity and the social impositions that might provide a conventional life, he cannot take Helene's route and devitalize himself, making an identity of custard's infantile smoothness. Where Helene suggests the limits of rationalization, Shadrack is irrationality given flesh:

Twenty-two years old, weak, hot, frightened, not daring to acknowledge the fact that he didn't even know who or what he was . . . with no past, no language, no tribe, no source, no address book, no rug, no bed, no can opener, no faded postcard, no soap, no key, no tobacco pouch, no soiled underwear and nothing nothing nothing to do.

(Part 1, p. 10)

In essence, his struggle, like Helene's out of the fearsome sexual and racial inferno of the Sundown House, is an effort to make an order in a hostile, frightening, and uncontrollable world. As Helene's failure is revealed to Nel in the wetness of the soldiers' eyes, Shadrack's is shown to him in the dark waters of a toilet bowl. But where Helene corsets tremors in rigid respectability, Shadrack admits his panic, embraces it as the irreducible core of his identity. The ritual he invents when he returns to the Bottom is called National Suicide Day, an attempt to "order and focus experience" by "making a place for fear as a way of controlling it. . . . If one day a year were devoted to [death and dying], everybody could get it out of the way and the rest of the year would be safe and free" (part 1, p. 12). Holding out January 3 as an annual occasion licensing people "to kill themselves or each other" (part 1, p. 12), Shadrack offers a model of release for the forces aroused but repressed by Helene's smile on the train. His social order complements Helene's apparently very different one in that both rest on the need for self-destruction. For the Bottom, as for Nel, the surface texture of life continues apparently unruffled. But Shadrack's doubtful ceremony, like Nel's precarious understanding of her own identity, is suspended in the book's structure and waits for Sula as a catalyzing agent.

Eva Peace, Sula's grandmother, is the third ironic guardian-figure Morrison provides as part of the machinery of life in the Bottom. Like Helene and Shadrack, Eva is forced to grapple with the destruction of the frame around her life: her husband Boyboy abandoned her in the cold winter of 1895, leaving her alone in a house with three children, "$1.65, 5 eggs, 3 beets," and, like Helene and Shadrack, "no idea of what or how to feel" (part 1, pp. 27–28). Having used the last of her food, a fingerful of lard, to give her son an enema, she confronts the emptiness before her and takes action. Leaving her children, she disappears for eighteen months and returns, finally, "with two crutches, a new black pocketbook, and one leg" (part 1, p. 30), her physique diminished but her reputation enlarged. The legend that grows around her suggests that she deliberately allowed a train to amputate her limb so that she could get the insurance money which would both provide for her family and allow her to be powerful instead of helpless. Galvanized by rage and mutilation, she takes charge of her world. She builds a house and moves her offspring into it. She takes in boarders, and homeless children whom she renames so compellingly that they are known ever after as "the deweys"; although they do not really resemble each other, no one is able to tell them apart.

Although she appears less vulnerable than either Helene or Shadrack, Eva, too, is compromised. Her power, like theirs, is founded on a contradiction; it depends on that very negativity it aspires to deny. Like Helene, Eva refuses explicitly to acknowledge she is "custard"; like Shadrack, she tries valiantly to arrange what threatens her into a manageable compass. Her missing leg and the status her wound confers upon her make her saga the personal equivalent of the more depersonalized romance of National Suicide Day. But, like the others', her effort too is limited by the social terms and private feelings which called it into being. Helene's conventionality masks a real dissolution of personality. Shadrack's rite is a struggle to appease an unquellable violence by externalizing it and assigning it a predictable place. Both figures are artists whose creations fail because they rest on fractured egos. Eva's energies also are ultimately frustrated, precipitating the defeat she has tried desperately to evade. When Plum, the son whose life initially summoned up Eva's strength, returns to the Bottom from the same war that destroyed Shadrack's sanity and created the men who exposed Helene, he comes as a junkie. Nothing Eva can do, no power that she can claim or conjure with, can alter his condition. Plum seeks the oblivion of heroin as a way station on the underground journey he really wishes to take: back to the safety of his mother's womb. Because Eva's power is limited she can reject such perversion of the natural order only by further perversion. Since she cannot fit him for life, Eva drags herself up to Plum's room at the top of the house and with hieratic authority, washes him not in the waters of life, but in kerosene, which she sets alight. Lacking the power to put things right, Eva, like Helene and Shadrack, can summon up merely enough strength to obliterate what she cannot finally control. In death, Plum is baptized, given an identity he never had in life. Eva's words are his epitaph:

"I birthed him once. I couldn't do it again. . . . I would have . . . let him if I'd've had the room but a big man can't be a baby all wrapped up inside his mamma no more; he suffocate. I done everything I could to make him leave me . . . but he wouldn't and I had to keep him out so I just thought of a way he could die . . . not all scrunched up . . . but like a man."

(Part 1, p. 62)

The crumpled webs of possibility provided by Eva, Shadrack, and Helene provide the context for reading Sula's relation to the Bottom, and particularly her connection with and effect on Nel Wright. These three—the priestess, the shaman, and the guardian of the hearth—define the Bottom's imagination; they share, despite their obvious differences from one another, a quality that is essentially static, reactive, and devious. Finding the world as it is unbearable, they strive to create an identity that will mask their need to live outside its borders. None actually confronts the surrounding circumstances or attempts to alter them. Their sterility is evidenced in their inability to pass on the strategies that have guaranteed their own personal survival. Helene stakes all, appropriately for her, on a wedding: Nel's to Jude Greene. But the marriage rests on a lie, on Nel's doing for Jude what Eva realized could not be done for Plum, on one human being acting as another's permanent shelter and making of "the two of them together . . . one Jude" (part 1, p. 71). Eva's creativity was meant to serve Plum, "to whom she hoped to bequeath everything" (part 1, p. 38), but had the cataclysmic consequences already described. And the only time Shadrack succeeds in getting the townspeople to immerse themselves in the enacted ritual of National Suicide Day, the immersion is literal: his followers fall into the river and drown.

Sula begins by sharing the isolation of her forebears, "a loneliness so profound the world itself had no meaning," a "solitude . . . that . . . had never admitted the possibility of other people" (part 2, p. 106). But unlike Helene and Eva, and unlike Shadrack (to whom she is most closely related and with whom the book's structure and imagery persistently associate her), Sula's devices avow rather than repress the essential desolation of her life's experiences and begin from this admission the struggle for a new formulation of relationship. She repudiates Helene's community and Eva's power as hypocritical in the first instance and corrupt in the second. Her ruthless energies express a need to find a private core of authentic identity that, reflected in another, might knit these fragile filaments into a new social fabric. It is this need that none of the other rituals addresses because, denying the actual terms of life, they destroy both privacy and the capacity to create a self that can join freely with another. Sula, then, must speak for a love which violates the safe disguises of the surrounding community, one that is necessarily anarchic, dangerous, full of risk and hazard. Loosing her imagination to play upon her needs, Sula invents her relationship with Nel: a new emblem to represent the limits of an old order and the foundations of a new one.[9]

After the discovery of her essential "me-ness" on the train, Nel adopts Sula as a kindred being. In the summer of their twelfth year, the two girls mingle their "adventuresomeness . . . and . . . mean determination to explore everything that interested them," and "in the safe harbor of each other's company . . . abandon the ways of other people and concentrate on their own perceptions of things" (part 1, p. 47). Nel stops pulling her nose, ceases to care about straightening her hair, as she and Sula venture into consciousness. "Because each had discovered years before that they were neither white nor male, and that all freedom and triumph was forbidden to them, they had set about creating something else to be. Their meeting was fortunate, for it let them use each other to grow on" (part 1, p. 44). Two schemers sharing a single delight, sex is "the thing that clotted their dreams" (part 1, p. 43). But sex as generalized connection rather than narrowly physical activity, as companionship and not solitude incompletely shared, as the union of two positive forces rather than the negation of a negative, requires a context. And Sula's world is fallen, ruined; love has been rendered an impossible luxury, for reasons which are historical and existential even more than they are sexual. Sula's mother, Hannah, asks Eva: " 'Mamma, did you ever love us' "; Eva can only reply: " 'No. I don't reckon I did. Not the way you thinkin' '" (part 1, p. 58). Eva's encounters with life's malevolence have made it impossible for her to gratify her daughter's yearning for a personal commitment from someone who can "play" with her: " 'They wasn't no time. Not none. Soon as I got one day done here comes a night. With you all coughin' and me watchin' so TB wouldn't take you off . . . what you talkin' 'bout did I love you girl I stayed alive for you' " (part 1, p. 60).

Sula's adventure, her quest for "the beautiful, beautiful boys who dotted the landscape like jewels" (part 1, p. 48) is blighted by her awareness of this vacancy at the Bottom's heart. Hannah's love, like Eva's, is impersonal, helpless to alter the fact that she doesn't actually like Sula as an individual. Hannah is punished for the indifference she both receives and transmits. While boiling water to blanch beans for canning, she is caught by flames and incinerated, her funeral pyre a twin to Plum's. The mutilated Eva cannot save her; the unforgiving Sula will not. Stronger than Hannah, however, Sula refuses to die from lack of love. Being more honest than Hannah—or Eva or Helene—Sula struggles first to record love's absence. She and Nel originate a ceremony, a rite that begins by summoning erotic powers and ultimately proceeds to murder.

Sula . . . joined Nel in the grass. . . . In concert . . . they stroked the blades up and down. . . . Nel found a thick twig and . . . pulled away its bark until it was stripped to a smooth, creamy innocence. Sula . . . found one too. When both twigs were undressed, Nel moved . . . to the next stage and began tearing up rooted grass to

make a bare spot. . . . Sula traced intricate patterns . . . with her
twig. . . . Nel . . . poked her twig rhythmically and intensely into
the earth, making a small neat hole that grew deeper and wider with
the least manipulation. . . . Sula copied her, and soon each had a
hole the size of a cup. . . . Together they worked until the two holes
were one and the same. When the depression was the size of a dish-
pan, Nel's twig broke.

(Part 1, pp. 49–50)

The twig's breaking signifies most obviously the inadequacy
of maleness, its impotence in a world where white boys work
and black ones must use women to provide "some posture of
adulthood" and "someone to care about [their] hurt" (p. 71).
But the placement of the entire scene immediately after Sula's
discovery of her mother's betrayal suggests ways in which this
failure is generalized. Eroticism is blocked, all love—not merely
heterosexuality—is denied. What began as an act of lyricism
and a celebration of life becomes a desecration, a violation.
The broken twigs are thrown into the hole. Other objects
follow:

Nel saw a bottle cap and tossed it in as well. Each then looked around
for more debris . . . paper, bits of glass, butts of cigarettes, until all
of the small defiling things they could find were collected there.

(Part 1, p. 50)

Sula and Nel's initial collaboration has produced no monument to life, fertility, and promise; rather, they have dug
themselves a grave, a cesspit.

Although she acknowledges this darkness, Sula refuses to
let it swallow her. Instead, seizing the arms of a little boy
whom Morrison provides as bait and sacrifice, she swings him
out far above the river, drops him, and watches while he
drowns. Chicken Little's sunken body makes "a closed place
in the water" (p. 87). Through this device, all the Bottom's
"closed places" are named. Previously, they existed as secret
recesses where individuals buried knowledge of their impoverishment and hid from the rage such awareness kindles. Sula's
terrifying action bares this fury, embraces the awfulness of

what she is prepared to admit about herself and her world, accepts even the necessity of murdering another as the only possible substitute for her own entombment.

Shadrack and Eva share Sula's knowledge of her act. Eva repudiates it: " 'Me, I never would've watched. . . . It's awful cold in the water. Fire is warm' " (part 2, p. 145). She should know; she offered two children to its snug embrace. Having done so, she excuses herself: Plum's death and Hannah's belong to them, not her. Eva, for all her power, is merely the world's agent, the enforcer of things as they are, not of things as they might become. Her survival involves an acceptance of brutality, but, unlike Sula, she denies her own participation in it. Shadrack seeks to make Sula a participant in his sacramental variant, welcoming her to a world which is permanently frightening and unbearable: "She had a tadpole over her eye (that was how he knew she was a friend—she had the mark of the fish he loved.) . . . But when he looked at her face he had seen also the skull beneath, and thinking she saw it too—knew it was there and was afraid—he tried to think of something to say to comfort her" (part 2, p. 134). Telling Sula " 'always,' " he seeks to guard her from change and decay "so she would not have to be afraid of . . . the falling away of skin, the drip and slide of blood, and the exposure of bone underneath. He had said 'always' to convince her, assure her, of permanency" (part 2, pp. 134–35).

Such fixedness is precisely what Sula does not want. Chicken Little is Sula's talisman against Helene's and Eva's chosen immobility and Shadrack's broken retreat. If Shadrack and Eva live, to some extent, outside the town's norms, their excesses nonetheless sustain the Bottom as much as Helene's posture does; they all seek to purge a disorder they can finally neither admit nor accept. To Sula, they are

spiders . . . who dangled in dark dry places suspended by their spittle, more terrified of the free fall than the snake's breath below. . . . If they were touched by the snake's breath . . . they were merely victims and knew how to behave in that role. . . . But the

free fall, oh no, that required — demanded invention . . . a full surrender to the downward flight if they wished to . . . stay alive. But
alive was what they . . . did not want to be. Too dangerous.

(Part 2, pp. 103–4)

Invested in danger and invention, loving the free fall as the
only honorable state, Sula appeals to Nel to participate with
her in this new communion, to accept destruction as a prelude to generation. But Nel, too, pulls back. Of the death of
Chicken Little, she wants to say " 'I did not watch it. I just
saw it' " (part 2, p. 146). Rejecting the challenge implicit in
Sula's feeling that "Nel was the first person who had been real
to her, whose name she knew, who had seen as she had the
slant of life that made it possible to stretch it to its limits"
(part 2, p. 103), Nel represses "any sparkle or splutter she had"
(p. 72). Where Sula kills Chicken Little in a gesture that expresses her sense of life's contamination, Nel marries Jude and
caters to his pain. Responding to the "shame and anger" (part
1, p. 72) Jude feels at his own "blank spaces"—the absence in
his life of any camaraderie, the distance between himself and
"something real, something he could point to" (part 1, p. 70)—
Nel moves away from Sula and accepts a spider's love "which
over the years . . . spun a steady gray web around her heart"
(part 2, p. 82).

Divorced from Nel, Sula leaves the Bottom, returning only
after a decade's travels have convinced her that the world is
everywhere alike, that every place she visits holds "the same
people, working the same mouths, sweating the same sweat,"
offers "the same language of love, the same entertainments of
love, the same cooling of love" (part 2, p. 104). For Nel, however, Sula remains restorative: "It was like getting the use of
an eye back, having a cataract removed. Her old friend had
come home. Sula. Who made her laugh, who made her see old
things with new eyes, in whose presence she felt clever, gentle
and a little raunchy" (part 2, p. 82). Attempting again, as she
had on the long ago day by the river's edge, to fuse her energies with Nel's, Sula sleeps with Jude. Once more, Nel with-

draws in horror. Jude was her possession. Belonging to her, he anchored her, gave her a fixed position in the Bottom's community. Unable to abandon this fixity, Nel now joins the ranks of those who regard Sula as evil incarnate, a force to be outlasted because, like other such forces, it cannot be annihilated or accepted.

At this point Sula retreats. Estranged from the one person she had hoped to convert to her gospel of contingency, she tries to make her peace with the forms the world has made available to her. As though trying to undo the work of twenty years, she abandons heroic enterprise, turns back to the world that existed before Chicken Little's death illuminated her life, and falls in love with Ajax, one of the beautiful boys whose presence had haunted her innocent dreams. Rejoicing in his acceptance, which seems to include her status as someone "both tough and wise" (part 2, p. 110), Sula experiences one brief and unique moment where her power of creation seems to be celebrated and confirmed. Ajax now, not Nel, becomes the creature of Sula's invention, a magnificent artwork, a statue made of gold and marble.

Then I can take a chisel and a small tap hammer and tap away at the alabaster. It will crack then like ice under the pick, and through the breaks I will see the loam, fertile, free of pebbles and twigs.

(Part 2, p. 112)

Fused with him, she attempts to use the power that killed Chicken Little to make something living, something free, something that does not participate in deadness or destruction:

I will put my hand deep into your soil, lift it, sift it with my fingers, feel its warm surface and dewy chill below. . . . I will water your soil, keep it rich and moist.

(Part 2, pp. 112–13)

Having created Ajax, Sula succumbs to the need to possess him, to protect him, to diminish him—and herself as well. He leaves, and Sula measures her temptation, discovers the depth of her own first lies. She never even knew his real name: no ancient hero who could assume the burden of her own existence, he is merely Albert Jacks. The beauty Sula had sought to impose on her creation is only an ornamental falsehood, and her equally false relationship to him represents her one attempt to deny that, in the Bottom, the only permanence is death. He is her retreat from the terror of the free fall, her illusion that a smile can be preserved away from "cigarette butts and bottle caps and spittle" (part 2, p. 116), her equivalent to Helene's disguised custardness, Eva's permitted power, Shadrack's mythologized festivity. With him, Sula sees, she has been reduced to a paper doll, one of those victims who will, so easily, learn to play her role. Even had he stayed, Sula finally admits, their union was imperiled: "Soon I would have torn the flesh from his face just to see if I was right about the gold and nobody would have understood about that kind of curiosity" (part 2, p. 117).

Pausing, her energies exhausted, Sula laments: " 'There aren't any more new songs and I have sung all the ones there are' " (part 2, p. 118). If gold is only acrid, alabaster chill, and loam's sweet smell like death's, Sula, too, must die. But death, appropriately, ironically, secures her final victory. For her absence—in death, in permanence—ultimately transforms both the town and Nel within it. Removing Sula from the scene, Morrison reveals that all that had held the community together was the force of its citizens' opposition to the threat she represented. With her gone, the Bottom itself must bear the bitter burden she had carried for them:

Mothers who had defended their children from Sula's malevolence (or who had defended their positions as mothers from Sula's scorn for the role) now had nothing to rub up against. The tension was gone and so was the reason for the effort they made. Without her mockery, affection for others sank into flaccid disrepair. . . . They returned to a steeping resentment of . . . burdens.

(Part 2, p. 132)

They recognize the falsity of the hope that had sustained them, the hope "that kept them picking beans for other farmers;

kept them from finally leaving as they talked of doing; kept
them excited about other people's wars; kept them solicitous
of white people's children; kept them convinced that some
magic 'government' was going to lift them up, out and away
from that dirt, those beans, those wars" (part 2, p. 137). While
Sula was alive, the town hid this knowledge from itself, projected it onto her. What she accepted, they need not admit.
Her death forces the town to honor Sula's knowledge as its
own. The Bottom—and the false conventions that sustained
it—falls into the closed place in the river, as Chicken Little
had fallen when Sula first flung him away from her. National
Suicide Day is at last enacted.

Sula's vision of the impossibility of unconsciousness, the
illegitimacy of the design the Bottom had endorsed, is validated by the book's conclusion. Yet her death is no simple
testimony to failure and vacancy. Her presence still seems to
haunt the hills above Medallion, "a dark woman in a flowered
dress doing a bit of cakewalk" (part 1, p. 4), mixing laughter
with pain, affirming the pain the laughter might otherwise obscure. And, most important, Sula finally survives in Nel, in
her forced admission that the meaning of Sula's life has permanently altered the categories of existence, in the acknowledgment that when Chicken Little died Nel "didn't . . . feel bad
. . . it felt good to see him fall" (part 2, p. 146). The book concludes with Nel crying out Sula's name, as the spider web she
wove to smother her heart in convention breaks and scatters
"like dandelion spores in the breeze" (part 2, p. 149). Sula is
dead, but her mission is accomplished. She has destroyed the
world of falseness and illusion she was born to and created
something living in its place. Her artwork, realized now at
last, is the formation of someone who can accept the world as
it really is without illusion, without guilt. In Nel, Sula has left
behind, at last, a friend, another woman who can begin to
carry on where she left off.

Sula is the dark prophet of her novel, the seer whose bleak

visions make others conscious of the sins they mistook for salvation. Although Janie Mae Crawford Killicks Starks Woods, the hero of Zora Neale Hurston's *Their Eyes Were Watching God*,[10] presents a more benign surface than Morrison's character, her powers are equally cosmic; and her energies, no less than Sula's, are focused on the need to destroy and reconstruct the assumptions that hold her society together. The positive print of Sula's negative, Janie blooms where Sula blasts. In her exercise of self-creation, Janie, like Sula, ritualizes the movements of her life and makes narration itself an act of heroism. Used by Hurston as Morrison uses Sula, Janie transmits the effect of her life to one other person, a chosen woman, an alter ego; in *Their Eyes Were Watching God*, Pheoby Watson plays the role Nel Wright Greene occupies in *Sula*.

Both Morrison and Hurston rest their abstract alterations of the institutional forms that structure personal relations on a model of internal resistance bred from imagination and private interchange. In the richly vivid language that displays its pattern, Janie's story fulfills the heroic outline we have already examined in detail in preceding chapters. Although *Their Eyes Were Watching God* demonstrates a greater measure of faith in the social possibilities of heterosexuality than *Sula*, Hurston's book shares Morrison's emphasis on the emblematic significance of connections between women, on female heroism establishing its descent through a line that is culturally distinct from what has been allowed to masculinity. The coalescence between Janie and Pheoby replaces in this fiction, as Sula and Nel's does in Morrison's, the older model of relationship through sexual complementarity and contrast manifest even in Janie's most successful relationship to a man.[11]

Hearing Janie's story moves Pheoby to reevaluate her own life, to assert her needs for joy and possibility, freedom and motion; Janie's tale allows Pheoby to grow, to change, to act. As "Pheoby's hungry listening helped Janie to tell her story" (chap. 2, p. 23), so Pheoby's last words to Janie make her own transformation clear: " 'Lawd!' " she says, breathing heavily,

"'Ah done growed ten feet higher from jus' listenin' tuh you, Janie. Ah ain't satisfied wid mahself no mo'. Ah means tuh make Sam take me fishin' wid him after this. Nobody better not criticize yuh in mah hearin''" (chap. 20, p. 284). Creating her life as a contemplative trope, Janie, even more than Sula, points out the need to use words to alter actions, to make narrative itself participate in transformation. She begins her story to Pheoby by joyously asserting "'Ah been a delegate to de big 'ssociation of life. Yessuh! De Grand Lodge, de big convention of livin' is just where Ah been'" (chap. 1, p. 18). She concludes with a warning about the proper usage of her tale:

"Talkin' don't amount tuh uh hill uh beans when yuh can't do nothin' else. . . . It's uh known fact, Pheoby, you got tuh *go* there tuh *know* there. Yo' papa and yo' mama and nobody else can't tell yuh and show yuh. Two things everybody's got tuh do fuh theyselves. They got tuh go tuh God, and they got tuh find out about livin' fuh theyselves."

(Chap. 20, pp. 284–85)

Despite the similarity of their goals, Janie and Sula differ in the sources of their energies and the details of their aspirations. No less implacably opposed to prevailing norms and standards than Sula, Janie is concerned more with reforming her community than with destroying it. Janie's world—Eatonville, Florida, and the nomadic agricultural settlements of the Everglades—is as black as Sula's and from the point of view of the culturally dominant white society, as marginal and restricted. Hurston, however, validates the possibilities implicit in this alterity by having Janie discover a life that need not exist in cramped reaction to white models, with their need for a hierarchy grounded most representatively and explicitly in the subordination of the female to the male. All the rigidities—including this one—against which Janie rebels at the beginning of the book are seen by Hurston as legacies of slavery, systems of illegitimate inheritance imposed on black society here, as in the Bottom. In rejecting them, Janie reorganizes her world and redefines the trajectory of its relationship to the values located in both whiteness and maleness. Not a simple recovery of something lost, Janie's life is a discovery of primary and inherent potency. As such it offers a compelling model of possibility for anyone who hears her tale.[12]

Sula's vision—or Morrison's—yokes sexuality to destruction, asserts the ultimate loneliness of life to reveal the falseness of ameliorating conventions. From the very beginning of *Their Eyes Were Watching God*, Janie's revelation is less fractured, more redemptive. In Sula's universe, women's wombs are contaminated, and connection between love and any positive expression of sensuality impossible. Although Janie's life is as riven with contradiction and denial as Sula's, Hurston nevertheless insists on a view of existence as potentially luxurious, rapturous, and nurturant. Janie's spirit is incarnated in "a great tree in leaf with the things suffered, things enjoyed, things done and undone. Dawn and doom was in the branches" (chap. 2, p. 20). This tree, a pear whose creamy blossoms open in perpetual desire, is Janie's characterizing image. Its mellow fecundity metaphorically counters the stark sterility of Morrison's world.

A life in bloom, a union in nature of bee and flower, is given to Janie as both endowment and invention. It becomes her proposition for a new self growing in a new society, her foil to the deathly vision of social marriage that has, in past books, thwarted heroism's future. Sula's garden, dug with Nel, became a garbage dump, a memorial to waste and rot and death. Janie's tree, in contrast, flourishes through her insistence, in the initial absence of any supporting evidence, that human life, social life, can be forced to flower, that dreams have their own fertility. Suggesting a world existing outside of Janie as well as within her, the vision of the pear tree moves Janie to search for correspondences. It calls her "to come and gaze on a mystery" (chap. 2, p. 23). It stirs her "like a flute song forgotten in another existence and remembered again. . . . The rose of the world was breathing out smell. . . . It connected itself with other vaguely felt matters that had struck her outside observation and buried themselves in her flesh. Now they emerged and quested about her consciousness" (chap. 2, pp. 23–24).

Witnessing Janie's stirrings, her grandmother, Nanny, sets herself in opposition. Sentience is attacked, knowledge imperiled. Where Janie longs to sink and stretch, "to be a . . . tree in bloom" (chap. 2, p. 25), Nanny is wilted, withered, parched "like the standing roots of some old tree that had been torn away by storm" (chap. 2, p. 26). Opposing Janie's dream of growth, Nanny offers a nightmare founded on desolation, nourished in privation:

"Us colored folks is branches without root. . . . Ah was born back due in slavery so it wasn't for me to fulfill my dreams of whut a woman oughta be and to do. Dat's one of do hold-backs of slavery. But nothing can't stop you from wishin'. You can't beat nobody down so low till you can rob 'em of they will. . . . Ah wanted to preach a great sermon about colored women sittin' on high, but they wasn't no pulpit for me. Freedom found me wid a baby daughter in mah arms, so Ah said Ah'd take a broom and a cook-pot and throw up a highway through de wilderness for her. She would expound what Ah felt. But somehow she got lost offa de highway and next thing Ah knowed here you was in de world. So whilst Ah was tendin' you of nights Ah said Ah'd save de text for you. Ah been waitin' a long time, Janie, but nothin' Ah been through ain't too much if you just take a stand on high ground lak Ah dreamed."

(Chap. 2, pp. 31–32)[13]

Nanny's love, like Eva's in *Sula,* is consumed in a struggle for success. It is grounded in her sense and her fear that "de nigger woman is de mule uh duh world" (chap. 2, p. 29). Victory, to her, is not the result of ecstatic union and relationship, but rather something measurable, material. For her, colored women will sit "on high" when, granted the putative privileges of whiteness, they can be enthroned on porches and need neither act nor speak.

Married to Logan Killicks, the much older man who is Nanny's choice for Janie's husband, Janie complains, as Hannah did in *Sula,* that some vital emotion is missing from her life. Nanny's reply, like Eva's, is scathing:

"You come heah wid yo' mouf full uh foolishness on uh busy day. Heah you got uh prop tuh lean on all yo' bawn days, and big protection, and everybody got tuh tip dey hat tuh you and call you Mis' Killicks, and you come worryin' me 'bout love. . . . Lawd have mussy! Dat's de very prong all us black women gits hung on. Dis love! Dat's just whut's got us uh pullin' and uh haulin' and sweatin'. . . . Better leave things de way deh is. . . . Wait awhile, baby. Yo' mind will change.

(Chap. 3, pp. 41–43)

But it doesn't. Instead, Janie's saga records her fidelity to her original view, her sense that she is different from her grandmother, that slavery's legacy of deprivation and imitation is historically outdated and categorically vicious. She makes this point to Pheoby:

"[Nanny] was borned in slavery time when . . . black folks didn't sit down anytime dey felt lak it. So sittin' on porches lak de white madam looked lak uh mighty fine thing tuh her. Dat's whut she wanted for me — don't keer whut it cost. Git up on uh high chair and sit dere. She didn't have time tuh think whut tuh do after you got up on de stool uh do nothin'. De object wuz tuh git dere. So Ah got up on de high stool lak she told me, but Pheoby, Ah done nearly languished tuh death up dere. Ah felt like de world wuz cryin' extry and Ah ain't read de common news yet."

(Chap. 12, p. 172)

However comprehensible Nanny's attitudes may be, given her particular historical circumstances, Janie comes to despise them and Nanny with them. Nanny's limits, in Janie's view, have more to do with fear and a narrow desire to embrace safety than with any necessary, or even desirable, fate.

Some people could look at a mud-puddle and see an ocean with ships. But Nanny belonged to that other kind that loved to deal in scraps. Here Nanny had taken the biggest thing God ever made, the horizon . . . and pinched it in to such a little bit of a thing that she could tie it about her grand-daughter's neck tight enough to choke her. She hated the old woman who had twisted her so in the name of Love.

(Chap. 9, p. 138)

Nanny's bound horizon is Janie's equivalent to Sula's world of spiders. Janie's struggle, like Sula's, goes beyond the per-

sonal. Its significance is enhanced because Hurston connects
Janie to the potential power of creation. She is all humanity
attempting "to climb to painless heights from [a] dunghill"
(chap. 7, p. 119), a "mud-ball" like the rest of us, but trying
valiantly "to show her shine" (chap. 9, p. 139). Seeking the
horizon, she is in search of the uncontainable root of communitas: "people; it was important to all the world that she
should find them and they find her" (chap. 9, p. 139). Knowing "things that nobody had ever told her," she understands
"that God tore down the old world every evening and built a
new one by sun-up" (chap. 3, p. 44) and desires to appropriate
that power in her life. The glory of Janie's undertaking
emerges in Hurston's quite literal association of Janie's magnitude with God's. A redemptive figure asserting that "the
dream is the truth" (chap. 1, p. 9), she seeks this unity in life,
in love, in language, in narration.

Her first two marriages, like so many we have seen before
(including Sula's thwarted efforts with the fatal Ajax), betray
this destiny. The grotesque conventions of these deathly
unions test her; they are concrete manifestations of the forces
that oppose her quest. Despite Nanny's hopes that life with
Logan Killicks would spare Janie the mule's burdens, Logan
seeks precisely to command his wife's labor when he cannot
dictate to her spirit. Leaving him, Janie strikes out for the first
time on her own. Staking all on "change and chance" (chap. 4,
p. 50), pursuing "flower dust and springtime sprinkled over
everything. A bee for her bloom" (chap 4, p. 54), Janie tries to
reconcile her "old thoughts" with the "new words [that]
would have to be made and said to fit them" (chap. 4, p. 55).
Although her next husband, Jody Starks, seems to speak "for
far horizon" (chap. 4, p. 50), he is disappointingly no more
fit than Logan to "represent sun-up and pollen and blooming
trees" (chap. 4, p. 50). What appears at first to be a certain
spiritual grandeur—a desire to inspire the world with novel
energies—dwindles, until Eatonville, the town that Jody
builds, is simply another version of Nanny's enclosure in the

white folks' yard. Like the Bottom, its values only pretend to be an alternative to tyranny and resignation. A white master is no longer needed to impose these standards, for Jody, with his desire for bourgeois respectability, wealth, and political power, becomes their new enforcer. Jody is, in fact, no more interested in Janie than Logan was. He wants from her what Logan wanted: a wife whose will conforms to his, a possession whose value will enhance his status. Recognizing these sad facts, Janie is diminished, dulled. Her marriage bed "was no longer a daisy-field for her and Joe to play in . . . She wasn't petal-open anymore with him. . . . She had no more blossomy openings dusting pollen over her man, neither any glistening young fruit where the petals used to be" (chap. 6, pp. 111–12). She is beaten down, entrapped, literally forbidden to speak, and spiritually numbed. Allied with Logan and Nanny before him, Jody too solicits Janie's death.

Janie almost succumbs. Over the years, while this marriage endures, the fight leaves Janie's face. She fears that it has left her soul as well. Nanny's lesson almost succeeds in becoming Janie's motto: " 'Maybe he ain't nothin'. . . . but he is something in my mouth. He's got tuh be else Ah ain't got nothin' tuh live for. Ah'll lie and say he is. If Ah don't, life won't be nothin' but uh store and uh house' " (chap. 7, pp. 118–19). She learns to live confined "between her hat and her heels" (chap. 7, p. 118), taking from her husband only "what she didn't value" (chap. 7, p. 118). Beneath this restricted surface, Janie's emotions survive as a subterranean stream. Like Edna Pontellier, she learns to separate her outer life of conformity from her questioning, questing interior. She stores up grudges. She waits. And one day, she strikes out. She finds her voice and, using it to scald Jody, she strips him of his maleness, of his position in the community he has made, and ultimately of his life: " 'You big-bellies round here and put out a lot of brag, but 'tain't nothin' to it but yo' big voice. Humph! Talkin' 'bout *me* lookin' old! When you pull down yo' britches, you look lak de change uh life' " (chap. 7, p. 123). He slaps her, but the power of his arm is in no way adequate to restore the balance he set between them. No longer his sweet child-bride, Janie becomes for Jody what Sula was for the Bottom: a witch ravening his vitals, a force invincible and supernatural. Believing that the food that Janie cooks is somehow poisoning him, Jody seeks out a "root-doctor" to protect him from her charms.

In their last moments together, Janie articulates for the first time in speech, not in reverie, in public argument rather than private grievance, what has gone wrong between them. In so doing, she rekindles her old flame.

"Ah ain't gointuh hush. Naw, you gointuh listen tuh me one time befo' you die. Have yo' way all yo' life, trample and mash down. . . . you ain't de Jody ah run off down de road wid. You'se whut's left after he died. Ah run off tuh keep house wid you in uh wonderful way. But you wasn't satisfied wid me de way Ah was. Naw! Mah own mind had tuh be squeezed and crowded out tuh make room for yours in me. . . . All dis bowin' down, all dis obedience under yo' voice — dat ain't whut Ah rushed off down de road tuh find out about you."

(Chap. 8, pp. 133–34)

After studying Jody's death mask, Janie looks at her own face in the mirror and finds the dreamy girl now grown into a handsome woman, someone who can play, for a while, the widow's expected part at the same time as she savors her solitude. Like Sula's, her loneliness is disavowed by her community. But to Janie, it is a "freedom feeling" and a fine one. She burns her head rag, symbol of Jody's capacity to impress his authority upon her, withdraws into herself, and waits, mockingly, as proposals for yet another preposterous marriage collect disregarded around her.

Eatonville hopes that Janie will safely wed a certain undertaker. But Janie's interest is invested in another: Virgible Woods, Teacake for short. This third and final husband is equal to the intensity of Janie's need and vision; he is, at last, the bee to her blossom. Teacake scandalizes Eatonville. Disreputable, shaggy, unemployed, he teaches Janie to play checkers and to fish, takes her to dances and to ball games. A "glance from God" (chap. 11, p. 161), his mediating presence is the passage through which Janie acquires at last "de keys to de kingdom" (chap. 11, p. 165). The barren soil of Eatonville dust beneath their heels, the two depart for the Everglades and a life that is Eatonville's antithesis. As Janie says to Pheoby: " 'Dis ain't no business proposition, and no race after property and titles. Dis is uh love game. Ah done lived Grandma's way, now Ah means tuh live mine' " (chap. 12, p. 171). In the narrator's terms, Janie's "soul crawled out from its hiding place" (chap. 6, p. 102) and finds, in fertile muck, a home at last.

The idyll of this life, however, is not the end of Janie's story. If it were, her tale would be, I think, more conservative, more sentimental, and finally less heroic than what Hurston actually offers us. Although the love that Janie and Teacake create between them counters the dead weight of marriage seen in preceding chapters and the sterile heterosexuality displayed in *Sula, Their Eyes Were Watching God* neither accepts the quietude of the old fairy-tale ending nor suffers the bitter, if productive, consequences of totally rejecting it. Teacake dies, victim of hurricane and rabies and a loving compulsion to save Janie. The water claims him as it claimed Edna Pontellier and Chicken Little and the doomed citizens of the Bottom and its surrounding town, Medallion. Janie kills him, resisting pity and choosing her own life over the needs of even a much-loved other. She survives her own immersion and its temptation to loss of self. She escapes the rushing waters which seem to be used consistently throughout the fictions previously examined to represent the ego's distintegration, however attractively or seductively disguised.

In making Janie literally and doubly responsible for Teacake's death—Janie shoots him because he is rabid, and he is diseased because he saved Janie from the dog that would otherwise have bitten her—Hurston continues and intensifies a motif begun when Jody died. Janie's actions provoke weaker souls around her to see her, with some justification, as monstrously destructive. It is true that Janie is not ultimately responsible for Jody's internal decay and that she had no real choice when she killed Teacake, but these explanations, though rational, hardly seem sufficient to weigh against a double charge of murder. By accusing Janie of an act of slaughter, Hurston seems to be drawing deliberate attention to her hero's power—highly, and possibly negatively, charged—and warning us away from a sympathy that would diminish Janie by making her too easily assimilable. From society's point of view, there are always good reasons to regard the heroic character as dangerous. The resolution of heroism embraces risks. This is the sense that Teacake's friends acquire, that finally they must accept Janie's deeds as necessary, not only so they can think well of her, but equally important, so they can think well of themselves.

Janie's status at the end of *Their Eyes Were Watching God* is unprecedented, whatever its structural resemblance to other endings we have seen. What Janie has, she shares with no other character we have considered: radiance; a complex and unshakable optimism; a capacity to stand alone without thereby abandoning a fully realized and never betrayed connection with another. Mortality does not measure the extent of Janie's connection to Teacake. But Janie could never have returned with him to Eatonville; his world is defined perpetually by its distance and its difference from Eatonville's bounds. Yet it is only by returning alone to the town which had so nearly defeated her, by telling her story to Pheoby Watson and transforming Pheoby's life, that Janie's tale gains its final meaning. In shabby overalls, her hair cascading down her back, Janie in Eatonville is an image of an option never before dreamed of, much less given flesh. Neither cramped nor bitter, she goes beyond the rigid limits that resistance can define and establishes a new incarnation of freedom and possibility. Janie's life gains its final meaning not from her relationship to Teacake, but from the change this relationship and Janie's survival of its loss make for Pheoby and, moving outward from her, for the entire town. The book's concluding words speak of the need to fuse the dream of love with a movement larger than the union of two people, however blessed. Janie and Teacake are not examples to be imitated, but impulses to be honored as variously as life affords the opportunity.

> "Love ain't somethin' lak uh grindstone dat's de same thing everywhere and do de same thing tuh everything it touch. . . . It's uh movin' thing, but still and all, it takes its shape from de shore it meets, and it's different with every shore."
>
> (Chap. 20, p. 284)

Janie and Sula are artists who find their art in life. For both characters, imagination begins in introspection, in solipsistic vision unreflected in public convention. Initially a mirror, creativity in Morrison's and Hurston's texts becomes a window, a way of organizing distant vistas. Defining the need to break down and discredit an old society and outlining the contours which might establish a new one, their imaginations discover a place for looking out as well as in. By conspiring with a chosen other to produce an altered understanding of communal identity, Sula and Janie distinguish their necessary egotism from narcissistic self-absorption.

In her epic novel *The Dollmaker*,[14] Harriette Arnow extends this narrative strategy to include a figure, Gertie Nevels, who is much more literally an artist than either Sula or Janie, and whose position within her primary community is, in consequence of her creative status, apparently both more privileged and less conflicted than theirs. Whereas Sula and Janie create themselves as artists out of a basic need to oppose, confront, and finally reorganize their original worlds and must use their lives as media because they discover no other objects capable of taking their impressions, Arnow's hero, in comparison, seems at first to dwell in a world of abundant possibility. Gertie's birthplace, the small town of Ballew, Kentucky, is

filled with materials already shaped by the correspondence between Gertie's practical needs and the requirements of her
creative vision. Her home is her workshop and her gallery. Its
rooms display buckets, baskets, tools, and furniture that have
leapt into life under her crafting hand. Its walls are lined with
vessels full of food she has planted, gathered, and conserved.
To share supper with the Neveleses is to move inside the frame
of one of Vermeer's paintings and experience domestic serenity as a high art. And always, Gertie is the focal point, the figure who organizes the scene in preparation for a communion
in which she, too, will participate:

> Gertie, sitting at the foot of the table with a lard bucket of sweet milk
> on one side of her, buttermilk on the other, a great platter of hot
> smoking cornbread in front, and other bowls and platters within easy
> reach, was kept busy filling glasses with milk, buttering bread, and
> dishing out the new hominy fried in lard and seasoned with sweet
> milk and black pepper. It was good with the shuck beans, baked sweet
> potatoes, cucumber pickles, and green tomato ketchup. Gertie served
> it up with pride, for everything, even the meal in the bread, was a
> product of her farming.
>
> (Chap. 5, p. 91)

In contrast to *Sula* and *Their Eyes Were Watching God*,
which both begin after the books' primary communities have
been split by encounters that produce their heroes' rebellions,
Arnow's tale opens by celebrating Gertie's social integration.[15]
If security is inversely related to heroism, and if Gertie is as
totally encapsulated within a stable and admirable society as
she appears to be, she would not need to make the kind of
wrenching self-assertion that marks the first steps of heroic
enterprise. But appearances in *The Dollmaker* are deceiving.
In fact, Gertie and her society are neither idyllically situated
nor neatly matched. And Gertie's position, as artisan as well
as artist, is very much at issue. As the book unfolds, the Neveleses' house emerges not as a representative institution, but
as a last preserve of safety in a world torn from its moorings.
Setting her text during the Second World War, Arnow first
displays Gertie's dream of goodness exempt from time and

threat, then reveals that the dream's heart is rotten; history's tentacles are universally intrusive; even in Kentucky, Gertie's existence is embattled. Much of the poignancy, as well as the irony, of the book's first section comes from a narrative structure in which Gertie's capacity to irradiate domestic life confronts a world of hardship, ignorance, and privation.

Ballew's people are not bucolic shepherds, but impoverished farmers. Many of them, like the Nevels family, are sharecroppers whose long labors yield sparse rewards. Despite Gertie's productive sufficiency, the absence of money is felt on every page. Children suffer because doctors are unavailable, inoculations unknown, and the simple need for eyeglasses unimagined. Although the presence of the war is much more obviously felt and seen in Detroit, the city whose mechanized urban landscape ultimately claims the family, Ballew, too, has been invaded. Signs along the road call workers from the land. Little is sown, still less reaped. Schools are closed, mines shut, homes desolate. Even Gertie's greatest hope, that she can somehow manage to scrimp and save enough to buy a farm of her own, is contaminated by the war; her brother, Henley, has been killed in battle, and his life insurance, Gertie's inheritance, completes the sum she needs for a down payment on the Tipton Place. In all these ways, Arnow measures the naïveté of Gertie's wish to maintain herself, her family, and her community outside of the war's axis, immune from the encroachments of a very different world. A futile dream, her vision is also self-deceptive.

Even Kentucky's center contains a figure who is anathema to Gertie: her mother, Mrs. Kendricks. A spider worthy of Sula's worst imaginings, she winds Ballew into her web and seeks to ensnare Gertie. In her portrait of this woman, Arnow presents starkly and in high relief the mythic figure of the terrible mother. A woman who disguises rapaciousness as nurturance and preys on Gertie's fear of dispossession from the source of life, Mrs. Kendricks demands allegiance to the existing moral framework—in this instance, a particularly narrow-minded and joyless version of fundamentalist Protestantism—and, paradoxically, aggrandizes herself by insisting on her own weakness.[16] An antihero, a monument to stasis, she is monstrous in herself and in the strength of her opposition to everything her daughter desires to achieve. Mrs. Kendricks hates and despises Gertie for exactly those qualities that make her most valuable to us and to her world. She repudiates as unwomanly the strength that allowed Gertie to maintain her family's farm when her father was ill and her brother too young and small to be helpful. She rejects Gertie's capacity for laughter and pleasure as sinful. Hostile to Gertie's artistic talents, she regards as blasphemous the vision that Gertie hopes to capture in the block of cherry-wood she has been carving since before the book's beginning. Gertie can imagine a "Christ . . . ready to come singing down the hill, a laughing Christ uncrowned with thorns and with the scars of the nail holes in his hands all healed away; a Christ who had loved people, had liked to mingle with them and laugh and sing" (chap. 4, p. 64), but Mrs. Kendricks can see only damnation resulting from the vision and the attempt to model it in art. Surrounded by potted plants, pinched and root-bound (like Janie's Nanny), she lectures Gertie on her sinfulness, her gracelessness, her failure to be adequately "feminine." She chastises Gertie for preventing her husband, Clovis, from " 'maken big money down at Oak Ridge' " (chap. 9, p. 142) and urges her daughter to remember " 'the Bible where it says, "Leave all else an cleave to thy husband" ' " and " 'th words writ by Paul, "Wives, be in subjection unto your husbands, as unto th Lord" ' " (chap. 9, p. 141). Mrs. Kendricks's power to deflect Gertie's dream depends on her capacity to enforce standards professed by the entire community. After speaking with her, John Ballew withdraws his offer to sell the Tipton farm to Gertie. " 'We both got to do our duty,' " he admits, however sadly. " 'I cain't let a piece a land come atween a woman an her man an her people' " (chap. 9, p. 145).

On the surface of the plot, it is Mrs. Kendricks who pre-

vents Gertie from buying the Tipton Place and remaining forever in Kentucky. A slightly more sophisticated reading suggests that it is no more Gertie's mother who is finally the
enemy than it is truly the case that in achieving her wish
Gertie would gain a place uncontaminated by the war. What
defeats Gertie is her mother's vision lodged in Gertie's head.
If Gertie's internal stamina were the equal of her physical
strength, she could simply assert herself—correctly, we feel,
given Arnow's sympathy for Gertie and her measured hatred
for Mrs. Kendricks—and stand her ground. This done, the
book would then end, or write itself out in some entirely different way, for its basic premises would have been radically
altered. But what Arnow is at pains to point out throughout
Gertie's horrifying encounter with her mother, is that Gertie's
power even on her home ground is compromised. As she yields
to Mrs. Kendricks's commands, Gertie externalizes the promptings of her own conventionalizing conscience and projects the
blame for all her future misfortunes back upon the mother
who betrayed her. Undermined by her inability to resolve the
conflict between her mother's wishes and her own, she is destroyed as well by the internal inconsistencies of her own aspirations. Only by leaving Kentucky and embarking on the
hero's journey away from an inherited moral schema, can
Gertie begin to discover the true scope of her own powers and
identity. In Kentucky, Gertie may be physically unfettered,
but her psychic life is shadowed there as much as in Detroit by
the insecurities and sense of incapacity that no amount of
physical labor can begin to eradicate.

Kentucky, as revealed in these details, is a place both dislo-
cated and repressive. A world now composed primarily of
women, it is not a self-sufficient community like those seen in
the last chapter, but a society fragmented by the departure of
its men. Gertie's offer " 'to be th man in this settlement' "
(chap. 6, p. 102) highlights the inadequacy she intended to obscure, by heightening awareness of her difference from the
husbands, sons, and fathers that the war has stolen or seduced

away from the town's productive life. The assistance Gertie
offers the other women who remain behind emphasizes her
difference from them and inadvertently supports their sense
of primary dependency, their incapacity—women's incapacity—to reshape their lives to fit the needs of an altered world.
In relation to the normative standards of her home, Gertie's
position is anomalous, the same way Sula's and Janie's stances
are anomalous within the overly rigid and oppressive confines
of their communities. Gertie's wish "to live and be beholden
to no man, not even to Clovis" (chap. 9, p. 139) cannot be dis-
entangled from her awareness that its gratification must depend on "the war and Henley's death" (chap. 9, p. 139). Gertie
longs to keep the two worlds separate, but Arnow demonstrates what Gertie cannot yet admit: that her status at the
book's beginning, like that of the soldiers and workers who
have already left the town, is actually an artifact of war, a
defiance of the community's values, a contradiction of her
own cherished beliefs. Insofar as Gertie's art—her carving and
the vision of joyous communitas which animates it—expresses
her hopes for her future and her family, it competes directly
with Kentucky's standards and must remain unfinished until
such time as those standards change, along with her relationship to them. Insofar as her work complies with Kentucky's
terms, it is debased. Whittling, is how Mrs. Kendricks describes what Gertie does, whittling and foolishness. But as her
unfinished statue reveals the unadmitted terms of Gertie's actual communal position, its very incompleteness provides the
model for her life.

Isolation within her original community prepares Gertie for
her journey to Detroit. Her bodily strength, her protective
power over her family's life, are momentarily sufficient, but in
a larger sense inadequate. Physically heroic, Gertie is psychologically impotent. Brawn and grit confer no privileges upon
her; she cannot refuse to go to Detroit, possess the farm she
yearns for, carve her block into a figure that will unite her desire with her community's evaluative standards. The order

that might endorse such yearnings does not exist where Gertie seeks it. Kentucky is no more able to contain Gertie than the Bottom and Eatonville were able to hold Sula and Janie. Gertie's struggle, like theirs, focuses on a need to let go of the inappropriate strictures of an old life, while simultaneously defining the terms of a new one. Because Gertie is initially so enmeshed in the values of the place that bred her, her struggle to break free is even harder and more difficult. As much as Arnow inscribes the appeal of Gertie's lost world—its relative freedom from a monetized economy, its capacity to produce objects whose beauty is the surplus of their utility—*The Dollmaker* finally demonstrates why Gertie's departure from it constitutes a triumph.

Arnow's text records Gertie's efforts to come to terms with this truth. In learning to distinguish Kentucky from Eden, Gertie redefines her strength and becomes the architect of a world that seems harsher than Kentucky's only because it is not idealized. Logically, such growth need not depend on Gertie's literal removal to Detroit. But her sense of her birthplace as a world apart, an island of certainty and predictability organized around the ancient rhythms of the land and her own capacity to live in harmony with nature, resists revision as long as she remains there. Gertie must leave home—as the hero must always undertake such a journey—in order to admit to herself the limits of her original framework. Gertie's initial faith is unable to encompass the new world that the war has created, and it masks the fact that her vision of home never even accounted for the realities of the old world. Gertie's sense that remaining in or returning to her point of origin would give her access to a New Jerusalem reflected in the windows of the Tipton Place glowing gold in the long rays of sunset combines nostalgia with delusion. The book, then, records Gertie's double displacement, a dislocation *in* Kentucky precipitating an exile *from* it. It is Gertie's total dispossession, her inability to align her vision with the facts of a world grown to include Kentucky, Detroit, and the battlefields of Europe and Asia, that is represented by her unfinished statue. Perpetually amorphous, ambiguous, and incomplete, this carving is no more unresolved in Detroit than it was long before Gertie set foot on the outbound train. When she destroys this statue by hacking apart the wood which embodies it, Gertie demonstrates not the defeat of her vision, but rather the recognition that it must be articulated through some other medium.

Without minimizing the scope of Gertie's losses, Arnow removes the shields that buffer her character's awareness. The book's final scene—Gertie's destruction of her statue—matches the intense resolve of its opening—her saving of her youngest child's life (she performs a tracheotomy and forces a car full of soldiers to stop and take her to the doctor's office)—but is remarkably more complex and less interrupted by passages recording Gertie's fear that powerful others will impede her progress. In *The Dollmaker*'s closing pages, Gertie, her three remaining offspring, and a gang of children from the alley where they live, take the wood, its identity still hidden and indeterminate—it may be a man, a woman, Christ, Judas, Gertie's dead daughter Cassie, or Cassie's imaginary playmate Callie Lou—to the scrap-wood lot. Gertie has made up her mind to sacrifice the statue because she has been offered a commission to carve commercially and needs material to do the job. Using the wood she has intended for her statue, she reinvests her energies, gains possession of money we have seen her earn, and, for the first time, becomes more powerful than any who surround her. Watching her action, her audience suffers, but Gertie's determination binds her grief: "She swung the ax in a wide arc, and it sank into the wood straight across the top of the head; and she stood so, the ax motionless, deep in the wood" (p. 599). The split timber cries and complains; Gertie is silent. Finally, the lumberman looks at the place where a face might have gone, had the statue remained whole, and asserts defeat: " 'Christ yu meant it tu be—butcha couldn't find no face fu him' " (chap. 39, p. 599). Gertie's last words—the book's concluding statement—refuse such acquiescence and speak the truth Detroit has finally taught her. Offering a glance that mixes wonder with pain, she contradicts the lumberman. " 'No,' " she says. " 'They was so many would ha done; they's millions an millions a faces plenty fine enough—fer him. . . . Why, some a my neighbors down there in th alley—they would ha done' " (chap. 39, p. 599). If this statement is true, and nothing but our own sentimentality as readers can cause us to deny it, we must accept, with a fortitude that matches Gertie's, the redirection of her energies. No longer consumed and frustrated by a desire to render her spirit's vision in a single piece of art, she can accept even the destruction of this art—and all art of its kind—and its replacement by gaudy toys crudely cut by a mechanical saw. Even her whittling knife is no longer a sacred instrument; it can be used, as Clovis used it, to murder, as well as to create. What engages Gertie now is the life of Detroit, the life that still remains in the alley where she lives. This world, more diverse than any Gertie could have imagined in Kentucky, a place whose competing ideologies must destroy it unless some humanizing force can be found to overarch it, is the material *The Dollmaker* leaves open at the end of the book to Gertie's organizing capacities.

The move to Detroit has introduced Gertie to an infinitely more complicated universe than the one she left behind. Where Kentucky was socially, religiously, and politically homogeneous, Detroit connects Gertie to a world of "others": black people, immigrants, Jews and Catholics, Communists and union organizers, the first members of any of these categories she has ever seen. Encountering them, she must learn to live with them in a place where her mother's hectoring letters are futile missiles from a place increasingly remote and irrelevant. If the city, with its flaring smokestacks, hideous noises, chaotic floods of people and machines, looks and feels like Hell, it becomes Gertie's task to find a way to knit her fate together with that of the other uprooted wanderers who find themselves there, alone and alienated in a strange land far from home. Gertie's old community is dead, the victim of a military assault that took its men and turned its landscape into a battlefield. Gertie must alter the dimensions of her vision, surmount her longing for a return to a home that never was, so that she can begin to build a new community in Detroit's dilapidated houses and deadly streets.

Gertie's dilemma, like Janie's and Sula's, is centered in the discrepancy between her imaginative vision and an intransigent and disordered world. Throughout much of *The Dollmaker,* Gertie tries to resolve this conflict by materializing her essence in discrete external objects: her carvings, her domestic paraphernalia, the Tipton Place. If, in Detroit, Gertie can no longer cook or cultivate, care for her home, or protect its inhabitants, she can at least still carve. Her artworks guard her internal sense of a continuing self from the extrinsic forces that threaten this identity. She resists Clovis's plea that she mechanize her art, in order to maintain a sense of her essence as separate from and permanently resistant to the world that actually surrounds her. Her individual carvings, however lovely, signify not Gertie's engagement with her new community—though, in fact, many of its members are responsive to her efforts—but rather her inability to deal directly with the terms of the life that she is living. For the most part, she models objects she remembers from Kentucky. The one exception to this nostalgic rule is the crucifix she creates in response to a request from her neighbor, Victor. Identifying his need for an emotional and psychic reference point with her own, she uses the figure of the suffering, defeated Christ as a physical metaphor. Capable of uniting Gertie and Victor, despite the differences in their ethnic and religious backgrounds, it objectifies them both as victims whose salvation must come from heaven, if at all. Gertie fears that Detroit has swept away every productive skill that had previously given value to her life; her retreat to the details of her carving signifies her diminished existence.

Arnow manages Gertie's confrontation with her own eva-
sions through the death of Cassie, the child to whom she is
closest, sharing her commitment to imaginative delight, and
whose invented playmate, Callie Lou, seems to be analogous
to all of Gertie's art. Callie Lou, however, unlike Gertie's artworks, is permanently and inherently disembodied. A figure
of pure instrumentality, Callie Lou's very evanescence makes
her available to Cassie as a means of coping with the world,
not fleeing from it. To Cassie, the skill of Gertie's carvings
mattered little. What connected her to Gertie was their shared
capacity to honor what could never be made visible, their mutual participation in a world where invention altered reality
and so made it bearable. When Gertie tells Cassie that Callie
Lou must be abandoned so that Cassie may seem "normal" in
Detroit, Cassie, unlike Gertie, cannot see the prescription as
part of an acceptable, if painful, division between inner truth
and outer life. Using her own art to make a bridge on which
lost, fugitive, and submerged selves could join with one another, Gertie has unwittingly ceded the rest of the world to
the forces of destruction. The victim of a train accident that
takes her life, Cassie is Detroit's pawn. But as the victim of a
vision that fails to connect the realm of art to the needs of
life, she is Gertie's sacrifice, a tragic scapegoat. Gertie's treatment of Cassie and Callie Lou manifests the still unacknowledged contradictions in her own character, her inability to
create an acceptable fusion of inner and outer reality.

Wrestling with this fact, with the inadequacy of her compromise in the face of Cassie's death, brings Gertie to the
brink of insanity and suicide. Detroit's hellishness pales before
the demons loose in Gertie's mind. This encounter with ultimate darkness, with the limits of a known self and identity,
marks all heroic narratives. Its appearance heralds one of two
possible outcomes: surrender, on the one side; renewed and
successful struggle, on the other. Because Cassie's death is so
horrible and Gertie's participation in it is so brilliantly
painted, any understanding of Gertie's further progress must

rest on a detailed analysis of this necessary moment in the plot's construction.

Prior to Cassie's death, Gertie has attributed all her troubles in Detroit to the fact that she obeyed her mother and abandoned what memory has transformed into a highly romanticized vision of her earlier state and circumstances. Lost in self-pity, she confines herself in a system of reactive postures and inadequate responses founded on her longing to escape from Detroit and reclaim her lost Kentucky home. In the urban world, the role played originally by her mother has been taken over by her husband, who blames her for refusing " 'to give in to bein like other people' " (chap. 24, p. 366). She listens "stony-faced and silent, helpless in the face of [Clovis's] words as in the face of her mother's" (chap. 22, p. 339).

Cassie's death first threatens to make Gertie's passivity a permanent condition. Her will paralyzed, she lies in bed and seeks oblivion. Her bed is like a grave, her life like death.

> She lay down and stared at the gray sheet; a solid sheet like ice, but never the same sheet, moving, always moving, a slow sliding that wouldn't stop. The day would be like that — a long gray thing sliding past. . . . A long business, and she was tired. . . . The sheet was grimy black. . . . She ought to change it, maybe even wash it, but she was too tired.
>
> (Chap. 28, pp. 420–21)

Wedded to her suffering, invested in her own disintegration, Gertie cannot summon up the energy to look outside.

> She wanted to look at the window again, but she was too tired. No, she wasn't tired; it was just that there was no reason at all why she should turn over and look at the window. The wall so close to her eyes was just as good.
>
> (Chap. 28, p. 427)

Utterly enervated, Gertie is pulled toward a state of permanent anaesthesia supported by the phenobarbital proffered by her addicted neighbor, Mrs. Anderson, who takes it for the same reason she offers it to Gertie: to blunt her sensibilities, bathe her awareness of inadequacy in a rosy self-forgetful glow. Mrs. Anderson sees Gertie as her sister in affliction, a twin who has suffered the same loss of identity and alienation from artistic aspirations, a woman whose birthright has been stolen away by irresistible others.

It is only when Gertie can no longer escape this clear image of her own pitiful impotence, when she accepts it as defining all her behavior since the book's beginning, that she can at last begin to grow. Cassie's death and burial, the irrecoverable loss of the money Gertie had hoped to use to establish life in Kentucky again at the war's end, have marooned Gertie in Detroit. Admitting this fact, she realizes that her previous views and desires have been infantile illusions.

> She sat still and straight in a too small chair; her mouth a bleak straight line of determination under eyes that were bewildered as a lost child's eyes, some strange child who, even as it begs to find the way home, knows there is no finding the way, for the home and all other things at the end of the way are lost.
>
> (Chap. 27, p. 418)

Standing accused at the bar of her own judgment, Gertie admits that it was she, and not her mother, who actually went to Detroit, she and not some anonymous voice of authority who deprived Cassie of Callie Lou, she who destroyed the safety of her daughter's world, as her mother had destroyed hers. This discovery, as agonizing as it is irrefutable, neutralizes the question of blame and guilt at the same time as it makes the issue of responsibility for what is left all the more compelling.

> "I didn't aim it that away. . . . I didn't send her off to be killed. I didn't aim to kill her when Mom made me come. It was Mom an —" Her voice was an incoherent screaming. . . . No, not her mother, herself, herself. . . . She ought to have stood up to them all.
>
> (Chap. 28, pp. 421–22)

In accepting responsibility for her own fate and complicity in Cassie's, Gertie invalidates Mrs. Anderson's charge—and her own former consolation—that a birthright can be lost to another's machinations. Homer Anderson didn't steal his wife's talents from her; no more did Mrs. Kendricks rob her daughter. The sense of having been unjustly wronged is as false a comfort as the numbness derived from a drug. As Gertie haltingly remarks to Mrs. Anderson, " 'We all sell our own—but allus it's easier to say somebody stole it' " (chap. 29, p. 440).

Drawn to life once again, Gertie attempts to reassert herself in the only way that has been possible and consistently gratifying before. But, reinvesting herself in her art, she finds in the unknown body prisoned in the wood only the figure of her immanence. Interposed between her self and outer reality, it simultaneously summons and denies her:

The man in the wood at first seemed far away, walled off like all other life . . . the knife fumbled, a lost life hunting a lost man. . . . But gradually the thing in the wood came closer and yielded itself, and chips and shavings fell. The hair grew, taking up the whole world, everything in the world; and there were moments like a drowsing dreaming when she and the wood were alone . . . in her mother's house. . . . Then would come the remembering, and the knife would be lost again while she was helplessly fumbling.

(Chap. 27, pp. 417–18)

Seeking in the wood an alternative to narcosis or literal self-destruction, Gertie finds in it only a slightly less lethal substitute for both. It is her "refuge" (chap. 29, p. 445) as much as the pink medicine is Mrs. Anderson's. Having rejected the diverting drug, she must also, finally, reject the solace offered by the block of wood.

What calls Gertie back to life is not her artwork, however necessary it has been as a mediating step, but her long delayed recognition of the life actually going on around her. It is springtime in the Alley, no less than in Kentucky. And Gertie has work to do here no less than there. Digging post holes, planting gardens, making toys, Gertie is part of the fragile communitas the Alley's women are patching together out of the disorderly fragments set down in mutual antagonism at the war's beginning. In contrast to the factories and the assembly lines where workers are still exploited and bitterly divided from each other, the Alley's harmony—female and domestic—constitutes a genuine alternative to the largely masculine capitalist hierarchy. A network of small and private gestures, it includes Mrs. Daly, who has conquered her phobic hatred of Protestants, foreigners, and hillbillies to a degree sufficient to allow her to wash the dye from Wheateye's hair with Roman Cleanser, to rescue Gertie's pots when Clovis has thrown them away, and even to make a bouquet for Mrs. Saito, a Japanese-American, but no longer an enemy at the war's end; and embraces the mother of Clytie's friend Iva Dean, who makes Clytie's graduation bouquet "out of delphinium spears and pink rosebuds, just as nice as the one she made for Iva Dean, doing it in the same unasking way as she had made the white thin dress and petticoat that Clytie wore" (chap. 30, p. 468). When Gertie meets Mrs. Huffacre, Cassie's former teacher, she discovers that Mrs. Huffacre, too, loved Cassie and appreciated Callie Lou. This revelation causes Gertie to reevaluate her vision of the school as simply another of Detroit's factories. Instead, the teacher's concern for each of her numerous charges seems to Gertie like God's interest in " 'the sparrer bird' " (chap. 30, p. 471). " 'I'd think God would have an easier time watchen all th sparrers fall,' " she says, " 'than you—with so many little youngens—thinken on one' " (chap. 30, p. 471). The community shares each singular creation. As Mrs. Schultz tells Gertie: " 'You grow some nasturtiums and I'll come smell them' " (chap. 29, p. 446).

Gertie's friend, Max, has left the Alley in pursuit of a "dream," a bigger world, a place somewhere else magically free from the restrictions of her husband's Polish Catholic heritage, a vision like the one that Gertie has now abandoned of freedom defined by a lack of external restrictions. Detroit's realities resist all such romanticizing impulses. They include murder and factionalism and Gertie's awareness that the war's end brings "no rejoicing, no lifting of the heart that all the planned killing and wounding of men were finished. Rather it was as if the people had lived on blood, and now that the bleeding was ended, they were worried about their future food" (chap. 32, p. 495). But at the book's end, Gertie stands in the city for the first time with money in her pocket and with work that makes her self-supporting.

In Detroit, Gertie has a status and an independence she never had in Kentucky; her bond with her new world is based on a shared perception of the altered realities of personal and communal life. Understanding, now, the terms of this place, admitting the beauty of its molten steel, as well as the squalor of its assembly lines, Gertie acknowledges its misery but also its capacity for life. Because she is finally able to embrace contradictions, rather than wall herself away from them, Gertie realizes that it is not the impulses that made her art that must be rejected, but only her sense of art as being a realm apart from daily life. If art and life belong to the same world, art needs no separate incarnation to contain it. Callie Lou's impalpable identity finds expression in the games of the children living in the alley. Gertie ought not to have respected Clovis's orders, as she ought not to have acquiesced to her mother's before him, but only Cassie's death and Gertie's decision to abandon her crutch—the statue—could teach her the hard lesson of independence and focus her vision on its proper medium. Her final view comprehends that the alley is "big enough and more . . . for Callie Lou . . . for the alley and the people in it were bigger than Detroit" (chap. 29, p. 436).

Gertie's power is more diffused than that of the two characters whose stories have preceded her in this chapter. Her life is not an artifact, a crafted thing that can be passed on whole to transform a chosen other. Yet, rhetorically, her narrative appeals to us all, omitting only the intermediary term of another character found within the text itself. And the communal structure that is left at the book's conclusion is, like that in *Sula* and *Their Eyes Were Watching God,* still expressed by means of the creation of a communitas represented by female characters. In the end, Gertie Nevels becomes a figure like Sula Peace and Janie Crawford: a woman, a hero, an artist whose medium is life.

Chapter 8

Alternative Mythologies

The Metaphysics of Femininity in *The Woman Warrior, Mrs. Dalloway,* and *The Memoirs of a Survivor*

The violence of the antagonism against the theory of matriarchy arouses the suspicion that it is . . . based on an emotional prejudice against an assumption so foreign to the thinking and feeling of our patriarchal culture.

Erich Fromm, *The Forgotten Language*

It is one thing, Helen, to slay Death,
it is another thing to come back
through the intricate windings of the Labyrinth;

. . .

we are together,
weary of War,
only the Quest remains.

H. D., *Helen in Egypt*

When the hero has become the artist, what worlds are left to conquer? In purely secular and social terms, the answer, I think, is: none; we are at one end of a representational line. The shift from the actor's role to the creator's, the identification of imagination as a source of social redefinition, permits a theoretically infinite set of particular narrative alterations which might display the passions and preoccupations of the woman hero. Once the heroic figure is free to invent new modes of human intercourse, she moves from the periphery of a hostile society to the center of a new communal form.

Impelled by her yearning to construct a self independent of culturally constructed norms, the woman hero, like her male counterpart, has upset the tyranny of social fact and revealed its contingency. Sula's, Janie's, and Gertie's final worlds revise both the representational systems available to fiction and the typological categories that shape a reader's response.

Because the culture whose fictive evolution we have been examining has derived female identity from an equation linking limited aspiration and circumscribed activity to institutionalized heterosexuality, the woman hero's energies have been systematically devoted to nullifying these conjunctions and the conclusions they require. Since the culture has imposed biological restrictions asymmetrically on the two sexes, the woman hero's quest has searched, more often than the male's, for a shaping gesture that might disconnect the worlds of love and reproduction. This task accomplished, the character can re-form (and thus reform) the social world to endorse her intuition that love is truly communal and affiliative only when it is freed from a compulsory entanglement with propagation and with sexuality in its narrowest sense. As a result, particularly in the works examined in the last two chapters, a loose network of egalitarian and reciprocal relationships has evolved to replace a system of opposing dyads. A focus on a transforming but inherently open friendship has supplanted the closed complements of death and marriage; fiction's frame has been rearranged to reflect this conceptual revision.[1] That this cultural and formal task has fallen to the woman hero says little about innate "femininity," and perhaps even less about sexuality, but tells much about the restrictive and exclusionary categories in terms of which Western culture has historically defined itself and against which the hero has necessarily rebelled.

The secular world requires no more metamorphoses of Psyche. But the secular world is not the one that Psyche finally inhabits. As Psyche, in her tale, ascends to Olympus, transforming earth by altering the heavens, so the hero always finally walks with the gods. The most mundane societies sustain themselves by myth as well as logic; humanity will accept as revelation truths whose existence ordinary life obdurately refuses to demonstrate. The epistemological border between our customary habits, on one side; and our beliefs about their origin, meaning, and moral status, on the other; is as genuine and as heavily fortified as the more earthy frontier that separates one form of social life from another. Although we think of the novel as a supremely worldly narrative mode, its plots have always been shaped by beliefs which survive in spite of the fact that they are rarely enacted or that they yield problematic results within the society in question; the proposed readings of *Clarissa, The Scarlet Letter, Jane Eyre, Middlemarch,* and *Jude the Obscure* establish this point and indeed depend upon it. Every fiction we have examined shares an assumption that the forces embodied in female heroism directly affront not just a certain social substructure but a divine superstructure within which society rests. Against the ineffable and the intangible, evidence, proof, reason, demonstration—all are powerless. Against a myth, one must send another myth.[2] Heroism's dialectic thus necessitates a metaphysic.

A figure in opposition to particular social structures, however legitimate her objections, however valuable the reorganizations that she offers, can be indefinitely accommodated within a basically unchanged society, providing that her reforming energies are maintained within a static and unresponsive cosmological frame. As a purely exceptional figure, the woman hero can, as we have seen, offer much in the way of local reform. Revealing contradictions within the structure of things as they are, she can bring society's mechanisms to a halt. Teasing out flaws in society's fabric, she can find the threads for weaving a new tapestry.

But the birth of a wholly revolutionized order can never be realized by a figure whose existence is wholly circumscribed by the plane of social reality. A break with the totality of the existing structures enmeshing and entangling the woman hero requires the articulation of a vision merging social action with some larger realm of being. This realm—the place where every social tale originates—shapes our lives' plots, determines the significance of our actions, provides the myths by which we live. Such myths organize our social view by locating the flux of daily life within a larger and more enduring order of reality, a realm where life's facts are apprehended as the shadows of eternal mysteries. The actions of the woman hero enter the realm of cultural history and evolution only when they can be read as supporting and reinforcing transcendent values. Lacking such validation, she and her followers—her society, her audience, ourselves—are doomed to live forever in a world where positive gestures are poised eternally between fight and flight. In permanent battle, the only rest is within a state of siege. Where faith offers the only source of nourishment, forces denied it must ultimately starve. So long as the rhythms of desire contradict the expressions of belief, the hero's followers are like the slaves let out of Egypt, exiled in the desert, unfit to enter the land that has been promised.

Heirs of their artist predecessors, the principal figures in these last fictions—*The Woman Warrior, Mrs. Dalloway,* and *The Memoirs of a Survivor*[3]—alter the quest's direction. Located in very different social worlds, they are connected to one another by their authors' collective sense that the creative energy that flows into their heroes' lives springs from a source beyond society. For Kingston's "I," who finds herself in a world of ghosts—in a California that is not wholly American, in a community that is not wholly Chinese—this source is the legendary realm of Fa Mu Lan, the woman warrior, and beyond her the whole shadowy sphere brought to being in the stories offered as exempla by Brave Orchid, the hero's mother. For Clarissa Dalloway, inhabitant of a world whose impoverished and empty forms seem able only to flash life's sterility back into the face of society's "perfect hostess," Woolf provides a glimpse of a parasol, dropped "like a sacred weapon

which a Goddess, having acquitted herself honourably in the
field of battle, sheds" (pp. 44–45), and a snatch of song sung
by a nameless, ageless derelict, a woman with "the voice of an
ancient spring spouting from the earth; which . . . roars and
creaks and moans in the eternal breeze" (p. 122). The domain
of the Goddess, created lightly and with laughter, shelters the
voice that sings "with an absence of all human meaning" (p.
122) and counters both the ordinary assessments of Clarissa's
dominion and the "pale light of the immortal presence" (p.
26) that identifies its Christly deity only as "the scapegoat, the
eternal sufferer" (p. 37). Lessing's nameless narrator seems to
live in the smallest world: a neat and comfortable, if shabby,
flat in the midst of a decaying city. Beyond her apartment,
however, just out of reach on the other side of the wall, there
is another world, composed of all the images of blight that
have produced the disorder the narrator sees everywhere
around her, but containing also the possibilities of growth.
Organizing this shadow-space is an unseen, but identifiably
female, "presence," a "rightful inhabitant" whose essence ob-
sesses and ultimately absorbs the narrator and the remnants
of her society, summoning them beyond themselves into the
world that emerges when all walls have collapsed.

Similar and similarly remarkable in each of these three instances are two authorial assumptions: first, that the cosmic
realm that borders on our own and promises redemption belongs to a female Creator; and, second, that Her power enters
our society through the agency of a mortal woman. No longer
God's vessel, Mary has become God's sole earthly expression;
the divinity that makes this choice can clearly no longer be
conceived as male. The heavenly mansion formerly entrusted
to patriarchy's God, the legislator of hierarchies modeled on
the image of fatherly authority, is now leased to a maternal
tenant who changes it according to her own blueprint. The
threat that cosmic paternity inherently poses to female heroism
prompts this final conjuring of a feminine divinity.

From fictions fascinated by the need for daughters to escape their crippled and crippling mothers, we move to tales concerned with figures who are themselves both mother and daughter. Inheritors of a divided legacy, they make peace with the maternity patriarchy has corrupted and discover the power that resides in the newly cleansed image. This power supports the central figure's continuing quest for an expressive gesture that might convey her force throughout a social realm. More important, as this power infiltrates society, its existence and its status envelop all particularized alterations in the social structure so that those various shifts are conceptually connected. Individual rebellious gestures thus merge, deriving communitas from a new theory of the bond between earthly life and a mythically sustaining frame.

The narrative strategies of Maxine Hong Kingston's fictional "memoir," *The Woman Warrior*, develop from the point emphasized in the last chapter: that artistic aspiration provides the most appropriate model for evoking female heroism's generative capacities. This model is compelling because it is both socially available and metaphorically refined: using the artist as paradigm of creation suggests that our traditional aesthetic, linking female regeneration to biological reproduction and the sanctity of marriage, is an impoverished literalization. In a freer, less socially inhibited structure, God the propagator and procreator gives way to God the inventor. The imagination replaces the womb as the structure's central icon.

In the case of Kingston's "I," social confusion is explicitly connected to the loss of a mythic structure. The daughter of Chinese parents who emigrated to California, Kingston's narrator finds herself in limbo. Neither Chinese nor American, she begins her quest at one remove from the language and representational systems of both worlds. Unrooted, unfixed, she is to us by now a most familiar figure. But her dislocation is vaster than any we have previously seen, for it describes not just her social and psychological positions, but her intellectual and moral disorientation as well. Outside the frameworks that contain society and give human life its meaning, she resembles a Jane Eyre who arrives at Thornfield not from the sanctified, if stultifying, Lowood, but from some much more distant country of the mind.

Her relation to her mother, Brave Orchid, partly mirrors this dislocation. Because she was born in China and grew up there, Brave Orchid, unlike the narrator, has a clear sense of her origins. But since she must survive in California, she sets the terms of her daughter's social confusion and unease. Brave Orchid, like the narrator and the other women we have so far examined, having matured within a system that imposes extraordinary limits and restrictions on women, might predictably resemble the typical maternal figures bred there. We are prepared to see her as some version of the Bad or Terrible Mother. As an agent of defeat and capitulation, Brave Orchid could counsel her daughter to accept repression in order to survive.

In *The Woman Warrior,* Kingston brilliantly reconceives this portrait. Brave Orchid becomes the model for the narrator's new invention of herself, the seed around which the pearl forms. In Kingston's text a reconceived mother-daughter relationship creates an imaginative bridge suspended between the two figures and sustained, initially, by the mother's power. Once this rearrangement takes place and the mother is established as legitimately strong, the daughter can rely on her to foster courage rather than repress it. When the narrator observes that she "had been in the presence of great power, my mother talking-story" (pp. 19–20), she connects herself as a maker of tales to a numinous maternal inheritance. Later, she explicitly describes both this linkage and the contours of the strength shared between two women. Totemic companions—"I am really a Dragon as she is a Dragon" (p. 109)—they are fierce in time of hazard.

My mother may have been afraid, but she would be a dragoness ("my totem, your totem"). She could make herself not weak. During danger she fanned out her dragon claws and riffled her red sequin scales and

unfolded her coiling green stripes. Danger was a good time for showing off. Like the dragons living in temple eaves, my mother looked
down on plain people who were lonely and afraid.

(P. 67)

Brave Orchid ushers the narrator into a realm of incantations, a shaman's realm where those who share a totem share a
spell. The stories Brave Orchid tells her daughter both recall
and exceed the sorts of stories familiar to us from our readings
of earlier fictions. Many of them, like the tragedy of No Name
Woman that begins the book, are cautionary tales. Indicating
the limits allowed to female identity within traditional Chinese
culture, such stories are the narrator's Sphinx-set riddles. What
is the proper response to the events of No Name Woman's
life? What is the narrator to make of the supposed fact that
her father had a sister who perished for the sin of conceiving
a child out of wedlock? Is she to glean from it the message that
" 'what happened to her could happen to you' " (p. 5)? Or is
she to find a more subversive meaning: "we failed if we grew
up to be but wives or slaves" (p. 19)? In admitting that the
story passed from mother to daughter establishes a line of inheritance—"unless I see her life branching into mine, she gives
me no ancestral help" (p. 8)—must the narrator embrace a
model that will teach conformity by making the price of rebellion mortally high? Or might she understand instead that
her aunt's life describes past female identity as a burial ground,
a bog of blighted sexuality, out of and against which she must
define some new alternative? Finally, and most interesting, is
Brave Orchid's account of her sister-in-law's destruction to be
read as fact or fiction? Everything that can possibly be gleaned
from the tale depends on its first telling. The narrator is unable to request more information because to do so she would
have to venture into a realm about which no one speaks. The
narrator's father will not admit that he ever had a sister; "it
is as if she had never been born" (p. 3). In declaring her existence, Brave Orchid claims control over a territory no one else
in the narrator's world will admit to consciousness at all. But

the nature of this world—whether it is fact or fiction—is always doubtful and unclear. In talking-story, Brave Orchid secures the right to determine the nature of reality, to blur the line between history and fable. The shapes that history takes in fable are, Brave Orchid's attitude conveys, the only shapes available. Against such fables, all that can be offered are other fables. And in each instance, as important as the structure of the fable itself is its interpretation.

It is thus Brave Orchid who sets the narrator off on her quest. Granted a cultural past displayed in female fabulation, the narrator is freed to write her future in the stories she can recast or invent. She reads the meaning of her life in fiction's codes. The process of fable making having been initiated by her mother, the narrator uses the story of Fa Mu Lan, the woman warrior who gives the book its title, to begin her progress. Here, the narrator sees herself directly in the remembered story. A victory saga, the warrior woman's epic life is another tale "to grow up on" (p. 5). Because Brave Orchid's inventions "tested . . . strength to establish realities" (p. 5), her daughter can appropriate the field of action and inspiration occupied by Fa Mu Lan and use it as the core of her own development. In Kingston's book, Fa Mu Lan's story is a first-person account: the narrating "I" replaces the more distant fictive "she." The record of Fa Mu Lan's heroic initiation has been incorporated into the narrator's own life, where it can grant both inspiration and control. In this account it is impossible to know with certainty what Brave Orchid told the narrator, what she invented, what she took as part of a received tradition, what is the result of a conflation of history and legend, and finally, what the narrator has simply made up for herself. What is important is the way in which the tale's function is inseparable from its form; the narrator's transmission, with her own commentary directing our responses, reveals the tale's significance in its relation to both teller and reader. A tale of shamanic initiation, the initiatory mythos of Fa Mu Lan's life exactly reflects the developmental needs of the surrounding fiction's hero. The figure elected by the gods as a candidate for magical transformation takes over and transforms the fiction's "I."

Fusing herself with Fa Mu Lan, the narrator, like all the figures we shall witness in this chapter, creates a shaping frame for female heroism which differs from that offered by the mythic structure of "Amor and Psyche" in being overtly and primarily concerned with the need to invest the hero's energies *directly* in the grand causes of social and metaphysical transfiguration. As long as Psyche's activities are netted in the structures of what can too easily be seen as a purely private romance, it is easy to overlook the connection between the terms of the partners' final relationship and a necessarily altered cosmic and social order. The connection, to be sure, is there; private communitas can only be guaranteed by a society prepared to reflect its terms as central to all human life; Psyche is granted immortality and godliness. But, as this book has so laboriously documented, the norms of social union are at such variance with the presumptions of cosmic marriage that the couple as emblem can scarcely signify either an improved or even an altered cultural strategy.

In the search for a replacement, Psyche's new incarnations require a mold that is both more generalized and less tainted by the assumption that femaleness is necessarily associated with subordination. Clarissa Dalloway's parties are war's antithesis, offering an alternative to her culture's defining structure; Lessing's narrator journeys beyond society's walls to find the source of a mythic spring whose waters might nourish social growth; so Kingston's "I" plots her journey away from the stale conformity and deadly repetition that is the choice of "wives or slaves" (p. 19) and engages in ritual battle for a new world order. As the two presiding elders suggest, her options are clear:

"You can go back. . . . You can go pull sweet potatoes, or you can stay with us and learn how to fight barbarians and bandits.

"You can avenge your village. . . . You can recapture the harvests the thieves have taken. You can be remembered by the Han people for your dutifulness."

(Pp. 22–23)

Where our earlier heroes have always had to reject duty in choosing action, our new ones are provided with a vehicle that neutralizes these former oppositions.

Vengeance is the swordswoman's task. Desiring to "[get] even with anybody who hurt her family" (p. 19)—the Chinese poor, imperially oppressed—the narrator, in the guise of Fa Mu Lan, undergoes tests and endures trials and privation for the sake of her caste and also her sex; among all those categorically oppressed, woman's lot is always the most afflicted, as No Name Woman's defeat reveals. Part of the retribution is literal: " 'I am a female avenger,' " (p. 43), the narrator declares triumphantly, revealing her identity to the fat baron she beheads. Equally important, however, the retaliation against past wrongs is metaphoric and verbal. The narrator sets off for battle with the image of "Kuan Kung, the god of war and literature riding before me" (p. 38). She defines her identity with Fa Mu Lan by means of the words tattooed on both their bodies.

What we have in common are the words at our backs. The ideographs for *revenge* are "report a crime" and "report to five families." The reporting is the vengeance — not the beheading, not the gutting, but the words.

(P. 53)

Initiation here is a multiple rite: a simultaneous induction into action, knowledge, language, and interpretation. It begins by emphasizing the traditional physical exercises productive of strength, grace, and bodily control. The narrator learns to soar above the dull plane of daily life, to survive in utter solitude, to endure fasts, and to journey to the dead land to discover and bring back the "fungus of immortality" (p. 25). She discovers that femaleness is necessary and not burdensome: "Menstrual days did not interrupt my training; I was as strong as on any other day" (p. 30). She is allowed to marry, to experience her sexuality, to bear a child, even to disguise her femaleness in male armor. Actions that in other texts would appear as dereliction and subversion are incorporated here into an emerging structure blending the feminine and the active principles. Having understood her first need and learned " 'how to be quiet' " (p. 23) within her own identity, the narrator is modest: she marches at her army's side, only riding "when we had to impress other armies" (p. 37). In her armor, she is seen as mighty, beautiful, and female by the villagers who are then willing to relinquish "their real gifts . . . their sons" (p. 36) to the figure who combines these attributes. Spurring her army on, she balances the competing claims of nurturance and anger and composes militarism into a living pageant, not a funereal cortege. Liberated from romance's thrall, Psyche is a warrior whose goal is life, not death:

I inspired my army and I fed them. At night I sang to them glorious songs that came out of the sky and into my head. When I opened my mouth, the songs poured out and were loud enough for the whole encampment to hear. . . . We sewed red flags and tied the red scraps around arms, legs, horses' tails. We wore our red clothes so that when we visited a village, we would look as happy as for New Year's Day. Then people would want to join the ranks. My army did not rape, only taking food where there was an abundance. We brought order wherever we went.

(P. 37)

Learning merely to hunt, to fight, and to conquer is a relatively early, relatively simple task. A test of physical survival, it involves "copying the tigers, their stalking kill and their anger" (p. 28). Tigers, the narrator remarks, "are easy to find" (p. 28). Taking aggression beyond itself, fusing it with festivity to make a unity of contradictions, is much harder. It requires "adult" wisdom, dragon's wisdom. ' "You have to infer the whole dragon from the parts you can see and touch,' " say the old couple who initiate the warrior into its mysteries. The dragon is large, as the universe is large, "so that there is room for paradoxes" (p. 29). The dragon's "voice thunders and jingles. . . . It breathes fire and water; and sometimes the dragon is one, sometimes many" (p. 29). And sometimes, as we have seen, the dragon who contains this suprahuman power and resolves refractory reality is the mother and the daughter of us all.

The image that illustrates this controlled tension, this conjunction of oppositions, is no marriage. Although it includes a couple, they are not locked into romantic immobility nor sexually mesmerized, but freely moving, ever changing, producing visions rather than children. The end point of the various tests—the climax of hunger, exhaustion, and conquest of death—is neither a battle nor a wedding, but this transformed relationship. As physical exhaustion makes the landscape a mirage, relief can come only when one submits to whirl and glitter, when one accepts the utter reality of the "new sights" (p. 26) one's eyes "invent" (p. 26). Then one spins like

two people made of gold dancing the earth's dances. They turned so perfectly that together they were the axis of the earth's turning. They were light; they were molten, changing gold — Chinese lion dancers, African lion dancers in midstep. I heard high Javanese bells deepen in midring to Indian bells, Hindu Indian, American Indian. Before my eyes, gold bells shredded into gold tassels that fanned into two royal capes that softened into lions' fur. Manes grew tall into feathers that shone — became light rays. Then the dancers danced the future — a machine-future — in clothes I had never seen before. I am watching the centuries pass in moments because suddenly I understand time, which is spinning and fixed like the North Star. And I understand how working and hoeing are dancing; how peasant clothes are golden, as king's clothes are golden; how one of the dancers is always a man and the other a woman.

(P. 27)

Beginning with a dancing couple, the narrator's vision expands, until she sees them as models of infinity and angels. All society, all time, all of human history is measured and freed in their swirling stillness. All former oppositions are resolved, contained, and given back in the dragon's embrace that unites Brave Orchid and Kingston's narratizing "I."

In her last act as a warrior, the narrator frees a group of women with bound feet who have been kept as chattel by a fat and evil baron. From a scurrying swarm of insects scarcely able to hobble away, they too become warriors, emblems of the narrator's power to inspire and mythologize. Riding as "women in black and red dresses" (pp. 44–45), they continue the narrator's work and devote themselves to improving the lot of those resembling their former selves, women who might otherwise have been forced to share their earlier destiny. Although the narrator says she is unable to "vouch for their reality" (p. 43), it is clear she is devoted to the image she has made of freedom loosed from bondage. Their story is one she will love to tell in the great hall where many will gather to "talk-story" in the "new year . . . the year one" (p. 45) of her rule. As the narrator is freed, so are all the foot-bound women whose tales will merge with hers in the legends she invokes.

The space between what might still be seen as a purely fictive realm and the world of a more ordinary reality is bridged for the narrator by two more tales, both of which involve Brave Orchid. One is a fable of success, telling how Brave Orchid vanquished a ghost that was plaguing the medical school where she had gone as a grown woman to make an independent way for herself after her husband departed for America. Here, Brave Orchid's tale suggests, is the literal experience that makes the world of Fa Mu Lan contiguous with ours. As the narrator observes, "[Brave Orchid] had gone away ordinary and come back miraculous, like the ancient magicians who came down from the mountains" (p. 76). While her sister students, terrified by the ghost, run away, Brave Orchid stays and fights. Addressing the spirit, she flexes her serpentine coils and asserts her power:

"You will not win. . . . You do not belong here. . . . When morning comes, only one of us will control this room, Ghost, and that one will be me. I will be marching its length and width; I will be dancing, not sliding and creeping like you. . . . There is no pain you can inflict that I cannot endure. You're wrong if you think I'm afraid of you. You're no mystery to me."

(P. 70)

Victorious in the end, Brave Orchid reproduces the particular benevolence of Fa Mu Lan toward those, especially women, whom society oppresses most. When she decides to buy a slave to be her assistant, she chooses a particularly clever child whom no one else had ever noticed, who—like the women with bound feet—proves surprisingly capable of cooperating with her liberator's plans and plotting her own course toward greater freedom. The escape from feminine captivity, not just the hero's but the follower's as well, is the point of this story and underscores again the significance of the narrator's imaginings in her account of Fa Mu Lan's adventuring.

Where Brave Orchid fails, where the hero's strength runs out, it is because she is wrecked—as her next tale tells us—on the rocks of a female identity committed to its own immobility and muteness. The uninitiated must desire something beyond her appointed state; if she does not, all the hero's labors on her behalf are insufficient. In the case of her sister, the aptly femininely named Moon Orchid, Brave Orchid can bring her to America and urge her to assert herself as her husband's proper wife, at the very least his first wife, with the right to a status and position of her own. Brave Orchid can talk-story to her:

"You are the Empress of the East, and the Empress of the West has imprisoned the Earth's Emperor in the Western Palace. And you, the good Empress of the East. . . . must break the strong spell she has cast on him that has lost him the East."

(P. 143)

But Moon Orchid cannot take the story up and make it her own. Unable to incorporate heroism's requisites into the confines of her life, she sees herself as persecuted and victimized. Sunk in paranoia, Moon Orchid believes she is being plagued by mysterious Mexicans, even though Brave Orchid points out that her sister can't speak Spanish and so is hardly in a position to determine whether or not she is being tormented. Hearing this interchange between her mother and her aunt, the narrator is suddenly enlightened: "I decoded their speech. I penetrated the words and understood what was happening inside"

(p. 156). Moon Orchid's incapacity has made Brave Orchid her oppressor, a Mexican foreigner, a speaker of alien tongues.

Unlike the dragon who countenances paradoxes and tells many tales, Moon Orchid has only one story—the story of her failure—that she recounts "over and over" (p. 159) until monotony becomes catatonia and a final, deathly silence. In her infinite tedium Moon Orchid is deranged, in thralldom to a society she is powerless to overturn. The hero's shadow, she too has kindly impulses toward a community of women, but they, like her, are mad. Moon Orchid's tale is not the stuff out of which new life can come. Describing her companions—inmates, now, not students—as pregnant, Moon Orchid is incorrect and unwittingly ironical. Fecundity is an illusion; no births take place. Moon Orchid's story makes pregnancy an image of sterility. Endlessly repeated, its conclusion is no issue: Moon Orchid's death is her tale's true subject.

Just as the narrator reenacts her mother's shamanic initiation in her own tale of the woman warrior, so she must test her own proclaimed understanding of the thwarted relationship between her mother and her aunt by trying herself against another's stubborn silence. Frightened by the possibility that she, like her aunt, is dumb, the narrator seizes upon one more mute than she, as Brave Orchid seized upon her sister. Raging against this figure, the narrator identifies the mixture of femininity, passivity, and silence that frightens and appalls her and tests her terror by projecting it outward upon another:

She wore black bangs, and her cheeks were pink and white. She was baby soft. . . . She stood still, and I did not want to look at her face anymore; I hated fragility. . . . I hated her weak neck, the way it did not support her head but let it droop. . . . I wanted a stout neck. I grew my hair long to hide it in case it was a flower-stem neck. I walked around to the front of her to hate her face some more.

(Pp. 175–76)

The other girl's body is inanimate. Her skin is "like squid out of which the glassy blades of bones had been pulled" (p. 176); it is powdery "like tracing paper, onion skin" (p. 177); her fingers are like "bread sticks" (p. 176); her ears like "white cut-worms curled underneath the hair" (p. 176). She is an "'animal'" (p. 179), a "'seal'" (p. 179), a "'plant'" (p. 179). The humanizing charm the narrator both offers and wishes to extract is no princely kiss of love and peace, but an active answer to a frantic need. Talk, the narrator demands. Anything will do: a name, a greeting, a call for help, a cry of pain. But no words come, just sobs and snot. Lacking language, the other girl is literally "'nothing,'" inhuman and "'disgusting'" (p. 178). She goes home to her family where she lives her life in infantile dependency, "supported," "protected" (p. 182), not sent off to make her way with strangers and with ghosts.

The narrator responds to this traumatizing encounter with her own potential weakness—and with the terror of her strength—by withdrawing, getting sick. This is her literal testing time, the enacting of the ritualized retreat foretold in the earlier legend, the "potato-picking" the elderly couple warned her against. It is finally Brave Orchid who decides that her daughter must continue, must be pushed to understand how in life "talking and not talking made the difference between sanity and insanity" (p. 186). But because the small world of her own life has given her only the experiences of her mother's and her own incapacity, their tragic inability to make another speak, the narrator inverts Brave Orchid's role and sees her as the old impostor, the imposer of limits, the enforcer, not the breaker, of silence. She accuses her mother of cutting her tongue, feeling the gesture as alarming and hostile. While admitting the act, Brave Orchid transposes its significance:

"I cut it so that you would not be tongue-tied. Your tongue would be able to move in any language. You'll be able to speak languages that are completely different from one another. You'll be able to pronounce anything."

(P. 164)

With her "list of over two hundred things that I had to tell my mother so that she would know the true things about me" (p. 197), the narrator is like a Caliban who has learned language but knows only how to curse. Hurling her supposed transgressions against Brave Orchid's presumed rage, the narrator discovers that her mother is indifferent. The daughter's tales belong to her alone; Brave Orchid is "off with the people in her own mind" (p. 200). The narrator must come to terms with the fact of independence: there is "no higher listener. No listener but myself" (p. 204).

The narrator must tell her tales in an American world, a place of logic and simplicity, full of "plastics, periodical tables, t.v. dinners" (p. 204) and entirely without belief in ghosts. In this world, "mysteries are for explanation" (p. 204), and "a spirit in a skirt made of light" becomes simply "a voiceless girl dancing when she thought no one was looking" (p. 205). But, paradoxically, as befits a dragon, the discovery of a necessary solitude within a limited and unsympathetic world finally allows the narrator and her mother to collaborate with one another as creative equals. In the book's last section Brave Orchid tells the narrator, not a tale from childhood's recollected hoard, but a new tale offered from one "story-talker" to another. Its beginning belongs to the mother, its ending to the daughter. Brave Orchid's portion tells of her own mother, who loved the theater so much that she attended performances despite the danger that her house would be robbed when there was no one left to guard it. Taunting the fearful, she leaves her home open to the robbers, who perversely choose to strike the theatre audience instead. But the family escapes and returns "safe, proof . . . that our family was immune to harm as long as they went to plays" (p. 207). Imaginative faith is pushed back one generation further into the female ancestral line. Completing this tale, the narrator remarks that she likes to think that the performances her grandmother witnessed included the songs of Ts'ai Yen, a woman poet captured by primitive barbarians whose music was never accompanied by words. To match their melodies' intensity. Ts'ai Yen composes a group of songs whose Chinese phrases of sadness, anger, and exile are nevertheless understood by her entranced barbarian captors. A few of these songs, the narrator informs us, continue to survive. One of them, "Eighteen Stanzas for a Barbarian Reed Pipe," is still sung by the Chinese "to their own instruments" (p. 209). "It translated well," is the narrator's—and the book's—last sentence. And indeed, if we count back, we see that her tale, too, has eighteen sections, eighteen stanzas. She is our Ts'ai Yen; we are her barbarians. Finishing the tale her mother began, the narrator has translated it into terms that we can understand. The narrator's artistry connects us to the possibilities of Ts'ai Yen and Fa Mu Lan, offers us their images in both myth and practice, incarnates them as divinity and mortal, and so redeems us from our own unrealized captivity at the same time as she liberates herself.

The structural weight of *Mrs. Dalloway* is again a double burden, as it was in Kingston's text. In this case, the division crosses sexual lines and indicates a gulf no concluding unity can bridge. Two figures dominate the novel, Clarissa Dalloway and Septimus Smith; only one lives beyond the tale's end. Clarissa buys flowers, gives parties, and survives; Septimus returns from war, goes mad, and dies. This relation—of the perfect hostess and the shell-shocked soldier—sets two kinds of heroism against each other and measures the relative worth of the systems each supports. The multiple connections and disjunctions that sustain these figures in a complex web of social possibility and metaphysical assumption compose the book's defining structure.

Inventing Septimus Smith as both match and foil for Mrs. Dalloway, Virginia Woolf focuses our attention, not simply on the topics of individual isolation and interaction, but on the relationship between modes of social organization and larger systems of belief. Informed and supported by forces beyond themselves, the institutions that society erects are variously identified with one or the other of the book's two principals. Septimus is imprisoned in systems which tend toward solitude, fragmentation, abstraction, rigidity, and death; Clarissa makes her social role the basis of a possible escape into communion, harmony, spontaneity, and life. Wars and parties, shellshock and roses, authority and individuality, death and life, "manly" and "feminine," Christ in torment and a Goddess in serenity: counters, metaphors, or symbols, these are also, Woolf suggests, the literal facts resulting from society's choice of particular models. Thus, in *Mrs. Dalloway,* wars; madness; the love of suffering and pain; adherence to a hierarchical, authoritarian set of abstract values and organizational modes are linked to death, and frequently, if not exclusively, to a particular notion of cultural "masculinity." Conversely, parties; roses; joy; and the celebration of the unforced diversity of life are interwoven and embodied in various female figures, particularly Clarissa. The cosmology of *Mrs. Dalloway* proposes that real life is possible only when roses, parties, and festivity triumph over war, authority, and death. Clarissa's celebrations—ephemeral and compromised though they may be—are a paradigm of sanity, a medium through which energy can flow in a world which is otherwise cruel, judgmental, and frozen. In Woolf's world as in Kingston's, the values by which people live, the order in which they consent to arrange these values, determine the shape of both social and metaphysical structures.

Mrs. Dalloway inspects and indicts the chasm separating the dispassionate simplicities of human liberty from the self-serving machinations of systems, bureaucracy, and Acts of Parliament. Woolf identifies those constrictions in our notion of politics which make it so difficult to span this gap. Believing too much in abstractions, we are unable to observe the single case. Assuming that humanity is a collective entity, we "handle" individuals "efficiently" by obscuring the private self within the categorical mass. Our organizing structures must therefore necessarily operate at an enormous distance from our emotional and sensuous lives. In the name of "Proportion," we impose a standard that makes it "impossible for the unfit to propagate their view" (p. 150), begging the question of who assigns the categories, who determines which of us is "fit." We make endless revolutions and perpetually betray them by handing them back to the system which forced our original revolt. Confusing our impulse to unite with others with the desire to convert them to our views, we bless only "those who looking upward, catch submissively from [our] eyes the light of their own" (p. 151).

The resolution of this confusion must invoke something beyond an appeal to yet another revolution, must go beyond a shift in the assignment of social power to envision a society in which the possession of power, as it is usually defined, is no longer paramount. Our fear of a resultant anarchy must be soothed by displaying power's absence in gestures that are free and flexible, but not therefore chaotic. Clarissa's parties are Woolf's version of Kingston's eternal golden dance. Yet the very familiarity of Woolf's social world makes it—and its observers—resist such efforts at re-vision. It is difficult to imagine, much less accept, Clarissa as heroic because, like Clarissa's old friend Peter Walsh, we can imagine a host to be holy but inevitably see a hostess as trivial, if not insufferably vain. Even as we condemn war and hope for some alternative, most of us are not prepared to take seriously the notion that giving a party to celebrate life provides a model capable of generating new social or political alternatives. The idea that the gesture might manifest grandeur and precipitate convulsion seems at best stupid or naïve and at worst so blind to the conditions and possibilities of all but the most privileged as to reveal not simply a moral lapse but moral blindness. Unlike the artist, the party-giver has a low official status. Because Clarissa appears to embrace, rather than defy, a conventionally female identity, she seems an unlikely repository of heroism's rebellious isolation; her devotion to her parties seems an expression of snobbery and frustration.

The text works against this assessment. Exposing the sterility of society's norms, *Mrs. Dalloway* suggests that it is only when we turn our gaze away from the "large" public world, whose right to significance custom has legitimized, that we can discern the fugitive gestures of resistance. To the extent that the private realm—Clarissa's sphere of domestic felicity and parties—has been devalued and despised, it has also escaped the notice and evaded the restrictions that obtain in the space outside. What is unofficial and informal need not be policed and so can flourish unobstructed. Clarissa's "femininity" and the actions that express it signal not a passive acceptance of what is, but a willful refusal to surrender her behavior to the judgments of society at large. Her parties' essential uselessness is what makes them wonderful. In her essay "Women and Fiction" (1929), Woolf discusses the radical imaginative adjustment such premises require:

> For a novel, after all, is a statement about a thousand different objects — human, natural, divine; it is an attempt to relate them to each other. In every novel of merit these different objects are held in place by the force of the writer's vision. But they have another order also, which is the order imposed upon them by convention. And as men are the arbiters of that convention, as they have established an order of values in life, so too, since fiction is largely based on life, these values prevail there also to a very great extent.
>
> It is probable, however, that both in life and in art the values of a woman are not the values of a man. Thus, when a woman comes to write a novel, she will find that she is perpetually wishing to alter the established values — and to make serious what appears insignificant to a man, and trivial what is to him important. And for that, of course, she will be criticized; for the critic . . . will be genuinely puzzled and surprised by an attempt to alter the current scale of values, and will see in it not merely a difference of view, but a view that is weak, or trivial, or sentimental because it differs from his own.[4]

Shifting the angle of critical perception inverts our sense of the meaning of both Clarissa's identity and her relationship to her surroundings, and allows us to see her as an opposing self defined by her resistance to an encapsulating world. In *Mrs. Dalloway* this world appears as overwhelmingly embattled. Recovering from one war, obsessed with its memory and horror, it is even yet hurtling blindly onward toward the next. Although always a disaster, war in such surroundings is never a surprise. Thus, in the middle of London, on a beautiful June day in 1923, Peter Walsh finds his way through the city blocked, and looks up to see, out of the infinite things an author might have created as impediments to individual progress specifically "boys in uniform, carrying guns," who "marched with their eyes ahead of them . . . their arms stiff, and on their faces an expression like the letters of a legend written round the base of a statue praising duty, gratitude, fidelity, love of England" (p. 76). Watching the doleful procession as it marches out of view, Peter ponders what his world has put before him:

> They did not look robust. They were weedy, for the most part, boys of sixteen. . . . Now they wore on them unmixed with sensual pleasure or daily preoccupations the solemnity of the wreath which they had fetched from Finsbury Pavement to the empty tomb. . . .
> On they marched . . . as if one will worked legs and arms uniformly and life with its varieties, its irreticences, had been laid under a pavement of monuments and wreaths and drugged into a stiff yet staring corpse by discipline.
>
> (Pp. 76–77)

This meditation on the metamorphosis that young men undergo when they become imprisoned in the carapace of armor is part of a web of references that joins war, mechanism, and the sacrifice of humanity to an abstracting system; in association or in memory, this referential embrace includes almost every character in the novel, from Lady Bexborough and Clarissa's Uncle William at the beginning to old Miss Parry at the end.

Set against it is a competing imagistic cluster whose spiritual center Peter Walsh divines when the soldiers have passed him by and he can pause to rest his tired eyes. Wandering into Regent's Park, Peter sleeps on a sunlit bench. At its other end, a nurse sits knitting. Her figure replaces the soldiers and transfixes his imagination, giving emblematic form to "spectral presences which rise in twilight in woods made of sky and branches" (p. 85). Awaiting each of us at the end of life's long ride, this "giant figure" is "endow[ed] with womanhood" (p. 85) and fulfills Peter's "desire for solace, for relief" (p. 85), for something beyond the base reduction of humanity whose funerary spectacle he has just witnessed. The soldiers' world beyond the Park is sterile, populated by "miserable pigmies . . . feeble . . . ugly . . . craven" (p. 85). This figure, in contrast, grows from nature's fullness: from trees which connect the heavens to the earth; from the "troubled sea" (p 86), where she lollops like a siren in green waves and, rising from them, showers down "from her magnificent hands compassion, comprehension, absolution" (p. 86). Frolicking, carousing, she is ever young; yet her greenness melts imperceptibly into grey. She resolves oppositions, being both seductive mermaid and "the figure of the mother whose sons have been killed in the battles of the world" (p. 87). In all her manifestations, she shelters and reforms.

An "adorable emblem which only the recollection of cold human contacts forbids us to embrace" (p. 87), this figure is capable of earthly incarnation, although, when he meets her, Peter is not always willing to admit what he sees. In the embodiment of Clarissa, she is recognizable by her consistent efforts to melt the frigidity which immobilizes a society of soldiers. Attempting to believe that she need "fear no more the heat of the sun," Clarissa joins its powers—the powers of an identity that Peter Walsh found when the sun suffused him, too—to her own. Enduring the classic tests of the hero, Clarissa at her party ascends "pinnacles," offers her body to kindle flames, stands "drenched in fire" (p. 255). A fête is not an easy feat. Even Clarissa fears the flames which threaten her ego's "woodenness"; but fire refines what it does not consume. So, brandishing her torch, her self, Clarissa merges with the party's dying embers and kindles new identities. Mrs. Hilbery calls her " 'a magician!' " (p. 291). Described in the language that defines Peter Walsh's Goddess, Clarissa establishes a realm where divinity penetrates society:

Clarissa escorted her Prime Minister down the room, prancing, sparkling, with the stateliness of her grey hair. She wore ear-rings, and a silver-green mermaid's dress. Lolloping on the waves and braiding her tresses she seemed, having that gift still; to be; to exist; to sum it all up in the moment as she passed . . . laughed . . . with the most perfect ease and air of a creature floating in its element. . . . Her severity, her prudery, her woodenness were all warmed through now, and she had about her . . . an inexpressible dignity; an exquisite cordiality; as if she wished the whole world well.

(Pp. 264-65)

Defined throughout the book by her love of life, and by her capacity to preserve this attitude in the face of war, death, sickness, age, and the "constrictions" of her own personality, Clarissa uses her parties as a prism, a medium that discloses life's hidden colors and allows reality's refractions to make new combinations.

Here was So-and-so in South Kensington; someone up in Bayswater; and somebody else, say in Mayfair. And she felt what a waste; and she felt what a pity; and she felt if only they could be brought together; so she did it. And it was an offering; to combine, to create; but to whom?

An offering for the sake of offering, perhaps. Anyhow, it was her gift. . . . that one day should follow another . . . it was enough.

(Pp. 184-85)

This delight in the diversity "in people's eyes, in the swing, tramp, and trudge; in the bellow and the uproar: the carriages, motor cars, omnibuses, vans, sandwich men shuffling and swinging; brass bands; barrel organs . . . London; this moment of June" (p. 5) separates Clarissa from the soldiers and the God who stands above them pulling strings. Her world is as full of stories, as various, paradoxical, and adult as the world of Kingston's dragon. The soldiers, in contrast, are only boys monotonously uniformed, marching in commemoration of death, arresting life. When Clarissa walks through the city, she sees, seizes, and examines everything. Creating "every moment afresh" (p. 5), she is always in motion; she darts and wheels like a bird. Her retreat to the nunlike seclusion of her room is not permanent, but merely suggests heroism's necessary isolation, the sanctified space where energies' springs restore themselves, a refuge all the more important to a heroism that hazards contamination as much as Clarissa's. The chosen others on her guest list, the initiands her ritual transforms, are, after all, unprepared people at the heart of the system she is attempting to subvert. Accepting the burden of emergence, Clarissa risks a potentially destructive penetration of herself, even as she exercises the tact that will allow her to penetrate others but not impose herself on them.

Her stance and attitudes thus directly oppose those offered by the world which surrounds, contravenes, and undervalues her. On the street, for example, the presence of a certain long grey car arrests even Clarissa's movements and makes other individuals feel insignificant. Associating the car's power with the power of its occupant, the pedestrians, the civilians, view themselves as correspondingly diminished and inessential, life's audience not its actors. The explosion of the motor provokes thoughts of "the voice of authority" and of the dispiriting hymns required by "the spirit of religion . . . abroad with her eyes bandaged tight and her lips gaping wide" (p. 20). This institutionalized worship, unlike Clarissa's disestablished order, is connected with churches, with formal structures, with the Westminster of buildings and memorials—the Cathedral and the Tomb of the Unknown Warrior—with prescribed prayers and enforced rituals. It is contrasted with the Westminster that is home to the almost offhandedly spiritual Clarissa, whose only icons are a discarded umbrella, a group of chairs, a sewing needle.

Returning home, like "a Goddess, having acquitted herself honourably in the field of battle" (pp. 43–44), Clarissa improvises transitory celebrations whose powers and forms must always be freshly generated. Unlike Mrs. Dalloway, the human agency responsible for the agitation the car produces will not be known or penetrated until Judgment Day. Depersonalized, a literal *deus ex machina*, it neither offers revelation nor commands any personal attachment. Its communicants are "strangers" who "looked at each other and thought of the dead; of

the flag; of Empire" (p. 25). Impressive mechanism divorced
from specific individuals quickly becomes associated with figures embodying the power of the state—the Queen, the Prince
of Wales, the Prime Minister, and finally, significantly, Sir
William Bradshaw, the doctor who drives Septimus Smith to
suicide. The association, to be sure, provokes a communal response, but one that is characterized by mayhem rather than
festivity: "in a public house in a back street a colonial insulted
the house of Windsor which led to words, broken beer glasses,
and a general shindy" (pp. 25–26). Even Moll Pratt, who
"would have tossed the price of a pint of beer—a bunch of
roses—into St. James's Street out of sheer light-heartedness
and contempt of poverty" (p. 27) is prevented from doing so
by her regard for a constable, another symbol of the state's
authority and its power to immobilize and impress. The car's
significance moves along a route that goes from dissociation of
personality and power, to a reverence for power in the abstract, to fighting against and damming up life. While each
particular instance seems inconsequential, the scale of import
is easily enlarged. Thus amplified, the results become more
visible and more sinister, as in the case of Septimus Smith and
his tragic misalliance with the doctors Holmes and Bradshaw.

When Peter Walsh looks at the soldiers, he sees them first
as boys, then as corpses, and finally as artifacts, statues who
have renounced life in order to achieve "at length a marble
stare. But the stare Peter Walsh did not want for himself in
the least" (p. 77). Septimus Smith, too, might have preferred
to retain his capacity to blink and cry. But nobody asked him,
and, in any event, nobody cared what his preference was.
There was a war, and the war needed men. "Septimus was one
of the first to volunteer. He went to France to save an England
which consisted almost entirely of Shakespeare's plays and
Miss Isabel Pole in a green dress walking in a square" (p. 130).
Septimus represents the possibility of a heroism that might
overturn Clarissa's. As a young male outsider, he, not she, is
the figure conventionally chosen to embrace the culture's as-

pirations and lead society to the land of its desires. Septimus'
actual experience of war makes him unable to bear successfully the weight society has laid upon him. In attempting to
live out the heroism ordained by society, Septimus shatters his
identity. Its fragments cohere only intermittently—in hideous
shapes.

Hoping to unite society's need for war with his private
dream of something beyond slaughter that might make war
supportable by suggesting that its outbreak is a temporary oc-
currence, its ends its own destruction, Septimus is ambiva-
lently regarded. The idea that cultural expression should involve something other than murder or the satisfaction of
rudimentary necessities makes Mr. Brewer, Septimus's employer, as nervous as it later makes his doctors. Imagination,
in all their views, is not healthy. Miss Pole is not fit company
for a rising young clerk. Exercise is what's required, porridge
more to the point. And "in the trenches the change which Mr.
Brewer desired when he advised football was produced in-
stantly; [Septimus] developed manliness" (p. 130). Now only
the birds talk Greek. All of Western civilization—Keats, Shaw,
"Greeks, Romans, Shakespeare, Darwin" (pp. 101–102)—the
world whose monuments inspired Septimus by giving his
imagination form has died in battle and can now exert itself
only as part of the paraphernalia of madness.

"Manliness" is as much an artifact in *Mrs. Dalloway* as
"femininity" was in our earlier texts. Unlike Clarissa, Septimus can neither define himself nor discover a permissible
action that fits what he actually is. Instead, he must take his
identity to school for reeducation, transforming himself where
he cannot change society. Learning to be manly, Septimus discovers that feelings' freedoms, the very things for which he
supposed he fought, are not allowed to him. When his best
friend, Evans, "was killed, just before the Armistice, in Italy,
Septimus, far from showing any emotion or recognizing that
here was the end of a friendship, congratulated himself upon
feeling very little and very reasonably. The War had taught

him. It was sublime. He had gone through the whole show
. . . and was bound to survive. He was right there" (pp.
130–31).

Surviving, unfortunately, kills him; for Septimus is finally
unable to turn himself into a statue by a simple exercise of
will. He tells himself he cannot feel. He wishes himself into
insensibility. "He would shut his eyes; he would see no more"
(p. 32). He lies, for, like Clarissa, he does feel and shares the
language of his feelings with her. He is aware of

himself drawing towards life, the sun growing hotter. . . . The trees
waved, brandished. We welcome, the world seems to say; we accept;
we create. Beauty, the world seemed to say. . . . To watch a leaf
quivering in the rush of air was an exquisite joy. Up in the sky swal-
lows swooping, swerving, flinging themselves in and out, round and
round, yet always with perfect control as if elastics held them; and the
flies rising and falling, and the sun spotting now this leaf, now that,
in mockery, dazzling it with soft gold in pure good temper; and now
and again some chime . . . tinkling divinely on the grass stalks — all
of this, calm and reasonable as it all was, made out of ordinary things
as it was, was the truth now; beauty, that was truth, that was the truth
now. Beauty was everywhere.

(Pp. 104–5)

Of the person who can entertain these perceptions, it is
simply silly—or mad—to say he cannot feel. What is wrong
with Septimus is not that he has no feelings, but that his feelings are incongruous, literally out of place. Belonging to
Clarissa's world, as the text's language clearly indicates, they
must by definition fail to be manly and thus disqualify Septimus from the masculine role assigned to him by society, the
particular heroism it is prepared to accept from him. Where
Clarissa's social self flows limpidly into a Goddess's sustaining
embrace, the similarly "colossal figure" (p. 106) yoked to Septimus is a millstone, not a life preserver. Unnatural, uncele-
bratory, this being "has lamented the fate of man for ages in
the desert alone with his hands pressed to his forehead, fur-
rows of despair on his cheeks" (p. 106). Septimus's "joy," his
"astonishing revelation" (p. 106) that life contains a beauty

and an order that have survived the raids of his culture cannot break through the Wailing Walls his deity has thrown up
around him. To work redemptively, Septimus's metaphysic
depends on the deathliness of earthly existence; it requires
wars. As Septimus accepts the burden his divinity imposes, he
understands that he has been "taken from life to death" (p.
37), that he must flee the sun and lie like "a snow blanket"
(p. 37), that he is doomed to endure pain "for ever, the scapegoat, the eternal sufferer" (p. 37). He does not choose this fate;
it has chosen him, and he cannot escape it. Dying, he receives
stigmata; he is pierced by the spikes on the fence that guards
his landlady's front yard. Such is Septimus's penetration and
Christ's debasement in the world Woolf's fiction is trying to
establish.

Septimus dies because war has acted on his refractory and
dangerous feelings, trapping him between anguish and guilt
and offering him no release but death. He feels anguish because of the discrepancy between his intuition of the natural
world's beauty and his knowledge of the human world's corruption, and guilt because, despite this discrepancy, his belief
in goodness and beauty persists. He is tormented because he
thinks he cannot feel, self-accusatory because he wishes he
could feel, and mad because he cannot admit what, in fact, he
does feel. Tortured because he cannot love, he is condemned
in his own eyes because, in not loving, he has deserted fallen
humanity, betraying his own capacities, and betraying, as
well, his ideal of a humanity that values love. Yet he feels
equally sinful because he has, indeed, loved Evans and because
this love violates the standards of manliness which war has
taught him he must honor. If he truly had not felt anything
when his friend Evans died, then he would not need to punish
himself for lack of feeling: the ability even to imagine the
need for such punishment would be beyond his capacities. He
feels anger because he has fallen and has been deserted by
those toward whom he had looked for help—the government,
the doctors, his wife—anguish, because, as a deserter, he

should expect no better treatment, and guilt because he feels unable to live in such a coldly just world. His dilemma is the mirror image of the double bind that confounded the aspirations of so many of our earlier female heroes—imprisoned in a cultural framework of prescribed femininity as Septimus is confined by masculinity—and the obverse of the freedom Woolf allows Clarissa.

Septimus's madness, then, is not so much the result of his misperceptions as it is of his inability to reconcile the conflicting, but accurate, information he receives. What is worst, of course, is the failure of those around him to admit that they are implicated in these contradictions and that what they ask of Septimus is either a lie or, failing that, his death. There is a terrible logic behind Septimus's suicide. There is logic as well in the mental colloquy that precedes it, in Septimus's final assertion that in dying he is merely giving the world what it desires, and in Dr. Holmes's response: " 'The coward!' " (p. 226). In flinging himself "vigorously, violently down on to Mrs. Filmer's area railings" (p. 226), Septimus is truly taking the only action possible to him, escaping from his double bind by gratifying Holmes without also betraying his own vision of the possibilities of life.

To be a soldier, a man must be persuaded or, if necessary, compelled to surrender his private identity, his central core of self. He must leave home, put on a uniform, forget that those he kills are also individuals, and, hearing only the assigned tune, must march in the assigned rhythm to his predetermined and bloody destination. No one would do this, Woolf's novel suggests, if there were no social imperatives sanctioning both means and goals, diverting attention from the costs and consequences by appeals to what, in *Three Guineas,* Woolf identifies as "unreal loyalties." In *Mrs. Dalloway,* the doctors, Holmes and Bradshaw, embody these sanctions and imperatives. In an outwardly peaceful society, theirs is that cause that makes war not simply possible but inevitable. They leave one no choice, no room to maneuver against them.

One must, like Lady Bradshaw, succumb "to the craving which lit her husband's eye so oilily for dominion, for power" (p. 152), give up one's claim to a personal vision and so die to oneself; or, if one refuses, as Septimus does, one must literarily die and be condemned by the system that has caused one's death. Reduced to counters symbolizing "Proportion" and "Conversion," the deities they worship—for no one in this fiction is unconnected to some immaterial essence—Holmes and Bradshaw emerge harshly and without shadows because Woolf seems to see them literally as vampires who feast "most subtly on the human will" (p. 152). They have done to themselves what they wish to do to Septimus. Their existence demonstrates in fictional terms the linkage she treats more expansively in *Three Guineas,* a network that ties all forms of oppression to each other, that has at its roots a love of power, an egotistic craving to stamp the world out according to the pattern that exists in one's own head or, failing that, to obliterate the other patterns in the world.

Woolf is not denying Septimus's madness by showing how it is provoked by what society calls sanity. She is, rather, suggesting that for one trapped as Septimus is—unable to find either a form through which his feelings can be contained, or a mode of action through which they can be extended, one pressured by a society covertly demanding denial of both actual feelings and the necessity for feeling at all—dying in order to preserve the integrity of feeling may be preferable to living without any such possibility. Death is not, in these circumstances, a solution, but a declaration that solution was impossible. A solution would require the discovery of a mode of being that enhances feeling and that, in the novel, results in action or plot that can harmonize feelings by accepting their fluidity and multiplicity rather than by attempting to endorse some and banish others.

Mrs. Dalloway provides such a solution, such an action, such a plot through the figure of Clarissa, who loves life and seeks to honor her love in the parties she creates. Because she is a woman, she can enact a kind of heroism Septimus's manliness denies him. Her capacity to admit feelings and to shape their appropriate form in our limited existence—to "decorate the dungeon with flowers" (p. 117)—constitutes Clarissa's affirmation, her heroism, her separation from what Holmes and Bradshaw are and stand for in the book. Where Bradshaw proposes to deal with Septimus's suicide by legislating "some provision in the Bill" (p. 279), Clarissa contends that "the veriest frumps, the most dejected of miseries sitting on doorsteps . . . can't be dealt with . . . by Acts of Parliament" (p. 5). They love life, too, she feels convinced; they must, therefore, be allowed to live it as they feel it and not as some external agency would interpret it for them.

Woolf extends Clarissa's view to a chorus of otherwise unrelated women who appear in the text, not as fully developed characters, but as shadows or impressions representing Clarissa's sense of how people wish to proceed through the universe. We see Peter Walsh's compassionate Goddess, and the old woman singing in the street opposite the Regent's Park tube station, and Moll Pratt wishing to toss roses. We see Rezia Warren Smith building up a world out of odds and ends, appearing triumphant as "a flowering tree" (p. 224) but invisible to those "judges . . . who mixed the vision and the sideboard" (p. 225); and old Mrs. Dempster, touching, but indomitable.

Roses, she thought sardonically. All trash, m'dear. For really, what with eating, drinking, and mating, the bad days and good, life had been no mere matter of roses, and what was more, let me tell you, Carrie Dempster had no wish to change her lot with any woman in Kentish town! But, she implored, pity. Pity for the loss of roses.

(P. 40)

And most vividly, perhaps, we see Clarissa's recollection of her love for Sally Seton. The book's most intense moment, it is always available to Clarissa's memory

like a blush which one tried to check and then, as it spread, one yielded to its expansion, and rushed to the farthest verge and there quivered and felt the world come closer, swollen with some astonishing significance, some pressure of rapture, which split its thin skin and gushed and poured with an extraordinary alleviation over the cracks and sores!

(P. 47)

This savored love stretched on the frame of supporting female presences exposes the pitifulness of Septimus's denial of his similar feeling for his companion, Evans. Looking for those like himself to reinforce his impulses, Septimus, unlike Clarissa, finds only a void. What Clarissa feels, what all these women—mortal and mythic—experience is a love which, however rooted in private experience, ultimately transcends the limits of privacy. At the end truly impersonal, such love is unmarred by the self-regard and possessiveness that make Peter Walsh, for example, wish to embrace all women but only within the plot of his own romantic narrative, flawing his passion for Daisy as it distorted his earlier desire for Clarissa. It is this contortion that corrupts Miss Kilman's feeling for Elizabeth and is responsible for Clarissa's sense that most forms of worldly love have been forced to dwell too close to the shadow of Conversion's darkness.

Freedom, in *Mrs. Dalloway,* is measured by the extent to which individuals can manipulate their socially assigned and defined roles and provide a forum where submerged humanity may emerge into the light. At her party, Clarissa and Sally discover they have survived and still exist despite their customary labels of Mrs. Richard Dalloway and Lady Rosseter. The guests refrain from laughing at the Prime Minister, not because his political function makes him awesome, but because he is "so ordinary. You might have stood him behind a counter and bought biscuits. . . . And to be fair, as he went his rounds . . . he did it very well" (p. 261). Clarissa invites even Miss Kilman to be her guest, admitting her to be both more and less than a generalized "enemy" or an idea. As her way of coping with Septimus's suicide, recognizing his resemblance to her, Clarissa uses her party to resolve the contradictions that destroyed him.

Clarissa's heroism is marvelously simple, fittingly unsystematic: she would encourage us merely to "be as decent as we possibly can" and to do "good for the sake of goodness" (p. 118) even though our ethical notions are inevitably primitive and the world full of seemingly incomprehensible disasters. Finally, in those situations where a choice must be made, we can endorse the heart rather than the head, choose roses and not war. Such freedom, Woolf suggests, has a social origin; it is more easily available to women and can thus be more directly embodied in a woman hero, precisely because having less power in the public realm women have a correspondingly smaller vested interest in either publicity or power.

When Clarissa asks if her love for her roses doesn't somehow help the Armenians whom Richard has gone off to aid by Parliamentary maneuverings, we might easily hear the question as frivolous or even shocking. Suppose we indulge for a moment in a bit of forbidden abstraction and alter slightly the terms of Clarissa's interrogation, asking now not specifically about roses, but instead about what, in general, might help all who are "hunted out of existence, maimed, frozen, the victims of cruelty and injustice" (p. 182). The usual answers involve appeals to just those agencies—governments, churches, charities—Woolf's fiction has revealed as least supportive. *Mrs. Dalloway* invents and endorses Clarissa's party-giving as an alternative and offers the hostess as a figure of heroic contemplation, a benign divinity's earthly representative. In imagining such a figure, might we not reinvent the social and metaphysical structures informing our own lives, so that Clarissa's parties could extend themselves beyond the boundaries of a single house, a single evening, a small number of participants? And if we could, might we not then learn to value joy as much as we now treasure suffering and learn, as Woolf suggests in *Three Guineas,* that when the mulberry tree makes us dance round it too fast the only thing to do is sit down and laugh? If we admit that the perfect hostess has a history and a heritage that is honorable, political, and heroic, would this admission matter? Would the Armenians be helped?

I think quite possibly they would. We can say with certainty that the solutions offered by religion, romance, philanthropic projects, letters to the *Times,* military campaigns are well known and do not seem to have done the hypothetical Armenians much lasting good. These ways have been tried repeatedly, while the way of the hostess has been confined to the private house. *Mrs. Dalloway* suggests that we should open the door and let Clarissa out rather than deny that she ever existed or that we, women and men alike, might have anything to learn from her. Surely a society which reveres the "figure made of sky and branches" celebrated in Peter Walsh's vision is more promising than one organized around "all the exalted statues . . . the black, the spectacular images of . . . soldiers" (p. 77). Woolf is suggesting that we damn ourselves if, in constructing a view of the world, we deny a connection between politics and values which originate in feelings or destroy the link between religion and Psyche's need for pleasure. If we take Woolf's suggestion seriously, as we must if we admit Clarissa as a hero, we may well discover that it pushes us, as heroism always does, toward actions whose correctness appear as functions both of their difficulty and the rewards they bring.

In the years between *The Golden Notebook* (1963) and *The Memoirs of a Survivor* (1974), Doris Lessing seems to have been struggling not so much with her judgments about society's nature and its flaws as with the difficulties of representing the conclusions her inferences demand within a conventional novelistic framework. Her forte having always been the realistic novel, her power typically depended on massive accumulations of specific data drawn from every facet of our world. Marriage and familial relationships, artistic experimentation, radical politics, psychological probings all fell within her purview, held together by her insight and lucidity.

The realistic novel, with its commitment to logic, causality, and rationality was gradually strained beyond containment by Lessing's developing awareness that these commitments worked against the solutions she was beginning to define. The new wine threatened the old bottles.

In *The Memoirs of a Survivor,* Lessing's push beyond realism's border seems balanced by a style and surface chronology that create a superficially conventional formal structure. But, like *Mrs. Dalloway* and Kingston's fictive memoir, Lessing's tale is more fabulous than novelistic. A myth deriving power from its ability to make us believe in what we have never seen, *The Memoirs of a Survivor* also resembles Woolf's text and *The Woman Warrior* in never letting go of the filaments connecting an imagined world with the necessities of daily life.

Lessing begins with a bleak vision of a putrefying city, an impoverished place increasingly abandoned by its inhabitants. Official institutions and interventions are irrelevant to lives which are no longer customary; inexplicable shortages of goods and services proliferate; streets are filthy, water polluted, air unbreathable. In this unnamed place, existence is constricted into the smallest possible space and is concerned only with physical survival. Where is it, this unnamed city, and when is this unnamed time? Give the city any name. Call the time now, or now plus a year or two, or half a dozen. Like Lessing's characters, we read the newspapers, hear the television commentators, receive the government's attention, and feel as though there were a fever screen between our world and theirs. (Even as I write, Great Britain has exploded into riot, the Middle East is a scene of slaughter, and residents of the relatively small town where I work must boil their water to make it drinkable. How can such horror be neatly contained? Why are our lives so unaccounted for?) As Lessing's narrator observes: "We apprehended what was going on in ways that were not official. Not respectable. . . . The truth was every one of us became aware at some point it was not from official sources that we were getting the facts which

were building up into a very different picture from the pub-
licised one" (pp. 94–95). Just as children see beyond fairy tales'
disguises to their own inner landscapes, so we see ourselves in
Lessing's anonymity.

The book's narrator, like Kingston's "I," is nameless. Living
alone, cut off—except as an observer—from human contact,
she watches the street, witnesses crowds forming and departing. They leave for the country, people think, for some still-
existing haven; but, in actuality, no one knows their fates or
hears from them again. Such escapes, however abortive, feed
"a hunger, a need . . . a passion of longing for . . . good
bread, uncontaminated water . . . fresh vegetables; love,
kindness, the deep shelter of a family. And so we talked about
a farm . . . like a fable where we would walk hand in hand
together. And then 'life' would begin, life as it ought to be,
as it had been promised. . . . to everybody on this earth"
(p. 34). But as the old images of "life" and "farm" and "family"
have been discredited, so the idea of earthly shelter itself is
rendered untenable.

The narrator notices the families in her building, the pro-
fessional Whites and the Indians from Kenya, sees their
struggle to preserve, as she does, the fiction of normality:

While everything, all forms of social organisation, broke up, we lived
on, adjusting our lives as if nothing fundamental was happening. It
was amazing how determined, how stubborn, how self-renewing were
the attempts to lead an ordinary life. When nothing . . . was left of
what we had been used to . . . we went on talking and behaving as
if those old forms were still ours.

(P. 18)

Living in one of the last inhabitable neighborhoods, in one
of the last "good" houses, in one of the few remaining "decent"
apartments, the narrator has an excellent vantage point. In
her singularity, her insulation, her detachment and self-
sufficiency, she embodies one version of an imagined female
liberation. Responsible only to and for herself, she appears
able to record collapse without participating in it.

But this liberation, this solitude, is itself a form of death. Life must change direction in order to continue. And, if Lessing's image of society is accurate as vision, if not quite yet as literal description, then her solution, her move beyond the world and the logic which contains it seems oddly sensible. Rejecting the social and political strategies characteristic of her earlier fictions, Lessing moves, in *The Memoirs of a Survivor*, along with her narrator into an entirely new realm. In the living room of the narrator's flat there is a wall, painted white, but with the outlines of some floral-patterned wallpaper still faintly visible. This wall marks the boundary, not just between the apartment and the public corridor outside, but between one world and another. It encloses the narrator's diminishing margin of safety, but it is also like the shell which a chick must peck away in order to be born.

> I was putting my ear to the wall, as one would to a fertile egg, listening, waiting . . . and then I was through the wall and I knew what was there. . . . I did not go in, but stood there on the margin between two worlds . . . and . . . I felt the most vivid expectancy, a longing: this place held what I needed, knew was there, had been waiting for . . . all my life. I knew this place, recognized it.
>
> (Pp. 12–13)

Behind the wall, there is another apartment, dirty, disorderly, apparently empty. "The place looked as if savages had been in it; as if soldiers had bivouaced there. . . . The room might have been used as a butcher's shop: there were feathers, blood, bits of offal" (p. 40). Its displaced inhabitant, barely glimpsed, is cast adrift until such time as the narrator should accomplish her task of restoration, finish her labor of cleaning the room and removing the accumulated defilement, integrate her knowledge of the world's disorder with her apprehension of some other way of being. As the heroic task is envisioned here as woman's eternal job of housekeeping, so the unhoused Presence who has set the labors is envisioned as female. Another version of the Goddess at the heart of *Mrs.*

Dalloway, this deity also promises compassion and exists beyond the categories of rational judgment:

> On that morning when I was beginning to understand how much work needed to be done . . . I saw . . . well, what? But I can hardly say. Perhaps it was more of a feeling than something seen. There was a sweetness certainly — a welcome, a reassurance. Perhaps I did see a face, or the shadow of one. The face I saw clearly later was familiar to me, but it is possible that that face, seen as everything ended, appears in my memory in this place, this early second visit: it had reflected itself back, needing no more to use as a host or as a mirror than the emotion of sweet longing, which hunger was its proper air. This was the rightful inhabitant of the rooms behind the wall. I had no doubt of it then or later. The *exiled* inhabitant; for surely she could not live, never could have lived, in that chill empty shell full of dirty and stale air.
>
> (P. 14)

The walls of reality, Lessing suggests, are like so many eggshells; and we, in the decadence of our maturity, are no more than developing embryos waiting for our births.

Such visions are hallucinatory. They happen here, as they occurred to Peter Walsh and Kingston's "I," when consciousness is exhausted, lulled to sleep, when we can admit that its supporting walls make structures which lock us into custom, lock us out of exploration. The narrator (the hero, the reader) resists the seductions of the world her vision increasingly endows with more reality than her "ordinary" life possesses because she, like us, is rooted in the commonplace and half afraid of what she sees. Her loyalties are divided, her sense of the separation of realms initially supreme:

> When I was actually through that wall, nothing else seemed real; and even the new and serious preoccupations of my life . . . slid away . . . did not much concern me. And . . . looking back now, it is as if two ways of life, two worlds, lay side by side and closely connected. But then, one life excluded the other, and I did not expect the two worlds ever to link up.
>
> (P. 25)

The narrator's need to join the two worlds parallels Lessing's need to convince us of their equal status as both reality and metaphor. If we can accept her social world as having affinities with our own, despite the hyperbole of her descriptions, then we might be compelled to accord her vision equal status.

The first of the narrator's "new and serious preoccupations," Emily Cartwright and her enigmatic pet, Hugo, are acquired mysteriously, arbitrarily. A man, presumably the girl's father, simply turns up with them one day and leaves them: " 'there's no mistake. She's your responsibility. . . . Look after her' " (p. 15). This event, accepted as inevitable, is an act of fate, not probability, and is another indication of the book's true logic. The arrival of Emily and Emily's animal transforms the narrator's apartment from a place coolly withdrawn from experience and growth into a mythic staging ground. The shaman's rite initiates the young into the tribe's accumulated wisdom; the shaman's world is never confined purely to the human.

The presence of Emily and Hugo forces the narrator into new involvements with both the life of the pavement and the life behind the wall. Unable either to withdraw or to plot easy escape, the narrator begins to connect her life and society's history with the two worlds she discovers behind the wall. These she labels the personal and the impersonal.

The impersonal scenes might bring discouragement or problems . . . but in that realm there was a lightness, a freedom . . . and the knowledge of the possibility of alternative action. . . . But to enter the "personal" was to enter a prison, where nothing could happen but what one saw happening, where the air was tight and limited, and above all where time was a strict unalterable law.

(P. 42)

The personal scenes mirror the developmental history of femininity within our culture. Seeming to be about Emily, they open in the narrator's view to include Emily's mother, the narrator herself, any woman. The distortions of growth, the deadly repetitiveness of action within this space—always either a bedroom or a nursery—the debasement of life within such tiny confines are in part responsible for its separation from the greater freedom of impersonality and for the exile of the female owner from her ruined habitat. Life in this realm is characterized by "a tyranny of the unimportant, of the mindless. Claustrophobia, airlessness, a suffocation of . . . aspiration" (p. 43). The entire range of familiar horrors is catalogued: the cycle of hostility between men and women, parents and children; the distrust of physical expression; the degradation of sexuality; the feelings of bitterness, helplessness, and guilt. To enter here is to hear always "frenetic laughter, squeals, protests" (p. 87), to see "colours . . . flat and loud as in old calendars" (p. 87). It is

a hot close place, everything very large, over-lifesize, difficult: this was . . . the child's view that I was imprisoned in. Largeness and smallness; violence of emotion and its insignificance — contradiction, impossibilities were built into and formed part of the substance of whatever one saw when that particular climate was entered. It was a bedroom. . . . with . . . two beds: father's and mother's beds, husband's bed and wife's bed.

                                                                    (P. 87)

In this world, a child cries perpetually "in innocent despair," as its mother recites an endless litany: " 'You are a naughty girl, Emily, naughty . . . disgusting, filthy, dirty' " (p. 146). Searching desperately for the sobbing, undiscoverable Emily, the narrator finds another weeping child: "Emily's mother . . . her tormenter, the world's image" (p. 152). Such, Lessing suggests, is the source and the nature of all the terrible mothers our past texts have revealed, those women who repress their daughters' energies, steal their souls, try to dispossess them of their heroism. And behind her personal instantiation stands the larger figure of the Terrible Mother, the grand composer of compulsion and incarceration that the unseen Presence redeems, unmakes, reshapes. Horrible because infantile, the personal world is ruled by a queen who is herself a slave.

Defined by "Heat. Hunger. A fighting of emotion," its inhabitants cry out "for the little crumbs of food, freedom, variation of choice which were all that could reach this hot little place where the puppets jerk to their invisible strings" (pp. 152–53). By finding a pair of crying children and comforting them—Emily's mother behind the wall, Emily in front of it—the narrator succeeds in breaking the cycle and providing a growing point where consciousness and history finally intersect, where knowledge alters the shape of time.

But the narrator does not make this journey entirely by herself; for heroism, to be recognized as such, requires followers, disciples, those who submit themselves to change according to the new pattern established by the hero. As long as Emily does not journey through the wall she cannot participate in the narrator's new wisdom. Emily's early relationship with the young man, Gerald, merely recapitulates the ancient irresolutions of romance:

> old thoughts, about stale social patterns. Yet one had them, they did not die. Just as the old patterns kept repeating themselves, re-forming themselves even when events seemed to license any experiment or deviation or mutation, so did the old thoughts which matched the patterns. I kept hearing Emily's shrill, overpressured voice: "Where's Gerald, where is he? as she stood in her woman's place, combing nits and lice out of the . . . children's heads, while Gerald was probably planning some expedition to capture supplies from somewhere.
>
> (P. 136)

This imprisoning pattern cannot change for Emily until she too walks outside her world's reality, discovers for herself the disorder that its conventions have attempted to disguise, takes on and shares part of the narrator's burden. Stepping into a late autumnal landscape on the wall's far side, Emily tries desperately to sweep up the leaves that have fallen through her house's broken roof, ponders the eternal nursery's sterile whiteness, discovers the source of the form that has given shape to the encounter between Gerald and herself. Just as the bedroom the narrator described contained two figures, male and female, so Emily is not her nursery's only child. Forced to admit the existence of a brother, not only another being but one vastly and unfairly more privileged than she, Emily is also forced to love what the nursery world has made it inevitable she would rather hate. Like the world which drove Septimus Smith to madness, Lessing's reflection of society's heritage contains contradictions that cannot be recognized within the system as it stands. The nursery world compels "a passionate violent protective love that had at its heart a trick and a betrayal, heat with a core of ice" (p. 140). This twisted emotion does not die when nursery days are over, but continues inappropriately to limit the terms of all heterosexual relations, including Emily and Gerald's.

In contrast to the personal world's domestic and sexual monotony, the realm of the impersonal is composed of a seemingly endless number of rooms and changes each time the narrator visits it. These chambers too are in ill repair. But however discouraged the narrator may be at the difficulty of her job, her feeling is "nothing like as bad as the shut-in stuffiness of the family, the 'personal'; it was always a liberation to step away from any 'real' life into this other place, so full of possibilities, of alternatives" (p. 64). Still, "in inheriting this extension of . . . ordinary life," the narrator is fearful that she will not be able "to carry through" (p. 64). If progress here is not continuous, there are, nevertheless, moments of extraordinary satisfaction when a room is actually made clean and beautiful and appears again to be like the "inside of a cleaned-out eggshell" (p. 66).

In impersonality, the narrator is no longer confronted with only unmoving, immobilized images. Instead "there was a continuity to what I did, a future, and I was in a continuing relation to . . . the . . . beneficent presence" (p. 66). A group of people is glimpsed living here in the "soberest and most loving co-operation" (p. 80) trying to fit the fragments of their lives to some grand, harmonic pattern, to solve a puzzle, find a literal figure in the carpet:

It was like a child's game, giant-sized; only it was not a game; it was serious, important, not only to the people actually engaged in this work, but to everyone. . . . I entered the room; I stood on the carpet looking down . . . at its incompleteness, pattern without colour, except where the pieces had already been laid in a match, so that parts of the carpet had a bleak gleam . . . and other parts glowed up, fulfilled, perfect. I, too, sought for fragments of materials that could bring life to the carpet, and did in fact find one, and bent down to match and fit. . . . I realised that everywhere around, in all the other rooms, were people who would in their turn drift in here, see this central activity, find their matching piece. . . . The room disappeared. . . . But I knew it was there waiting; knew it had not disappeared, and the work in it continued, must continue, would go on always.

(Pp. 80–81)

The events taking place in the twin worlds behind the wall thus comment on the events taking place in the narrator's reality. Impersonal chaos reflects social disintegration, history's decline, life's falling away from the structures of some ideal order still dimly discernible but scarcely remembered. It even appears that this space "until so recently full of alternatives and possibilities, had absorbed into [it] something of the claustrophobic air of the realm of the 'personal,' with its rigid necessities" (p. 158). A deformed society befouls even its dreams, and a sleeping reason encounters the monsters it has created.

As the narrator's comprehension of these intersecting realms behind the wall develops, so events in the outside world also progress. Emily leaves the apartment to go out on the street and join Gerald. Salvaging junk and waste materials, they set up elaborate systems of barter and exchange; they rebuild machines to purify the fouled air; they grow their own food; they shelter, care for, and employ their own domestic animals; they attempt to rediscover in the shards of earthly life the roots of the wondrous fecundity the narrator has discovered in the impersonal realm behind the wall: "gardens beneath gardens, gardens above gardens . . . the plenty of it, the richness, the generosity" (p. 161). The narrator, who initially sees the new alliances as primitive throwbacks, "nuclei of barbarism, . . .

people . . . huddled together in groups and clans whose structure evolved under the pressures of necessity" (pp. 105–6) comes to respect them as "an orderly crowd . . . able . . . to settle . . . disputes and differences quickly and without bad feeling" (p. 118).

Through the characters' struggles and failures—Emily's and Gerald's, as well as the narrator's—we, as readers, are made aware that freedom from hierarchy, the desired goal of all communitas, must be more than a notion, more than an attractive idea approved by abstract theorists. Emily and Gerald, who began with the naïve hope that external pressures alone would be strong enough to eliminate "that old nonsense, people in charge telling people what to do, all that *horrible* stuff" (p. 132) find they are mistaken. The new world they design comes all too quickly to resemble the old world that they hoped to leave behind. "On the one hand, you're a good little girl, a bad little girl, and institutions and hierarchies and a place in the pecking order; and on the other, passing resolutions about democracy, or saying how democratic we are" (pp. 132–33); Lessing's concentration on betrayed revolutions and on the fatal error of separating our ideologies from the most private realities of daily life resembles Woolf's. For Lessing too the achievement of a truly new form of social organization, a sheltering but noncoercive structure, depends upon an alteration in our epistemology, our way of understanding thought's nature and imagination's goal: "As for our thoughts, our intellectual apparatus, our rationalism, and our deduction . . . it can be said . . . that . . . as we sit in the ruins of this variety of intelligence, it is hard to give it much value" (p. 82).

In this context, Lessing's use of Hugo, Emily's pet, is most instructive. It is important to regard Hugo as a real animal, as well as a hairy symbol. For, paradoxically, it is only when seen as completely animal that he has symbolic status. The narrator comes to view the permanence, dignity, and fidelity of Hugo's attachment to Emily as embodying modes of thought, perception, and relationship that humanism and the claims of progress have devalued. If human love grows from the nursery's passions, shames, and guilt, Hugo's feeling for Emily is a model of nobility and discipline. Neither an externally imposed duty nor a disguised personal need, Hugo's love ironically reveals the vacancy at the heart of traditional social images of human interconnectedness.

Lessing's world is one where all such images have been invalidated or destroyed, and so must be reimagined. There is no "natural" love, just as there are no "natural" families. Emily's father abandoned her, and in the streets children roam homeless and alone. Despite an awareness of the oppression that seems implied in the very idea of the family (as this structure has been revealed not only here, but in so many of the other fictions we have examined), the needs for shelter, nurturance, intimacy, and reproduction persist. The family's failure to fulfill these needs does not eradicate their existence, but makes the need to find some compensating form all the more imperative. Lacking this, Lessing's text suggests, the children spawned by society become a group of virtual demons. Gerald discovers one such band living in empty subway tunnels, returned to modern life's version of the cave from which we trace our human evolutionary line. Hobbesian infants, lacking even the most rudimentary forms of social commitment, they destroy everything in their path and prey on everyone. Unlike animals—unlike Hugo—they have no loyalties, no friendships, and no memories. They are cannibals, murderers born from the family's death throes.

By the end of the book, the walls by which society defines its existence to itself have thinned to the point where they offer no more shelter. The building in which the narrator, Emily, Gerald, Gerald's animals and his pack of scary children have sought refuge is a dead machine. Everyone else has departed. These last survivors too must leave. But there is nowhere left to go: "There was silence from . . . the places so many people had set off to reach. . . . No word ever came back, no one turned up again on the pavements and reported" (pp. 210–11). They go, therefore, into the only available space: behind the wall, into the impersonal world made accessible by the hero's labors. Only enacted vision offers a way out. Only by accepting the hero's imperative can we follow her beyond the falling structures of our world into a new reality, adopting her faith in a shaping presence that exceeds and reorganizes our rational perception of a finite world.

Emily, Hugo, Gerald, all make this choice; even Emily's parents are liberated at last from the hideous confines of the personal space, the personal past, and the psychological and social structures it has imposed. As the wall itself had been an eggshell which they have broken through, so now they see another egg which opens before them in another act of birth. And leading the voyagers into "another order of world altogether" is a woman, the One who was the half-seen true inhabitant of the multifaceted impersonal world, the One the narrator had been seeking all this time, the unity that always stands at the end of the hero's eternal voyage of discovery. This One, merging finally with the narrator herself—her face has seemed familiar to the narrator because it is, of course, her own—frames the group that opens one last time to welcome and include even Gerald's children, they who "came running, clinging to his hands and his clothes . . . [following] quickly on after the others as the last walls dissolved."

The realms that reign supreme at the conclusions of Kingston's, Woolf's, and Lessing's fictions are suffused with feelings that flow from the central female character, the heroic woman, and expand to include the entirety of the postulated world. Kingston's art, Woolf's parties, and Lessing's literal step beyond our planet's borders depend equally on the incarnation of a new cosmological force, a feminized divinity which can honor and sustain their hero's varying quests to make a new order, a new species of earthly communitas. Psyche's labors, previously ventured against a metaphysic that supported society's repression of female identity by holding it up against a norm legitimized by patriarchy's God, are not thereby concluded. But, transferred to a new symbolic mode that reflects a radicalized and feminized metaphysic, her ongoing quest to shape communitas from the dead ends of the known community will now involve the assumption of one less burden. The struggles of the old heroes produced this alteration; the forms new fictions will devise must take account of the profound revolution they accomplished.

Notes

Prologue: The Labors of Psyche:
Women Heroes and Patriarchal Culture

1. Numerous works describe heroism's characteristic structures. Most prominent among these are: Joseph Campbell, *The Hero with a Thousand Faces,* 2nd ed., Bollingen Series 17 (Princeton: Princeton University Press, 1972); *The Collected Works of C. G. Jung,* trans. R. F. C. Hull, Bollingen Series 20, 20 vols. (Princeton: Princeton University Press, 1953–1979), especially *Symbols of Transformation,* vol. 5 (3rd ed., 1967) and *The Archetypes and the Collective Unconscious,* vol. 9, pt. 1 (2nd ed., 1968); Erich Neumann, *The Origins and History of Consciousness,* trans. R. F. C. Hull, Bollingen Series 42 (Princeton: Princeton University Press, 1970) and *The Great Mother: An Analysis of the Archetype,* trans. Ralph Manheim, Bollingen Series 47 (Princeton: Princeton University Press, 1963); Lord Raglan, *The Hero: A Study in Tradition, Myth, and Drama* (1936; reprint ed., New York: New American Library, 1979); Otto Rank, *The Myth of the Birth of the Hero and Other Writings,* ed. Philip Freund (New York: Vintage, 1959).

   Feminist modifications of theories that regard heroism as an exclusively male preserve are provided by: Carol P. Christ, *Diving Deep and Surfacing: Women Writers and Spiritual Quest* (Boston: Beacon Press, 1980); Mary Daly, *Beyond God the Father: Toward a Philosophy of Women's Liberation* (Boston: Beacon Press, 1973); Carolyn Heilbrun, *Reinventing Womanhood* (New York: Norton, 1979); Carol Pearson and Katherine Pope, *The Female Hero in American and British Literature* (New York and London: Bowker, 1981); Annis Pratt, *Archetypal Patterns in Women's Fiction* (Bloomington: Indiana University Press, 1981); Ann Belford Ulanov, *The Feminine in Jungian Psychology and in Christian Theory* (Evanston, Ill.: Northwestern University Press, 1971).

2. See also Daly, *Beyond God the Father*; Stanley Aronowitz, *The Crisis in Historical Materialism: Class, Politics, and Culture in Marxist Theory* (New York: Praeger, 1982), pp. 45–72; and Sherry B. Ortner, "Is Female to Male as Nature is to Culture?" in *Women, Culture, and Society,* ed. Michelle Zimbalist Rosaldo and Louise Lamphere (Stanford, Calif.: Stanford University Press,

1974), pp. 67–88. All discuss the triangular relationship among women, nature, and culture in terms evocative of Victor Turner's account of marginal systems and relationships (see text, pp. 5–7 and note 6). Ortner suggests that women are always seen as occupying an "intermediate position" between culture and nature and argues that "we may envision culture . . . as a small clearing within the forest of the larger natural system. From this point of view, that which is intermediate between culture and nature is located on the continuous periphery of culture's clearing; and though it may thus appear to stand both above and below (and beside) culture, it is simply outside and around it" (p. 85). Daly sees the creation of a new kind of cultural consensus as dependent on the positive valuation of marginality, the creation of a "new space . . . an open road to discovery of the self and of each other. The new space is located always 'on the boundary' . . . of patriarchal institutions, such as churches, universities, national and international politics, families . . . on the boundary of all that has been considered central" (pp. 40–41).

3. The presence of a hero tends to turn subordinates into functional heroines. Thus, when the hero is female, surrounding males may take on the heroine's role.

4. D. H. Lawrence, *Women in Love* (1921; reprint ed., Harmondsworth, England: Penguin, 1960), p. 167.

5. This interpretation differs significantly from the one Kate Millett proposes in *Sexual Politics* (Garden City, New York: Doubleday, 1970), pp. 262–69. For interpretations closer to my own, see: Janice Harris, "D. H. Lawrence and Kate Millett," *The Massachusetts Review* 15 (1974): 522–29; Roger Sale, *Modern Heroism: Essays in D. H. Lawrence, William Empson, and J. R. R. Tolkien* (Berkeley, Los Angeles, London: University of California Press, 1973); and Evelyn H. Hinz, "*Women in Love* and the Myth of Eros and Psyche," in *D. H. Lawrence: The Man Who Lived,* ed. Robert B. Partlow, Jr. and Harry T. Moore (Carbondale: Southern Illinois University Press, 1979).

6. *The Ritual Process: Structure and Anti-Structure* (Harmondsworth, England: Penguin/Pelican, 1974) and *Dramas, Fields, and Metaphors: Symbolic Action in Human Society* (Ithaca and London: Cornell University Press, 1974). These titles will be abbreviated as *RP* and *DF&M*; further references will be given parenthetically within the text.

7. This rhythm is not anomalous, but typifies the hero's character. As Robert Scholes points out in *Structuralism in Literature: An Introduction* (New Haven and London: Yale University Press, 1974), the hero is normally "not an agent but a patient. . . . There are no actantial figures basic to all fiction. There is only that strangely passive creature, the subject/hero, and the functions that shape his existence" (p. 110).

8. Although cultural assumptions do not absolutely prohibit the use of male characters to subvert patriarchal norms, such use would inevitably "feminize" a male character. The term "feminize" here carries no pejorative connotation; it merely describes those qualities our particular culture assigns generally to women. For further discussions of cultural assignments of sexual traits and of the relationship between sexual division and the definition of culture, see: Clellan Ford and Frank Beach, *Patterns of Sexual Behavior* (New York: Harper & Row, 1972); Margaret Mead, *Sex and Temperament* (1935; reprint ed., New York: Morrow, 1963); and Gayle Rubin, "The Traffic in Women: Notes on the 'Political Economy' of Sex," in *Toward an Anthropology of Women*, ed. Rayna R. Reiter (New York and London: Monthly Review Press, 1975), pp. 157–210.

9. The term "strategy of containment" is borrowed from Fredric Jameson, *The Political Unconscious: Narrative as a Socially Symbolic Act* (Ithaca: Cornell University Press, 1981), but used here in a different critical sense and in relationship to narratives whose concerns Jameson does not consider.

10. *Crisis in Historical Materialism*, p. 218.

11. In his full and detailed commentary, *Amor and Psyche: The Psychic Development of the Feminine—A Commentary on the Tale by Apuleius*, trans. Ralph Manheim, Bollingen Series 54 (Princeton: Princeton University Press, 1971), pp. 57–161, Erich Neumann also makes many of these points. His interpretation differs from my own in requiring Psyche, as a woman, to stop short of full heroic achievement. Preoccupied with Psyche's femininity, Neumann, in my view, distorts his portrait of her heroism. For another reading of the tale and Neumann's commentary on it, see Rachel Blau DuPlessis, "Psyche; or Wholeness," *The Massachusetts Review*, 20 (1979): 77–96.

12. See also Daly, *Beyond God the Father*, pp. 169–74.

13. *The Madwoman in the Attic: The Woman Writer and the Nineteenth-Century Literary Imagination* (New Haven and London: Yale University Press, 1979).

Chapter 1. Psyche's Progress: The Heroine's World as the Hero's Maze

1. Herman Melville, *Moby Dick; or, The Whale*, ed. Charles Feidelson, Jr. (Indianapolis: Bobbs-Merrill, 1964), p. 249).

2. See Ian Watt, *The Rise of the Novel: Studies in Defoe, Richardson, and Fielding* (Berkeley and Los Angeles: University of California Press, 1965), pp. 93–134. For two full and interesting readings of Defoe's text in terms that show the fidelity with which his

creation adheres to the reality of eighteenth-century female life, see Miriam Lerenbaum, "Moll Flanders: 'A Woman on her own Account,'" in *The Authority of Experience,* ed. Arlyn Diamond and Lee R. Edwards (Amherst: University of Massachusetts Press, 1977), pp. 101–17; and Nancy K. Miller, *The Heroine's Text: Readings in the French and English Novel, 1722–1782* (New York: Columbia University Press, 1980), pp. 3–20.

3. For a series of fascinating explorations of *The Wide, Wide World* and a host of other, for the most part long-forgotten novels by nineteenth-century American women see Nina Baym, *Woman's Fiction: A Guide to Novels by and about Women in America, 1820–1870* (Ithaca and London: Cornell University Press, 1978). Reading many of the same texts Ann Douglas reads in *The Feminization of American Culture* (New York: Knopf, 1977), but from a different angle, Baym applauds their subversive moments, while Douglas condemns their overall conservatism.

4. In chapter 2 of *Woman and the Demon: The Life of a Victorian Myth* (Cambridge, Mass., and London: Harvard University Press, 1982), Nina Auerbach gets a lot of play out of the metaphoric association that many nineteenth-century artists made between women and queens.

5. See chapter 6 of Elaine Showalter's *A Literature of Their Own: British Women Novelists from Brontë to Lessing* (Princeton: Princeton University Press, 1977), which performs the same service for a group of largely ignored novels by British women that Baym does for American novels. The quotations from Braddon are taken from Showalter's text.

6. *Rise of the Novel,* p. 142, where the quotation from *Roxana* also appears.

7. *A Literature of Their Own,* p. 152 and chapter 5 generally.

8. For a full account of these parallel declines in early nineteenth-century New England, see *The Feminization of American Culture,* especially chapters 1, 2, and 4.

Chapter 2. Lilies That Fester: The Divine Compromise in *Clarissa* and *The Scarlet Letter*

1. Samuel Richardson, *Clarissa; or, The History of a Young Lady* (Oxford: Shakespeare Head, 1930), V, letter 21, p. 241. Further references will be given by indicating volume, letter, and page parenthetically within the text.

2. Nathaniel Hawthorne, *The Scarlet Letter* (New York: Norton, 1961) "The Custom-House," p. 11. Further references will be given by indicating chapter and page parenthetically within the text.

3. For a view of Clarissa that never moves beyond her status as a

conventional woman unable to break with conventional judgments, see: Norman Rabkin, "*Clarissa*: A Study in the Nature of
Convention," *The Journal of English Literary History*, 23 (Sep-
tember, 1956): 204–17.

4. The *locus classicus* for literary discussions of the relationship between women and money is Virginia Woolf's *A Room of One's
Own* (New York: Harcourt, 1929). Ellen Moers's *Literary Women:
The Great Writers* (New York: Doubleday, 1976) is suggestive
and illuminating on the importance of money for female authors
and concern with money as a subject in women's writings. I would
alter Moers's view somewhat and suggest that money is important
for women heroes regardless of the sex of their creators.

5. The best discussions of the relationship between Clarissa's pre-
dicament and the economic imperatives of a newly bourgeois
world remain Christopher Hill, "Clarissa Harlowe and her
Times," *Essays in Criticism*, 5 (1955): 315–40; and Ian Watt, *The
Rise of the Novel: Studies in Defoe, Richardson, and Fielding*
(Berkeley and Los Angeles: University of California Press, 1965).

6. Contemporary feminist analysis has made us acutely aware of the
intertwining of personal and political life and has enabled us to
see the patterns of this relationship even in texts that, like
Clarissa, precede our own time by more than two centuries. The
most eloquent statement of this thesis is Virginia Woolf's *Three
Guineas* (London: Hogarth, 1938).

7. On the participation of women in Clarissa's downfall, see Judith
Wilt, "He Could Go No Farther: A Modest Proposal about Lovelace and Clarissa," *PMLA*, 92 (1977): 19–32; and Janet Todd,
Women's Friendship in Literature (New York: Columbia University Press, 1980), pp. 25–46. Arabella's actions here parallel
those of Psyche's sisters in "Amor and Psyche"; in both cases, female conservatism and hostility toward the challenge represented
by the heroic woman ultimately advances the cause of her heroism
by forcing her to act in ways which make a return to conventional
society impossible.

8. Leo Braudy's essay, "Penetration and Impenetrability in *Clarissa*,"
in *New Approaches to Eighteenth-Century Literature*, ed. Philip
Harth (New York and London: Columbia University Press, 1974),
pp. 177–206, sees Richardson's main theme as the desire to remain or become self-sufficient, "the efforts of individuals to discover and define themselves by their efforts to penetrate, control,
and even destroy others while they remain impenetrable themselves" (p. 186).

9. Here I go beyond Braudy's contention that "in the early novel,
men tend to be the main characters when vocation and society
are the main themes. The issue in such novels is often 'what place
in society is suitable to his merits?' In novels that have a woman
for a central character, the basic question is usually 'how is the

self to be realized, whether society exists or not?' " ("Penetration and Impenetrability," pp. 199–200); I see Clarissa's heroism as seeking to combine modes that representational and psychological convention habitually separate.

10. A useful analysis of Clarissa as a type of Christ is provided by John A. Dussinger, "Conscience and the Pattern of Christian Perfection in *Clarissa,*" *PMLA,* 81 (1966): 236–45.

11. The most detailed study of the relationship between Richardson's characters and the Puritan tradition is Cynthia Griffin Wolff's *Samuel Richardson and the Eighteenth-Century Puritan Character* (Hamden, Conn.: Archon, 1972). For another view which, unlike mine, accepts the Christian framework as offering a genuine resolution, indeed the only one possible, to Clarissa's dilemma, see Coral Lansbury, "The Triumph of Clarissa: Richardson's Divine Comedy," *Thalia: Studies in Literary Humor* (1978), pp. 9–17.

12. See Michael J. Colacurcio, "Footsteps of Ann Hutchinson: The Context of *The Scarlet Letter,*" *The Journal of English Literary History,* 39 (1972): 459–94. In this essay Colacurcio argues persuasively that Hawthorne deliberately evokes a parallel between Hester Prynne and Ann Hutchinson in order to suggest an anti-Puritanical historical tradition in which "female sexuality seems, in its concentration and power, both a source for and a type of individualistic nullification of social restraint" (p. 472).

Chapter 3. Heroes into Heroines: The Limits of Comedy in *Emma, Jane Eyre,* and *Middlemarch*

1. *Anatomy of Criticism: Four Essays* (Princeton: Princeton University Press, 1957), p. 163.

2. The editions used are as follows: *Emma,* ed. Ronald Blythe (Harmondsworth, England: Penguin Books, 1966); *Jane Eyre,* ed. Mark Schorer (Boston: Riverside, 1959); *Middlemarch,* ed. Gordon Haight (Boston: Riverside, 1956). Further references will be to these editions; page and, where appropriate, chapter numbers will be given parenthetically within the text.

3. For a discussion of the significance of the sea as an image of liberated space in Jane Austen's fiction, see Nina Auerbach, "O Brave New World: Evolution and Revolution in *Persuasion,*" *ELH,* 39 (1972): 112–18.

4. In *Essays on Sex Equality,* ed. Alice S. Rossi (Chicago and London: University of Chicago Press, 1970), p. 238.

5. Evelyn J. Hinz, in "Hierogamy versus Wedlock: Types of Marriage Plots and Their Relationship to Genres of Prose Fiction," *PMLA,* 91 (1976): 900–913, usefully distinguishes between the

legal conventions of "wedlock," which govern the treatment of marriage in novels and the more cosmic conventions of "hierogamy" which govern the treatment of the same subject in what Hinz refers to as "mythic narratives." In some ways the language Brontë uses here, and throughout *Jane Eyre,* suggests that she is working outside of the main novelistic tradition in the territory Hinz defines as mythic. It seems to me, however, that Brontë is attempting to straddle the two conventions, attempting, that is, to disguise the conflict between the two ideas of marriage. *Jane Eyre,* then, is finally an ambivalent narrative rather than a mythic one; its two-faced treatment of marriage is one indication of its ambiguous status.

6. C. G. Jung, *Symbols of Transformation,* trans. R. F. C. Hull, 2nd ed., Bollingen Series 20 (Princeton: Princeton University Press): 5, 356.

7. Ibid., p. 334.

8. Ibid., p. 391.

9. Hester Prynne similarly wanders—in the forest's maze with Arthur Dimmesdale and in the dark labyrinth of her mind. See especially chapters 13 and 20.

10. Mr. Rochester starts out with flashing eyes, but must be rendered short-sighted in order to be fitted into the conclusion of *Jane Eyre.*

11. In *The Mill on the Floss,* an earlier work, Eliot has her central female character turn these ferocious energies against herself: Maggie Tulliver dies. In *Daniel Deronda,* Eliot's last novel, Gwendolyn Harleth is even more implicated in the death of her husband, the fiendish Grandcourt, than Dorothea is in Casaubon's demise. At the end of *Daniel Deronda,* however, Gwendolyn does not remarry, and it is a measure of the shift in Eliot's vision and the increased possibilities she has allowed her plot that our response to this ending combines equal measures of pleasure and disappointment.

Chapter 4. " 'Weddings be funerals' ": Sexuality, Maternity, and Selfhood in *Jude the Obscure, The Awakening,* and *The Portrait of a Lady*

1. The editions used are as follows: Thomas Hardy, *Jude the Obscure* (New York: Dell, 1959); Kate Chopin, *The Awakening,* ed. Margaret Culley (New York: Norton, 1976); Henry James, *The Portrait of a Lady,* ed. Leon Edel (Boston: Riverside, 1963). Further references will be to these editions; page and, where appropriate, chapter numbers will be given parenthetically within the text.

2. *Dramas, Fields, and Metaphors: Symbolic Action in Human Society* (Ithaca and London: Cornell University Press, 1974), p. 13.
3. Ibid., p. 15.
4. Ibid., p. 16.
5. *Anatomy of Criticism: Four Essays* (Princeton: Princeton University Press, 1957), p. 44.
6. *Counter-Statement* (Berkeley, Los Angeles, London: University of California Press, 1968), p. 31.
7. Ibid., p. 124.
8. The sense of things being in flux characterizes late nineteenth-century fiction generally and is not restricted only to those works that consider the position of women or rely heavily on female characters. Marriage is one of many institutions perceived as collapsing under the weight of suddenly revealed internal contradictions.
9. I am using libido here to stand for energy in general, energy that is not restricted to sexuality, but that necessarily includes the sexual within its compass. As Jung says: "We would be better advised . . . when speaking of libido, to understand it as an energy-value which is able to communicate itself to any field of activity whatsoever, be it power, hunger, hatred, sexuality, or religion, without ever being itself a specific instinct" (*The Collected Works of C. G. Jung,* trans. R. F. C. Hull, Bollingen Series 20 [Princeton: Princeton University Press] *Symbols of Transformation,* vol. 5 [3rd ed., 1967] p. 137). Hardy, Chopin, and James widen the categories within which we may understand female virtue by including sexuality as a specific kind of female energy and by suggesting that the imposition of limits on any particular manifestation of psychic force necessarily constricts a being's entire expressive capacity.
10. For a full discussion of the theory of the "double bind," see Gregory Bateson, *Steps to an Ecology of Mind* (New York: Ballantine, 1972), pp. 194–227.
11. Ibid., p. 211.
12. For counter examples, the *loci classici* are Charlotte Perkins Gilman's "The Yellow Wallpaper" (1899; reprint ed., New York: Feminist Press, 1973) and, of course, Charlotte Brontë's portrait of Bertha Mason in *Jane Eyre.* The motif of madness in women's fictions has been fully explored in Sandra Gilbert and Susan Gubar's *The Madwoman in the Attic: The Woman Writer and the Nineteenth-Century Literary Imagination* (New Haven and London: Yale University Press, 1979).
13. The following cases are offered as examples of what I am calling "isolated" madness: Clarissa after Lovelace has raped her; Jane Eyre on the heath after she learns of the existence of Bertha Mason; Emma after she has insulted Miss Bates and fears that

Mr. Knightley will marry someone else; Dorothea after she learns of the provisions of Casaubon's will.

14. Cynthia Griffin Wolff, "Thanatos and Eros: Kate Chopin's *The Awakening*," *American Quarterly*, 25 (1973): 462.

15. Albert J. Guerard, *Thomas Hardy: The Novels and Stories* (Cambridge: Harvard University Press, 1949), p. 109.

16. If these evaluations are, as they may be, instances of irony, the critics have yielded too easily to the temptation to "rationalize" the texts in order to distance them from the reader and to spare themselves the need to take the heroes' aspirations seriously.

17. "A Case of Maternity: Paradigms of Women as Maternity Cases," *Signs*, 4 (Summer 1979): 608.

18. For a further discussion of this point, see Donald A. Ringe, "Romantic Imagery in Kate Chopin's *The Awakening*," *American Literature*, 48 (1972): 580–88.

19. This point is also pursued, although with a differing interpretation of its ultimate significance, in Wolff, "Thanatos and Eros," pp. 449–71 *passim*.

20. Wolff's "Thanatos and Eros" once again offers a wonderful reading of this scene, limited, however, by Wolff's conviction that Edna never gets beyond her longing for a prince to satisfy her needs.

21. For a contrasting narrative strategy illuminating the same point, see Gilman's "The Yellow Wallpaper."

22. A similar, though more subdued, pattern might be traced in *Jude the Obscure* as well. Sue's mother drowned herself in circumstances that remain ambiguous but seem connected with the general fatality that blights all Fawley marriages; Sue escapes the nunnery through water; and, as a child, Sue's energies persuaded her to go wading, for which enterprise she was severely punished.

23. In considering the ultimate disposition of Isabel's money, legal requirements come into play. As American citizens residing in Italy, Isabel and Osmond are subject to Italian law. The revised Italian Civil Code (1865) contained a provision protecting the property married women brought with them to the marriage. Thus, legally speaking, Isabel's money remains hers despite her marriage, unless she specifically signed it away in the form of a settlement on Osmond. James makes no reference to such a settlement; and, when one thinks about Osmond, it seems inconceivable that he should require anything so vulgar. Osmond's control over both Isabel and her fortune is a moral force; when this compulsion goes, there is no reason to believe Isabel incapable of taking charge.

24. James's treatment of Henrietta Stackpole, as this character evolves in relationship to Isabel, Ralph, and Mr. Bantling, seems to suggest an alternate way of resolving the conflict between sexuality

and autonomy. This alternative involves both a developed commitment to work as an expression of psychic autonomy and the
creation of another figure, in this case an adult male, capable of
accepting this commitment as part of the female character's innate endowment. Although James reveals the capacity to understand these psychological and formal requisites, his sense of Henrietta's possible heroic features is blunted by his envisioning her
as a largely comic character; her humorous possibilities constrain
her significance. Since James seems unable finally to take Henrietta quite seriously, the hint of a new kind of narrative possibility provided by Henrietta's equal commitments to both jour-
nalism and Mr. Bantling is not really fulfilled and must wait for
later texts, as we shall see in the next chapters.

Chapter 5. Psyche's Ascent: A New Earth, A New Heaven

1. In *The Resisting Reader: A Feminist Approach to American Fiction* (Bloomington and London: Indiana University Press, 1978),
   Judith Fetterley makes many of these same points as she revolu-
   tionizes our understanding of several canonical American literary
   texts.

Chapter 6. Love and Work: Reciprocity and Power in *The Odd Women, Daughter of Earth,* and *Gaudy Night*

1. Victor Turner, *Dramas, Fields, and Metaphors: Symbolic Action
   in Human Society* (Ithaca and London: Cornell University Press,
   1974), p. 38.
2. Ibid., p. 14.
3. The editions cited are as follows: George Gissing, *The Odd
   Women* (New York: Norton, 1971); Agnes Smedley, *Daughter of
   Earth* (Old Westbury, N.Y.: The Feminist Press, 1973); Dorothy
   L. Sayers, *Gaudy Night* (New York: Avon, 1968). Further references will be to these editions and will be cited parenthetically
   within the text.
4. For further comments on the historical and spiritual reality represented by Gissing's odd women, see Nina Auerbach, *Communities
   of Women: An Idea in Fiction* (Cambridge, Mass. and London:
   Harvard University Press, 1978), pp. 141–57.
5. Nina Auerbach's "Dorothy Sayers and the Amazons," *Feminist
   Studies*, 3, No. 1/2 (Fall 1975): 54–62, takes a rather different
   and, I think, incorrect view of the Shrewsbury community. Taking

the dons' fears about themselves as Sayers's revelation of their true natures, she overemphasizes their dislocation as "potty," sex-starved spinsters and utterly overlooks the community's capacity to function together for ends worthy of our admiration.

6. Full and eloquent expositions of this argument can be found in Dorothy Dinnerstein, *The Mermaid and the Minotaur: Sexual Arrangements and Human Malaise* (New York: Harper Colophon Books, 1977) and Nancy Chodorow, *The Reproduction of Mothering: Psychoanalysis and the Sociology of Gender* (Berkeley, Los Angeles, London: University of California Press, 1978).

7. Perhaps this view is overly simple, assuming too easily that all labor can be dignified by dedication and that the correspondence between occupation and talent need not be wrecked by social, economic, or ideological claims. Certainly, in present circumstances it is hard to see how coal miners, factory workers, or migrant laborers could be faulted for not having chosen their professions or for reacting to the terms of their lives with anger and frustration. It is equally clear, however, that Sayers is not really talking to—or of—these people, though a more socially complicated fiction would necessarily have to take them into account. Sayers is speaking of, and to, an elite, an heroic cadre, a class of educated women (to use Virginia Woolf's phrase) whose education and intelligence demand that they choose, and that they understand their choice and its consequences.

8. Such logically simple potentiality has proven singularly resistant to the lures of even the most contemporary imaginations. Sylvia Plath's *The Bell Jar* (London: Faber, 1966), for example, presents a particularly poignant counter image in Esther Greenwood's vision of the fig tree full of figs. Each is labeled as a possible or even desirable goal, but to choose here is to choose one only, and that one forever. So Esther starves amidst plenty.

9. Both Nina Auerbach, in *Communities of Women*, and Gillian Tindall, in *George Gissing: The Born Exile* (New York and London: Harcourt Brace Jovanovich, 1974), pp. 168–76, 195–201, 203–5, also comment on Gissing's subversion of heterosexual relationships so that these ultimately function in *The Odd Women* to strengthen the bond uniting women to each other. Tindall, however, goes beyond either Auerbach or myself in stressing the lesbian potential of Gissing's communal portrait.

10. I am not suggesting that a loss of heterosexual intimacy is necessarily a cause for mourning, but only that in these particular instances—Rhoda's rejection of Barfoot and Marie's rejection of her second husband, Anand—it is clearly meant to be seen as the price each woman has to pay for her heroic investment in the life of a larger community.

Chapter 7. Makers of Art, Makers of Life: Creativity and Community in *Sula*, *Their Eyes Were Watching God*, and *The Dollmaker*

1. For a discussion that considers further possible distinctions between what she calls social and spiritual quests, see Carol P. Christ, *Diving Deep and Surfacing: Women Writers and Spiritual Quest* (Boston: Beacon Press, 1980).
2. Introduction, *The Golden Notebook* (New York: Bantam Books, 1973), pp. xi–xii.
3. Ibid., p. xi.
4. The fact of gender is functionally important to *The Golden Notebook*, too. Although Lessing quite correctly asserts that her book is not simply "a tract about the sex war" (Introduction, *The Golden Notebook*, p. x), it matters that Lessing's hero is a woman, Anna and not Alan Wulf. The dilemmas Anna encounters, the solution she works out, are tied not so much to Anna's biological sex as to the circumstances that a human being who happens to be a member of that sex inhabits in our society. The book is unfairly limited by a critique that sees Anna as "only" a woman; but it is equally limited if a desire to see her as "simply human" obscures the fact that her status as cultural critic, her awareness of cultural dis-ease, in part depend on the vantage point afforded her by her culturally assigned position as a woman.
5. In considering this distinction between the oppositional relations thought to typify male writers' connection to their predecessors and the more affiliative countertradition women have evolved, it is useful to compare Harold Bloom's *The Anxiety of Influence* (New York: Oxford University Press, 1973) with Ellen Moers's *Literary Women: The Great Writers* (New York: Doubleday, 1976). The difference here is both historical and critical: Moers's and Bloom's analyses of psychological and historical data are colored by the sense that each has—as a self-consciously representative woman and man—of a self existing in the same relation to the texts described as the writers of these texts are seen to have to their larger contexts. Bloom's account describes and enacts the sort of egotism Lessing is trying to discredit, while Moers's notions of the relation of women artists to each other and to their separate culture seems closer to the relatively less ego-obsessed state Lessing admires. As Elizabeth Abel remarks in her essay "(E)Merging Identities: The Dynamics of Female Friendship in Contemporary Fiction by Women," *Signs*, 6 (Spring 1981), 413–35: "The female tradition Moers finds operative in the work of Austen, Eliot, Dickinson and others is characterized more fully by the search for resonant female voices than by the quest for originality" (p. 433). On this subject see also Mary Daly, "The

Bonds of Freedom: Sisterhood as Antichurch" in *Beyond God the Father: Toward a Philosophy of Women's Liberation* (Boston: Beacon Press, 1973), pp. 132–54.

6. *Sula* (New York: Bantam Books, 1973). All further references to *Sula* are to this edition; page references will be given parenthetically within the body of the text.

7. Robert Stepto, " 'Intimate Things in Place,' a Conversation with Toni Morrison," *The Massachusetts Review*, 19 (1977): 477.

8. Lack of ego hurts Anna Wulf as well. The existence of the entire book we know as *The Golden Notebook* depends, whatever our interpretation of the book's overall meaning, on Anna's return from the egoless state of the "Golden Notebook" section of the novel.

9. In regard to the significance of Sula's relationship to Nel for any proposed reading of Morrison's text, see also: Barbara Smith, "Toward a Black Feminist Criticism," *Conditions: Two* (1977), 25–44; Abel, "(E)Merging Identities," pp. 426–29; and Judith Kegan Gardiner, "The (US)es of (I)dentity: A Response to Abel on '(E)Merging Identities,' " *Signs*, 6 (Spring 1981): 436–42.

10. *Their Eyes Were Watching God* (Urbana, Chicago, London: University of Illinois Press, 1978). All further references are to this edition; page references will be given parenthetically within the body of the text.

11. Even in *Gaudy Night*, where the requirements of female heroism are seen as compatible with a particular heterosexual relationship, the general contradiction between the development of Harriet's heroism—as represented by a reworking of her culturally debased relationships to other women—and the typical ordering of heterosexuality in our culture is finessed rather than resolved. *Sula* and *Their Eyes Were Watching God* generate new cultural models by relying entirely on relationships created between two human beings who are identical—and identically devalued—in the traditional social model. (See Abel's "(E)Merging Identities" for a further discussion of the ways in which "identification replaces complementarity as the psychological mechanism" (p. 415) used to epitomize the ideal of human relatedness in a variety of texts, including *Sula*.) These relationships are as different from the usual formulation of the lesbian couple as from its heterosexual counterpart, in that they emphasize not sexuality but imaginative capacities. In the next chapter, we shall see this imaginative emphasis refined into a new metaphysic that replaces the old narrative focus on the couple with a new one on the single adult female within a cosmology that has dethroned the patriarchal God in favor of a shaping presence reflected in acts of pure imagination rather than in any particular set of structured social gestures.

12. The reader infers from the narrative strategy employed by both Hurston and Morrison that the ideal interpreter for these texts

is someone who is, if not biologically and culturally identical to Pheoby or Nel, certainly someone capable of being moved by Janie and Sula in ways analogous to the way they have been moved, and for analogous reasons. The hero as a type does not belong to a single gender or a single race, but the assignment of these limiting characteristics to a specific hero inevitably elevates the cultural status those characteristics represent.

13. In *Sula,* Helene Wright's grandmother offers Helene the same distorted vision, imposing, for the same reasons, the same set of emotional restrictions on her female charge.

14. *The Dollmaker* (New York: Avon Books, 1972). All further references to *The Dollmaker* are to this edition; page references will be given parenthetically within the body of the text.

15. For a view which accepts this premise and thus reads the book's account of Gertie's life in Detroit as depressing and defeatist, see "Joyce Carol Oates on Harriette Arnow's *The Dollmaker,*" *The Dollmaker,* pp. 601–8.

16. A great deal of work, both literary and psychological, has been done on this figure, including large sections of Erich Neumann's *The Great Mother: An Analysis of the Archetype,* Bollingen Series 47 (Princeton: Princeton University Press, 1963) and Otto Rank's *The Myth of the Birth of the Hero and Other Writings* (1914; reprint ed., New York: Vintage Books, 1959). One of the most interesting recent attempts to understand both the psychogenesis of this archetype and her cultural effects is Dorothy Dinnerstein's *The Mermaid and the Minotaur: Sexual Arrangements and Human Malaise* (New York: Harper Colophon Books, 1977). Dinnerstein suggests that in our society the mothering figure is "the overwhelming external will in the face of which the child first learns the necessity for submission, the first being to whose wishes the child may be forced by punishment to subordinate its own, the first powerful and loved creature whom the child tries voluntarily to please. . . . It is in the relation with her that the child experiences the earliest version of what will be a lifelong internal conflict: the conflict between our rootedness in . . . acute, narrow joys and vicissitudes and our commitment to larger-scale human enterprise" (pp. 28–29). In Dinnerstein's sense, Kentucky is quite as much a part of this figurative complex as Mrs. Kendricks.

Chapter 8. Alternative Mythologies: The Metaphysics of Femininity in *The Woman Warrior, Mrs. Dalloway,* and *The Memoirs of a Survivor*

1. Such friendships may include both sexes and need not exclude heterosexuality. *Gaudy Night, Their Eyes Were Watching God,*

and, to a lesser degree, *Daughter of Earth* bear on this point. Indeed, our capacity to share in the happiness of the couples at the end of *Emma, Jane Eyre,* and *Middlemarch* depends on our sense that these unions constitute exceptions to the norm insofar as the partners *are* each others' friends and equals. Such couplings become problematic—as I think they are in Austen's, Brontë's, and Eliot's texts—as soon as we are allowed to realize that the claims of marriage and the requirements of friendship are actually antithetical; in a friendship, after all, neither party must promise to obey. Because it is so difficult to represent an ideal mutuality in terms of a structure as ingrown with hierarchical assumptions as marriage has been within our culture, fiction has had to grope its way toward alternative formulations that emphasize the sameness or identity of the participants by making them the same sex.

2. Elizabeth Janeway makes this point repeatedly in *Man's World, Woman's Place: A Study in Social Mythology* (New York: Dell, 1971).

3. The editions used in this chapter are as follows: Maxine Hong Kingston, *The Woman Warrior: Memoirs of a Girlhood Among Ghosts* (New York: Knopf, 1977); Virginia Woolf, *Mrs. Dalloway* (New York: Harcourt, 1925); Doris Lessing, *The Memoirs of a Survivor* (New York: Bantam, 1975). Further references will be to these editions and will be given parenthetically within the text.

It may seem that the inclusion of Kingston's text violates the generic structure within which I have been working, since it appears to be an autobiography rather than a novel. While in many cases this objection would be significant, in this particular instance it is trivial, since the structures that organize *The Woman Warrior* are identical with those that organize the other works I am discussing. Kingston is setting out to create herself as woman, artist, and hero. To do so she must create a myth about her own origins that will legitimize her efforts. The "facts" she offers, if we take her text as autobiography, are extremely dubious. It is precisely their dubious and fugitive status that makes them significant to her, that makes them malleable in accordance with her needs. If *Jane Eyre* and *Daughter of Earth* are autobiographical fictions, then *The Woman Warrior* is a fit match for them by being a fictional autobiography.

4. In *Granite and Rainbow: Essays* (London: Hogarth, 1958), p. 81.

Index

Alcott, Louisa May, 5
Amor: myth about Psyche and, 10–14, 19, 92
Andrews, Pamela (character), 21–22
Antigone (character), 5
Apuleius: his version of myth of Psyche, 10–14, 19
Archer, Isabel (character), 27, 107–18, 157, 189; as precursor of modern female heroes, 132–40, 150–51
Arnow, Harriet, 190, 192, 220–35. *See also Dollmaker, The*
Aronowitz, Stanley, 9
Artist: social position of the, 49–50; not option given to Dorothea Brooke, 99; Edna Pontellier as, 126–32; communal role of female, 147–49, 177, 189–254
Atwood, Margaret, 19
Aurora Leigh (Browning), 150
Austen Jane, 65–72, 89, 91, 93, 100–02
Austin, Mary Hunter, 19
Autonomy: in relation to Clarissa Harlowe and Hester Prynne, 28–61
Awakening, The (Chopin), 14, 59, 105, 109–13, 117, 157; sexuality, maternity, and selfhood in, 123–40. *See also* Pontellier, Edna

Barfoot, Mary (character), 153–56, 160, 173
Bateson, Gregory, 114
Beauty. *See* Physical attributes
Beauvoir, Simone de, 6, 94, 150
Beyond God the Father (Daly), 188
Braddon, Mary, 24
Brecht, Bertolt, 6
Bridehead, Sue (character), 27, 108–18, 134, 140, 144, 189; issues of sexuality, maternity, and selfhood for, 118–23
Brontë, Charlotte, 5, 24, 65, 92, 94, 97, 101–02; *Jane Eyre* as her creation, 72–91. *See also Jane Eyre*

Brontë, Emily, 5
Brooke, Dorothea (character), 65, 91–103, 144, 189
Browning, Elizabeth Barrett, 150
Burke, Kenneth, 107

Children: significance of gender of, in novels about female heroes, 102–03, 140; their inhibition of their mothers' sexuality, 113–15, in *Jude the Obscure*, 120–23, in *The Awakening*, 123–32
Chillingworth, Roger (character), 50–52
Chodorow, Nancy, 165
Chopin, Kate, 108–12, 115–17, 123–34, 144. *See also Awakening, The*
Christian morality: in *The Scarlet Letter* and *Clarissa*, 29–61; its deleterious effects on Sue Bridehead, 108, 118–23; as a formative repressive force on Edna Pontellier, 124–25. *See also* Goddess
Clarissa (Richardson), 14, 238; female heroism in, 29–48, 56, 61; deathly marriage motif in, 110. *See also* Harlowe, Clarissa
Cleopatra, 5
Comedy: transforms female heroes into heroines, 62–103; formal elements in, 104–08
Communitas: defined, 13; Christian concept of, in *Clarissa*, 42–43, 47; found in women's work in *Gaudy Night*, 164–68; women artists' construction of, 192; as Jane Crawford's heroic quest, 215, 218–20; in *The Dollmaker*, 225, 233–35; spiritual foundation of, 241; its relation to its social context, 245; as portrayed in *The Memoirs of a Survivor*, 281; as goal in 20th-century literature, 283–84. *See also* Friendship

Consciousness: growth of, in heroic tales, 11

Crawford, Janie (character), 190–92, 210–20, 235, 237

Creation, female: as a communal act, 147–49

Dalloway, Clarissa (character), 148–49, 239, 245, 254–71

Daly, Mary, 188

Daughter of Earth (Smedley), 14, 146; love and work in, 152, 156–62, 168, 174–84, 186. *See also* Rogers, Marie

Davis, Natalie Zeman, 29

Death: its function in *Clarissa*, 45–48; its role in heroic plots, 45, 60; its associations with water in *The Awakening*, 127–32, in *The Portrait of a Lady*, 133; significance of Sula's, 208–09. *See also* Deathly marriage

Deathly marriage: as staple of female heroic plots, 26–28, 109–12, 114–16, 151; in "Amor and Psyche," 13; in *Clarissa*, 37–40, 46; in *The Scarlet Letter*, 50; in *Middlemarch*, 92, 101; in *The Awakening*, 113, 123–32; in *Jude the Obscure*, 118–23; in *The Portrait of a Lady*, 132–40; in *Daughter of Earth*, 156–60; in *The Odd Women*, 168–73; in *Their Eyes Were Watching God*, 212–17; open friendship as alternative to, 237

Defoe, Daniel, 21–22

Destruction: its link with heroism, in *Sula*, 192–209; in *Their Eyes Were Watching God*, 218–19; in *The Dollmaker*, 227–28, 230–33

Dickens, Charles, 144

Dimmesdale, Arthur (character): as heroine in *The Scarlet Letter*, 50–52

Dinnerstein, Dorothy, 150, 165

Dollmaker, The (Arnow), 14, 146, 191, 192, 220–35. *See also* Nevels, Gertie

Double-bind: between marriage and sexuality for women, 114; in *Daughter of Earth*, 177; Septimus Warren Smith's, 266

Drabble, Margaret, 145

Eiseley, Loren, 3

Eliot, George, 65, 91–102, 106, 107. *See also Middlemarch*

Emma (Austen), 14, 65–72, 89, 100–01, 107. *See also* Woodhouse, Emma

Eyre, Jane (character), 15, 102, 144, 171, 189; her rebellion, 22, 65, 72–91; compared to Dorothea Brooke, 92, 97–98; compared to Isabel Archer, 116–17; compared to Marie Rogers, 156, 160

Father-daughter relationships: in *Daughter of Earth*, 180–82

Female role models: absence of, in early 19th-century literature, 137. *See also* Mentors, female

Fitzgerald, F. Scott, 145

Flanders, Moll (character), 21–22, 24

Forgotten Language, The (Fromm), 236

For Whom the Bell Tolls (Hemingway), 144

Friendship: as alternative to deathly marriage, 237, 268–70. *See also* Communitas

Fromm, Erich, 236

Frye, Northrop, 62–63, 65, 107

Gaudy Night (Sayers): female work in, 14, 146, 152, 161–68, 184–87. *See also* Vane, Harriet

Gilbert, Sandra M., 14–15

Girls, The (LeSeuer), 146

Gissing, George, 16, 146, 152–56, 160–61, 165, 169–74. *See also Odd Women, The*

Goddess: her image in 20th-century fiction, 239–40; in *Mrs. Dalloway*, 255, 258–59, 261, 264, 274; in *The Memoirs of a Survivor*, 274, 277, 283

Golden Ass, The (Apuleius), 19

Golden Notebook, The (Lessing), 146, 190, 271

Grandmother-granddaughter relationships. *See* Women, relations between

"Grave of the Famous Poet, The" (Atwood), 19

Great Gatsby, The (Fitzgerald), 145
Gubar, Susan, 14–15

Hardy, Thomas, 108, 110, 112–16, 118–23, 134, 144. *See also Jude the Obscure*
Harlowe, Clarissa (character), 15, 63, 189; as victim of repressive social context, 29–48, 56, 61, 144; contrasted with Isabel Archer, 27, 134
Hawthorne, Nathaniel, 29–32, 48–61, 193, 194. *See also Scarlet Letter, The*
H. D., 236
Helen in Egypt (H. D.), 236
Hemingway, Ernest, 144
Hero: characteristics of, 4–16; as female artist, 236–54; importance of descendants to, 137, 278. *See also* Heroes, female; Heroes, male; Heroism
Heroes, female: characteristics of, 4–16, 33, 36–37, 46, in literature, 21–28; as alternatives to conventional female archetypes, 14–16; need for descendants of, 137, 278 (*see also* Mother-daughter relationships); artists as, 143–51, 189–254. *See also* Heroes, female comic; Heroism, female
Heroes, female comic: in *Emma*, 65–72; in *Jane Eyre*, 72–91; in *Middlemarch*, 91–101
Heroes, male: characteristics of, 4–16, in literature, 20, 21
Heroic plots: characteristics of, 45–46, 83, 226, 230–31
Heroine: characteristics of, 5–6, 13, 20, 105; changes in role of, 25–28; result of comedy's attempts to deal with female heroes, 62–103
Heroism: defined, 4–16; male and female, contrasted in *Mrs. Dalloway*, 254–71; Jane Eyre's rejection of, 86–88, 90–91
Heroism, female: how it functions in patriarchal context, 44–45; clear 19th-century conflicts with marriage, 105–40; its connection with maternity, 165–66; as artistic enterprise, 177, 189–235; 20th-

century arena for, 245
Hurston, Zora Neale, 148, 190, 192, 210–20. *See also Their Eyes Were Watching God*
Husbands: extermination of, in late 19th-century novels, 24–25; desire for reformed, 110

Iliad, The, 13
Immense Journey (Eiseley), 4
Isolation: Clarissa's, 36–37, 48; Jane Eyre's, 78–91
I Stand Here Ironing (Olsen), 146

James, Henry, 23, 107, 108, 171; his portrayal of sexuality and maternity, 110–12, 116, 132–40. *See also The Portrait of a Lady*
Jane Eyre (Brontë), 5, 14, 24–25, 59, 101, 107, 157, 238; transformation of hero into heroine in, 65, 72–91, 110. *See also* Eyre, Jane
Jerusalem the Golden (Drabble), 145
Joan of Arc, 5
Jude the Obscure (Hardy), 14, 108, 238; sexuality, maternity, and selfhood in, 105, 109–12, 114, 118–23. *See also* Bridehead, Sue
Judith (Bible), 5
Jung, C. J., 29, 80, 82–83

Kelly, Edith, 146
Kingston, Maxine Hong, 148–49, 239, 241–56, 275, 283. *See also Woman Warrior, The*

Labyrinth: as motif in *Middlemarch*, 92, 96
Lady Audley's Secret (Braddon), 24
Lawrence, D. H., 6, 7
LeSeuer, Meridel, 146
Lessing, Doris, 16, 245; alternative mythologies in *The Memoirs of a Survivor*, 149, 240, 271–83; her paradigm of the female artist, 190–93. *See also Memoirs of a Survivor*
"Liminars": defined, 7–8; as comedic heroes, 62
Little Women (Alcott), 5, 23
Love: its relation to power and heroism in "Amor and Psyche," 10–14; Jane Eyre's need for, 76–91; its

Love (*continued*)
  role in *Middlemarch*, 97–99; its
  link with work and community in
  20th-century novels, 152–87; its
  connection with friendship, 237,
  267–70, 281–82
Love Story (Segal), 144

Madwoman in the Attic, The (Gilbert and Gubar), 14–15
Mailer, Norman, 144
"Manliness": as useless artifact in
  Mrs. Dalloway, 255, 263–66, 268
Marginality: its importance for female heroes, 37; Hester Prynne's,
  53–54; Pearl's, 58–59
"Marginals": defined, 8
Marriage: in *Clarissa*, 34–35, 38–42;
  its function for heroic women in
  comedy, 62–65, 102–03; in *Emma*,
  71–72; in *Jane Eyre*, 77, 79, 84–85,
  89–91; as vocation in *Middlemarch*, 91–95, 97–99; as institution
  destructive of women's sexuality
  and autonomy, 105–40; in *Jude
  the Obscure*, 118–23, in *The
  Awakening*, 123–32, in *The Portrait of a Lady*, 132–40; as entrapper of women in *Daughter of
  Earth*, 147, 157–60, 176–77; work
  as alternative to, in *The Odd
  Women*, 153–56, in *Daughter of
  Earth*, 160–61; insignificance of,
  in *The Woman Warrior*, 246, 248.
  See also Deathly marriage
Maternity. *See* Children; Mother-child relationships
Memoirs of a Survivor, The
  (Lessing), 149, 239, 271–83
Men: relations between, in *Clarissa*,
  41–42
Mentors, female: in *The Awakening*,
  126–29; in *The Portrait of a Lady*,
  137–39; mothers as, in *The
  Woman Warrior*, 242–44, 251, 254
Mermaid and the Minotaur, The
  (Dinnerstein), 150, 165
Middlemarch (Eliot), 14, 107, 238;
  transformation of hero into heroine, 65, 91–103, 110. *See also*
  Brooke, Dorothea

Mill, John Stuart, 69, 100, 101
Mill on the Floss (Eliot), 23
Mrs. Dalloway (Woolf), male and
  female heroism contrasted in, 239,
  254–71, 272, 274. *See also* Dalloway, Clarissa; Smith, Septimus
  Warren
Money: its significance to the heroic
  woman, 33, 88; its importance in
  The Portrait of a Lady, 134–35
Moon: images of, in *Jane Eyre*, 80–82
Morrison, Toni, 148, 190, 192–210,
  212. *See also Sula*
Mother-child relationships: in *Jane
  Eyre*, 83–84; significance of child's
  gender in, 102–03, 140; redefinition of, by Dorothy Sayers, 165–66.
  See also Mother-daughter relationships
Mother-daughter relationships:
  240–41; in *The Scarlet Letter*, 58–60; in *The Portrait of a Lady*,
  134–40; in *Daughter of Earth*, 157,
  176–80; in *The Odd Women*, 174;
  in *Sula*, 196–98; in *The Dollmaker*, 222–25, 230–33; in *The
  Woman Warrior*, 242–44, 252–54;
  in *The Memoirs of a Survivor*,
  276–83. *See also* Goddess; Mother-child relationships; Women, relations between
Mythic structure: importance of,
  236–41, 283–84; in *The Woman
  Warrior*, 241–54; in *Mrs. Dalloway*, 258–59; in *The Memoirs of
  a Survivor*, 272, 274–75, 281

Nature, its rejection of women: in
  Clarissa, 46; in *The Scarlet Letter*,
  59; in *Jane Eyre*, 80–85
Nevels, Gertie (character), 147–48,
  190–92, 220–35, 237
Night and Day (Woolf), 145
Novel: as mythic genre and social
  metaphor, 19–28
Nunn, Rhoda (character), 146, 153,
  169–74, 184

Oakley, Ann, 120
Odd Women, The (Gissing), 160,

184, 186; importance of work in, 146, 147, 152–56, 161, 168–74. *See also* Nunn, Rhoda; Barfoot, Mary

Olsen, Tillie, 143, 146

Peace, Eva (character), 196, 199–205, 213

Peace, Sula (character), 189, 191–210, 212, 235, 237; compared with Janie Crawford, 211–12, 220

Pearl (character), 54, 58–61

Phelps, Elizabeth Stuart, 24–25

Physical attributes: importance of, to female heroes, 33

Piercy, Marge, 146

Pontellier, Edna (character), 140, 144, 157, 189; sexuality, maternity, and selfhood issues for, 108–17, 123–32; female mentor for, 137

Portrait of a Lady, The (James), 27, 105–12, 132–40, 151. *See also* Archer, Isabel

Power: its relation to love in "Amor and Psyche," 10–14; female heroes' claims to, 22–24; as an issue in *Clarissa* and *The Scarlet Letter*, 30–61; in *Emma*, 68–73

Pride and Prejudice (Austen), 19

Prostitution: in *Roxana*, 25; in *Daughter of Earth*, 158–60

Prynne, Hester (character): as victim of patriarchal religion, 29–32, 48–61, 63, 144; as artist, 189; compared with Sula Peace, 193, 194

Psyche, 247, 271; as female heroic paradigm, 10–14, 19, 92; limitations of, 245; deadly marriage motif in myth of, 110; her attempt to transform heroine into hero in contemporary literature, 143–49; as Goddess, 237–38; quest of, 283–84

Puritanism: the moral context for Clarissa Harlowe's and Hester Prynne's rebellion, 29–61

Quest, heroic: role of, 7; in "Amor and Psyche," 11–14; Clarissa's, 40; Dorothea Brooke's, 96–99; Harriet Vane's, 163; Janie Crawford's search for communitas as, 215; the woman warrior's, 241, 244–54;

nature of, in *The Memoirs of a Survivor*, 274, 283; nature of females', 237, 239, 241

Rape: its role in *Clarissa*, 43–44; in *Daughter of Earth*, 157–58

Reproduction of Mothering, The (Chodorow), 165

Richardson, Samuel, 29–48, 56, 60–61, 90, 144. *See also Clarissa*

Rochester, Edward (character): as Jane Eyre's mother, 84–85

Rogers, Marie (character), 99, 146, 156–61, 174–84

Role models. *See* Female role models; Mentors, female

Room of One's Own, A (Woolf), 143, 146

Roth, Philip, 144

Sayers, Dorothy, 147, 152, 161–68, 184–87. *See also Gaudy Night*

Scarlet Letter, The (Hawthorne), 14, 84, 110, 238; female heroism in, 29–32, 48–61. *See also* Prynne, Hester

Second Sex, The (Beauvoir), 6, 150

Segal, Erich, 144–45

Sexuality, female: its treatment in literature, 25–26; its link with domination in *Clarissa*, 38–45; as incongruous with maternity, 112–15; in *Jude the Obscure*, 118–23, in *The Awakening*, 123–32; marriage as warper of, 109–12, in *Jude the Obscure*, 118–23, in *The Awakening*, 123–32, in *The Portrait of a Lady*, 132–40; as revitalizing force in *The Odd Women*, 172–74; its link with women's victimization in *Daughter of Earth*, 175–83; its link with destruction in *Sula*, 193–94, 202–08, 212

Shadrack (character), 196, 198–202, 205

Shakespeare, William, 5

Showalter, Elaine, 26

Silences (Olsen), 143

Smedley, Agnes, 152, 156–61, 165, 174–84. *See also Daughter of Earth*

Smith, Septimus Warren (character), 254–71, 279

Sophocles, 5

Story of Avis, The (Phelps), 23–25

"Subjection of Women, The" (Mill), 69, 101

Sula (Morrison), 148, 191–210, 213, 218–21. *See also* Peace, Eva; Peace, Sula; Shadrack; Wright, Helene; Wright, Nel

Sun Also Rises, The (Hemingway), 144

Symbols of Transformation (Jung), 29

Tell Me a Riddle (Olsen), 146

Thackeray, William Makepeace, 22

Their Eyes Were Watching God (Hurston), 148, 191–92, 210–21. *See also* Crawford, Janie; Watson, Phoeby

Three Guineas (Woolf), 266, 267, 270

To the Lighthouse (Woolf), 147

Turner, Victor: 53, 62, 106, 152; definitions by, 7–8, 13, 37

Vane, Harriet (character), 147, 161–68, 184–87, 189

Vanity Fair (Thackeray), 22

Venus: her role in "Amor and Psyche," 10–14

Vida (Piercy), 146

Villette (Brontë), 24

War: Clarissa Dalloway's parties as antithesis to, 245, 254–71

Warner, Susan, 22–23

Watson, Phoeby (character), 210–11, 219–20

Watt, Ian, 21, 25

Weaning: as metaphor in *Clarissa*, 46

Weddings. *See* Marriage

Weeds (Kelly), 146

Weil, Simone, 13

Wide, Wide World, The (Warner), 22–23

Wives: in *Daughter of Earth*, 158–59. *See also* Marriage; Heroine

Wollstonecraft, Mary, 62

Woman of Genius, A (Austen), 19

Woman Warrior, The (Kingston), 148–49, 239, 241–54, 272

Women, relations between; in *Clarissa*, 36, 41; in *Emma*, 69–71; in *Jane Eyre*, 76, 82, 85, 86; in *The Odd Women*, 173; in *Daughter of Earth*, 177–78; in *Sula*, 202–10; in *Their Eyes Were Watching God*, 210–11, 213–14; in *The Woman Warrior*, 250–51; in *Mrs. Dalloway*, 268–70. *See also* Mother-daughter relationships

"Women and Fiction" (Woolf), 257

Women in Love (Lawrence), 6

Woodhouse, Emma (character): 15, 91, 102, 189; her transformation from hero to heroine, 65–72, 78, 89, 144

Woolf, Virginia, 143, 145, 146, 283; alternative mythologies in *Mrs. Dalloway*, 239, 254–71, 281. *See also Mrs. Dalloway*

Work: as means of restructuring patriarchal society, 145–49, 152–88

Wright, Helene (character), 196–202, 205

Wright, Nel (character), 196–209

Wuthering Heights (Brontë), 5, 23

About the Author

Lee Edwards is a graduate of Swarthmore College (B.A. 1962) and of the University of California at Berkeley (M.A. 1965) and at San Diego (Ph.D. 1969). The recipient of a fellowship from the National Endowment for the Humanities and the editor for six years of *The Massachusetts Review*, she has written more than a dozen papers and articles and edited four books of feminist criticism. Edwards taught at U. C. S. D. in 1965–66 and is now professor of English and Women's Studies at the University of Massachusetts at Amherst, where she lives.